Shall We Gather at the River

Shall We Gather at the River

E. Reid Gilbert

Copyright © 2011 by E. Reid Gilbert.
Cover art by Wanda Hein

Library of Congress Control Number: 2011913985
ISBN: Hardcover   978-1-4653-4806-7
            Softcover   978-1-4653-4805-0
            Ebook   978-1-4653-4807-4

All rights reserved. No part of this book may be reproduced or transmitted in any form or by any means, electronic or mechanical, including photocopying, recording, or by any information storage and retrieval system, without permission in writing from the copyright owner.

This book was printed in the United States of America.

To order additional copies of this book, contact:
Xlibris Corporation
1-888-795-4274
www.Xlibris.com
Orders@Xlibris.com
103513

"This story is dedicated to all those who have loved and . . ."

CONTENTS

Chapter 1 Waiting for Uncle Jimmie Sue's Headstone 9
Chapter 2 The Sharecroppers 15
Chapter 3 At Grandpa's Church 21
Chapter 4 Madeleen 27
Chapter 5 Visit to Madeleen's 41
Chapter 6 The Swimming Hole 49
Chapter 7 The Healing 57
Chapter 8 Down the Mountain 66
Chapter 9 Dinner on the Grounds 72
Chapter 10 Grounded 80
Chapter 11 Water Encounter 85
Chapter 12 Bringing in the Sheaves 95
Chapter 13 Haying 104
Chapter 14 The Rain Cometh 113
Chapter 15 The Barn Loft 119
Chapter 16 Corn Shucking 127
Chapter 17 The Revival Meeting 134
Chapter 18 Altar Call 141
Chapter 19 Back Home 146
Chapter 20 Breakfast at the Bennetts' 149
Chapter 21 Talking or Not Talking 158
Chapter 22 Christmas Gift 162
Chapter 23 Snow Cream and Snow Angels 167
Chapter 24 Mistletoe 173
Chapter 25 A Long, Cold Winter 180
Chapter 26 Gone 186
Chapter 27 Retracing the Path 193

Chapter 28 But Not Forgotten 201
Chapter 29 An Answer...206
Chapter 30 His Answer to Her Answer 210
Chapter 31 Last Rights...218
Epilogue...225

CHAPTER 1

Waiting for Uncle Jimmie Sue's Headstone

Its Easter time, so I thought I'd bring a bunch of sarvisberry flowers up to Uncle Jimmie Sue's grave and wait for the headstone which was to have been delivered this morning. He had died in the dead of winter, when they had to dig his grave with a backhoe (one of those infernal earth-digging machines) which he abhorred and declared that they would be "the ruination of us all" by displacing the work of several men, "what with pushin' whole mountains aside 'cause folks're in sech a all-fired hurry."

In the old days, when a grave needed to be dug it was well-nigh impossible to dig into the frozen earth with mattick, pick and shovel the appropriate "six feet under." They'd have to put the deceased in a backroom until the ground thawed a bit. Sometimes it might take even longer for the preacher to get there to hold the "sarvises" (funeral services). That would be about Easter time when the first of the woodland flowers would be poppin' out of the June berry trees, which were often called sarviseberry trees, because the flowers were timely for the spring funeral *sarvises*.

The berries didn't ripen until June, and as they were the first berries to ripen, they were then called June berries. Although quite small, they were the sweetest berries on the mountain. It'd take forever to pick enough for a pie, so the better judgment would be just to eat them when you'd pick them off the lowest hanging branches from the most convenient trees. The berries had no pits like cherries, so you could eat them as fast as you could throw them in your mouth.

Ruminating on the dual names of sarviseberries and Juneberries, I began this morning to consider the life of Uncle Jimmie Sue and his headstone, which he paid for with his own money.

He never had many earthly treasures, leaving behind after his passing on only a few marvelous mementoes of his craftsmanship both in wood and in metal. He had no insurance except his burial insurance, like all the rest of his family and neighbors. It seemed "only fitten" to provide resources for one's own "decent burial," thereby sparing the loved ones left behind from having to bear those expenses. That way everyone would be able to assure oneself of "havin' a say" in the manner in which one was to be "put away." It was said that Uncle Jimmie Sue had kept up his premium payments so well and for so long that he was even going to be getting a large memorial stone with an epitaph inscribed on it.

Today is a wonderful spring day, which I'm thoroughly enjoying while waiting with a bit of bitter sweetness for the monument truck to get here with Uncle Jimmie Sue's gravestone. It's been such a birdsong-filled morning that I headed out here to the graveyard long before the truck was appointed to arrive. This is the kind of morning Uncle Jimmie Sue would have enjoyed either to start on some project or maybe come here for an hour or so to think or meditate while whittling on a walking stick or some other thingamajig.

He had chosen this particular gravesite for reasons unbeknownst to anybody but himself, only I had kind of figured out what it was all about. It was right next to the metal fence which separated the white folks' cemetery from that of the "coloreds." Now, why would a body choose deliberately to be buried for all eternity down the hill here next to the woods and this close to the fence separating us from the coloreds.

Being a blacksmith, he'd even made some repairs on the fence down here, which I'd never noticed before. I believe those are little iron angels he put there on the fence. Everybody'd always considered him a little eccentric, sometimes downright *quare*.

There was always about him a kind of mystery with usually a mixture of compassion plus a great deal of mischief. Maybe he really had a double personality like the sarvisberries and June berries. You could enjoy the solemn beauty of the sarvisberry blossoms in springtime and the celebrational sweet fruit of the June berries in the summer. You might could say that a body could appreciate Uncle Jimmie Sue's neighborliness as well as laugh at his pranksteriness.

He seemed to like nothing better than to play a trick on a friend or a family member, but especially to outdo some high-falutin' outlander who'd wandered up the mountain from the flatland.

On the other hand his generosity seemed to have no bounds if he felt a body really needed something he could provide. It was said of him that if he thought you needed his shoes, he'd take them off and offer them along with the socks and declare, "Ah really wanted to go barefoot anyways."

Because of his restlessness, his jumping around from one job to another or his wandering off to sit and whittle without finishing whatever it was he was supposed to be doing, his grandma Sally had said that "He was just born tired an' never got rested." He knew when to take a "settin'-down rest" whether anyone else did or not. He'd heard about that little saying of hers, and it bothered him a bit, but didn't seem to change any of his ways of doing things. He respected his grandma a good deal and said that a little saying like that "oughtta be writ down sommers." I had never seen it in print anywhere nor had he, or so he said.

Actually, Uncle Jimmie Sue was really my great-uncle, and besides, his name wasn't Jimmie Sue, but was James Lafayette Bennett. There were so many James Bennetts in the community which their great-granddaddy had homesteaded three generations earlier that folks devised a way of distinquishing one James Bennett from another by giving him his mother's first name, which in Jimmie Sue's case was Great-Grandma Sue. So all of his life he was known as Jimmie Sue, which was a kind of acknowledgment that he belonged to her. Of course, I never did know her, but Uncle Jimmie Sue told me she lived to be a hundred and two.

It was a different situation with girls; they didn't have to get an extra name tagged onto their first name until they got married when they got not only their husband's last name but also their first name, such as Cousin Lizzie Bob, Aunt Bessie Tobe, etc. I'm sure that a psycho sociologist or somebody like that would have been intrigued with this strange way of nicknaming, but I just figured that it had to do with belonging to someone or to be along *with* somebody else in the family.

Uncle Jimmie Sue had done a number of things in his lifetime of blacksmithing, farming, cooking for a sawmill camp, tan barking and for a short spell, working—doing something or another—on the railroad. I remember him once saying about railroad travel, "If you can't enjoy the ride, the ticket ain't worth the price." I suspect he applied that to the whole human journey, as he certainly appeared to be enjoying his trip.

He would have also considered preaching and probably did, but his older brother, my Grandpa George Dowell Bennett, was a Primitive Baptist preacher, who earnestly believed in double-predestination and was always so dour that Uncle Jimmie Sue took notice of Grandpa's unusually doleful demeanor and said, "If that's what religion does for you, I ain't got no time for it." You see, he saw the "fullness of life" as the intention of the Good Lord. His fullness included a little fun: some dancing, rooster fighting, a taste for the spirits, a bit of fiddling—with some fiddling around—and a great deal of mischief-making or just plain tomfoolery.

He once told me, "Why, I just bet that I could preach as good a sermon as your Grandpap George Dowell, especially if I could have just a little toddy afore I was to step up into the pulpit." I dared not take him up on his bet, because he could never let a bet—particularly if it was a double-d-dare—go by without jumping wholeheartedly into the venture, whatever it might be.

No doubt but that he would go up to the pulpit come next Association Meeting day when the moderating elder would ask if there were any more preachers led by the Lord that morning to speak to the assembly.

I knew that he would welcome the chance, needing only the nudge of a wager with a "nip" of the spirits to set him off in that direction. So I kept my peace by simply agreeing that he might for sure be able to preach as good a stirring sermon as Grandpa.

Now the reason that I thought Uncle Jimmie Sue might have, under different circumstances, considered preaching, was a kind of mystery—almost something spiritual or otherworldly about him in his understanding of the "fullness of life." Although he wasn't much of a hand to quote scripture, he once, right in the middle of a conversation, said, "Thou shalt show me the path of life; in thy presence is the fullness thereof."

One day when Grandpa was trying to explain double-predestination to me I asked him about the time when lightning struck the church and everyone went running. I asked, "If it was the Lord's will for the church to be struck why didn't the church members stay in the church?"

Grandpa said, "That was just the Lord's extra message that his predestination for us right then was to get on home and get the milkin' done." I really couldn't argue with that.

On one occasion I overheard Uncle Jimmie Sue and Grandpa discussing religion, then arguing religion, then fussing and almost cussing about religion. Finally Uncle Jimmie Sue says, "Now Dowell, jest 'splain in plain words what you and them other preachers mean by 'double-predestination'?"

Granddaddy says calmly—almost too calmly—"Why, James, (He always addressed Uncle Jimmie Sue formally when they got on the subject of religion; him being the older brother and a presiding elder of the church) it's really quite simple. It just means that God A'mighty has already from the beginning of time predestined ever'thing for ever'body, an' what is to be will be whether it ever happens or not. 'According as he hath chosen us in Him before the foundation of the world, that we should be holy and without blame before Him in love: Having predestined us unto the adoption of children by Jesus Christ to Himself, according to the good pleasure of his will.' Ephesians 1:4 & 5." I would readily admit that Grandpa could out quote anyone with scripture. And of course this scriptural passage was crucial—in fact the very basis—of his theology.

After this pronouncement, he took one of those Primitive Baptist preacher's audible breaths, "uh . . . huh," which was a clear signal he was fixin' to launch off into a fulmination with full sails into his sermonic mode and dissertation on the matter, except that Uncle Jimmy Sue interrupted with, "Well then, Dowell, why don't you go and lay yoah head on the railroad track so's we can see if the Lord has willed from the time of Adam if he meant for you to be beheaded by a train today?"

Granddaddy glowered with an internal intensity, I had seldom seen except when he was in the pulpit, as he simultaneously stood up, picked up and put on his hat while announcing, "That'd be temptin' the Lord, an' it's not fittin' nor proper to tempt the Lord."

With that dramatic exit line he stalked out of the house, but not before Uncle Jimmie Sue yelled after him, "Now, Dowell, fer what reason would the Good Lord be tempted to cut your head off, especially on sech a nice day as today?" He always gloried in having the last word with Grandpa, particularly if it was pertaining to religion in some form.

After that, I never heard the two of them discuss anything more substantial than the weather or family or some unfortunate happening in the county . . . never touched on religion again, together, so far as I know.

I did wonder if and why the Good Lord might be tempted to appoint a train to come down the railroad track to decapitate Granddaddy, except him being so foolish as to lay his head on the track, thus deserving a heavenly trip to glory. I think Uncle Jimmie Sue mentioned the railroad track because of an unfortunate experience he'd remembered about it when he was a boy.

It seems that some of his older brothers, maybe even Grandpa, had convinced him one cold morning when they had to cross the railroad tracks on the way to school to stick his tongue on the track, claiming it tasted like licorice candy when the track got frost on it.

Uncle Jimmie Sue hesitated at first, but the memory of good licorice candy at Christmastime, inspired him, and his tongue stuck as strong as glue. All the older boys were whooping and hollering at Jimmie Sue's predicament, and I believe to this day that was one reason he was so determined to be the one playing jokes on other folks from then on.

I never did hear how he got his tongue unstuck before the Roanoke Special came by. But, as they say, "Boys will be boys." even if it be in the Good Lord's Book for one of them to be predestined toward a lifetime of preaching or the other a lifetime of moonshining.

Maybe Granddaddy's preaching was to expiate for some of his guilt for Uncle Jimmie Sue's tongue getting stuck on the cold steel railroad track that cold winter morning.

* * *

CHAPTER 2

The Sharecroppers

Uncle Jimmie Sue was born in High County, Virginia on December 23, 1860. It was several months before the start of the Civil War, often called the "War Between the States." Of course, he and his brothers were too young to fight in that war, although several of his uncles and cousins were drafted unwillingly into the Confederate Army. I say *unwillingly* because the way they figured it was that the war really wasn't their war—it was the war of the plantation owners, the slave holders, who wanted that war to preserve their way of life. They needed the continuation of the practice of owning other human beings to perpetuate their own political and economic power.

The mountain men had been fierce fighters in the Revolutionary War, but they were less enthusiastic about fighting the battles of wealthy landowners in the tidewater part of Virginia. Uncle Jimmie Sue had several kin folk who were constantly going AWOL and heading back to the hills to hide out away from the military authorities.

His Uncle Elbert, who'd have been my great-great uncle had gone AWOL, and a cousin, Charles Taylor, was his commander and kept sending letters to Uncle Elbert's wife, begging her to convince Uncle Elbert to come on back to the army or Cousin Charlie would have to come after him. That little game of cat-and-mouse continued until the end of the war, but Uncle Elbert was reported to have said, "I'll fight my wars, I'll follow my beliefs an' I'll choose what I want to do with my life, but I'll be damned if I'm gonna leave home to shoot at some northern Yankees so's the flatlanders down to Richmon' can keep on their highfalutin' ways of livin'."

It was generally acknowledged that if secession had been put up to popular vote in the whole South, the war would never have happened. As a matter of fact, several of the western counties of Virginia actually did secede from the state with the rationale, "If the state of Virginia can secede from the nation, the westernmost counties can secede from the state."

That action was the way President Abraham Lincoln declared West Virginia the 31st state in the union.

There were no slaveholders in the mountains, and very few "colored", which was the usual accepted word the mountain folk would use to refer to black folks. The Bennetts, especially, felt that to call the colored, *Negro* or *niggah,* didn't show enough respect for any of "God's children." It was generally understood that the few coloreds were primarily runaway slaves, and their sense of independence was thought of quite highly by mountainfolk, who were, themselves, assuredly independent-minded.

I wouldn't want to be misunderstood that there was no racial prejudice in the mountains against the colored folks; there was plenty and more than enough to go around, but it was more of a sense of "outsiders" than of "colored"—both of which were regarded suspiciously as they represented the unknown.

Although Uncle Jimmie Sue was only five when the war ended, he told me that he remembered when a Yankee soldier jumped the rail fence with his horse and dropped a little blue china cup with a broken handle. He said, "Papa found it an' brought it in fer us to see. We didn't know whether the handle broke when it fell to the groun' or whether it was already broke an' jest fell outta his saddle bag. We figgered the yankee had stole it from some of his war-lootin'. I hung onto it, jest fer a keepsake kinda thing."

Even though there were some colored families in the mountains, it was unusual for them to actually own any land for a couple of reasons: They were usually too poor to buy the land and even if they did have some money scrounged from years of hard work, they would still have to overcome local and state laws or petty officials who would erect all kinds of barriers against landholding by the coloreds.

After the war, the coloreds were promised forty acres and a mule, and the Yankee carpetbaggers flowed in to the South, in another kind of invasion, to enforce that and to take advantage of the disenfranchised white folks in various other ways—both financially and politically. However most of that activity was in the tidewater and piedmont areas. As usual, the mountain areas were pretty much ignored—or at least left alone.

Uncle Jimmie Sue's folks (Great-Grandpa Robert and Great-Grandma Sue) owned a nice fifty-acre farm with some good timber, pasture and fertile bottomland. Their place was comparable to other farms, but there were a few farms for sharecroppers, who were mostly colored.

Uncle Jimmie Sue told me that there weren't many coloreds in his family's neighborhood until he saw a colored sharecropper family moving in when he was fifteen. That would've been in 1875, only ten years after "Thet Ol' War" was over. It was so unusual to see non-whites moving in that the whole Bennett family went out in the yard to see them pass when Great-Uncle Simon yelled into the house, "Yawl come on out an' see the new fambly of sharecroppers comin' down the road."

The reason he reckoned they were sharecroppers was that only sharecroppers moved around from one farm to another. The landowners seemed to stay mostly put. They kind of belonged to the land. Some sharecroppers moved every year, but others would usually stay a few years and sometimes may stay not only long enough to raise several crops of tobacco but maybe also a whole crop of youngsters.

The Bennetts knew that Mr. Goins had a farm for sharecroppers and that he had found a new sharecropper family to move in, but they didn't know beforehand that the sharecroppers would be colored. Anyway, the way that Uncle Jimmie Sue told it, "We couldn't jest stand their gawkin' like a bunch of infidels, so Papa stopped the movin' party to interduce us to them an' find out who they might be an' to see where they might've come from."

There was a closer way to get to the Goins' place, if you were walking, but to get a mule and wagon over there on Sapling Ridge you'd have to go by the good road—well, now, but to say the 'good road,' it would mean the sand-clay road that narrowed down to two ruts by time you got to the actual house on the sharecropper farm.

The sharecropper family just had one mule pulling the mover wagon, that would also be the haying wagon, and the potato-hauling wagon as well as the go-to-meetin' wagon. Aside from the people, there was a lot of house plunder on the wagon—beds, and cabinets, tables and chairs and such.

Tied to the back of the wagon was a milk cow, and following close to her were four dogs: what looked like two beagles, a blue-tick hound and a redbone hound. The blue-tick was a bitch, and Jimmie Sue's black-and-tan stud dog, Rattler, was awful anxious to introduce himself by paying a whole heap of attention to her, sniffing carefully her backside.

Uncle Jimmie Sue thought, *You know them dogs don't pay nary a bit of 'tention to their differences of color—one bein' a blue-tick an' the other'n bein' a black-an-tan. I declare they do seem to have more important things on their minds than differences of color.*

Seated on the wagon seat were a middle-aged man and woman who introduced themselves as Levi and Lily Hilton. Two boys—one about fourteen, and the other maybe seventeen—were walking beside the wagon. They seemed awfully shy. They didn't introduce themselves, and Jimmie Sue didn't find out till later their names were Cletus and Clyde.

But the most striking of all the critters and people in the moving parade was a girl sitting in a rocking chair right behind the wagon seat. Jimmie Sue said, "Hit was a good thing there was a sideboard on the edge of thet wagon or thet rockin' cheer mighta fell right offen there."

She had a small girl in her lap, but all you could see of the little one was her face, because she was so wrapped up with a quilt. You could see part of one hand with a thumb stuck into her mouth. Her big brown eyes looked jest like a scared deer. It was difficult to tell what the older girl's age might have been.

She looked younger than the boys but simultaneously appeared older than her mother, the way she sat in that rocker, slowly rocking back and forth and holding on so tight to the little one as though she might be liable to fall out of the wagon or might could have been attacked by something or other. The older girl kept looking straight ahead as perhaps there might be something particularly special up the road. Every once in a while she'd shoo a fly away from the little girl's face.

Everybody got to talking except the girls, and the Bennetts found out the Hiltons were moving from the other side of Pierson, the county seat. The way they told it was that the landowner had cheated them twice out of most of their tobacco crop money.

Although the Bennetts never sharecropped, either by owning sharecropper land or sharecropping somebody else's land, they knew what the rules were with a few little different agreements between one fellow and another. But once the hands were shook on the arrangements, everyone was obliged to abide by the contract. Ordinarily the landlord supplied the house—rent-free—the seeds for the crops, what timber was needed for cooking and heating, and of course the land for the crops and even for a garden. The sharecropper would have to provide their own cow and mule. When everything was settled up at the end of the year the proceeds would be divided up, straight down the middle with the sharecropper getting half and the landlord keeping his half.

The Hiltons' previous landlord presumably kept more than his rightful share.

Uncle Jimmie Sue's mamma told the Hiltons to wait a couple of minutes for her to go get something. She grabbed a hold of George Dowell by the scruff of his collar and led him toward the house.

Directly they both came out with a bucket of water and a chocolate pie, which she'd just then taken out of the stove, and said, "Hyar, take this pie as a welcome present fer yoah new home. We can get the pie tin latah."

George Dowell, my grandpa, offered water to the newcomers and handed them the gourd dipper, which of course would ordinarily be shared with one person after another. The colored mother said, "Thanks for the watah, but we won't need the dippah, 'cause we got a tin cup fer our drinkin' watah."

She, no doubt, was aware how most white folks wouldn't dare put their lips on a drinking utensil where black folks' lips might've been.

Uncle Jimmie Sue went on, "You nevah seen such a look of surprise on the whole fambly's faces, when Mamma an' George Dowell offered them the pie an' watah. Even the girl in the rockin' chair smiled an' changed her look from down the road an' looked twarge me an' said, 'My name be Madeleen, an' this little one we call Sistah, but her name be Ruth named fer the Bible Ruth.'

"I don't know what I said. I'm not sure I said anything, I was so s'prised. There was some kind of mystery 'bout thet girl. I couldn't put my finger on it—not right then anyways. She wadn't dressed in no peculiar way. Of course, 'cause they wuz colored an' sharecroppers besides, they wouldn' be affordin' no fancy clothes."

Although it was a chilly day, and Madeleen had wrapped up her little sister so that a person could hardly see the child's face, her own wrapping's had seemed to have loosened up a little. Her dress had slipped down just a tad off of her right shoulder. You couldn't tell if she was just neglectful of her appearance or was somehow not bothered by cold weather. Jimmie Sue figured that she was just warm-natured.

Although he could sometimes be terribly forgetful, he somehow knew he was destined to remember that name—Madeleen— and the girl who belonged to the name. *An' why did the girl an' the name seem to go together?*

The way Uncle Jimmie Sue told it was that his mamma made sure that everyone was introduced, and when his little sister, Rosie, was introduced she waved to Ruth, who had already taken her thumb out of her mouth. The little girls waved to each other and Ruth's hand stopped waving in order to reach to that pie placed on the wagon seat between her folks.

Before anyone could stop her, she'd stuck her pointer finger into the pie meringue. Her mamma gave her hand a little pat and admonished her,

"Now, Sistah, you know we gotta wait fer ever'body to share at the same time. Ya know we don't like fer nobody to be a little piggy."

That poor little girl looked to the world like she was gonna cry, but when she drew back from the pie her whole hand was covered with meringue, because her mamma's little slap had knocked her hand into the pie topping. She then looked sure enough like she was gonna pucker up, til her mamma laughed and said, "Now, Sistah, what we gonna do 'bout thet smudged-up hand? You s'pose you oughta lick it clean?" And that's what she did, and everybody felt better about everything.

Later when the Bennetts were all talking about the pie incident, Great-Grandma Sue said, "It was right then an' there thet I knew what kinda folks, partickerly the parents, the Hiltons was."

Just before the new sharecropper neighbors left, Great-Grandpa said, "Yawl'll be crossin' a creek up ahead, an' thet'd be a good place to watah yoah mule an' cow. I'm sure the dogs will help theirselves to the watah." He went on to say, "Do yawl s'pose you could give us a hand next summer when 'baccer primin' time comes 'round? We could swap off work thet away, if yoah of the same notion."

They all agreed that swapping off work that way sounded like a good neighborly and business-like idea.

Uncle Jimmie Sue finished telling the story by saying, "The Hiltons thanked all of us, an' when they pulled away to head on twarge their new place, my head was plum' full of all kinds of confusions. *What was thet girl thinkin' all thet time, an' was she maybe a little slow, an' what was thet smile 'bout, an' why was I even worryin' 'bout it?*

Uncle Jimmie Sue admitted that he was really put out about his mamma giving away that chocolate pie, his most favorite pie in the *whole wide world*.

He finished his story by saying, "I then seen Rattler trottin' off right behind thet blue-tick bitch. I tried to whistle him back. He did look ovah his shoulder oncet, but never even broke his stride. He was really gettin' into this neighborly welcomin' thing.

"I knew he was like all them other stud dogs—after extendin' his welcome he'd be back home by supper time."

* * *

CHAPTER 3

At Grandpa's Church

Although there were several churches in the county, the one most of the Bennett family related to was the Sand Creek Primitive Baptist Church, which captured much of Granddaddy George Dowell's adult focus and energy. He was greatly respected in that faith community,

In the summer of 1940, Uncle Jimmy Sue and I attended one of the summer Association Meetings of the Upper Snow River Primitive Baptist Association, which would usually last a whole weekend, when folks and preachers from various Primitive Baptist congregations would be present—of course, there might be some unbelievers like Uncle Jimmie Sue and myself.

Scripture was normally the basis on which most of the sermons would be built—*Bible preachin'*. But there'd be no sermon notes or previous planning, for "If the Lord intends for you to have somethin' to say, He'll give the message to you at the appointed time an' hour," which was when a preacher would be asked by the eldest elder, "Has the Lord laid on yoah heart this mornin' somethin' for you to say?"

The idea that "abody would go to school off yonders sommers to study to be a preacher an' not wait on a word from the Lord, wadn't even worth mentionin'."

Quite often a dream might be a substitute for the actual scripture exposition, especially if it was a fresh dream, and more particularly if it was from the night right before the service. It was as though God A'mighty had directly conveyed to the preacher a message intended to be shared with the faithful flock as expeditiously as possible.

On that appointed Association Sunday, Brother Jarrell, one of the preachers on the pulpit platform, responded to the call to "come forward an' say somethin'." So he began to norate (narrate) a dream what had come to him in his sleep the night before.

The dream was about the "passin' on" of Brother George Dowell Bennett, who was also present on the dais and as grief-stricken as any of the other preachers or mourners worshiping that morning. The young preacher, having just recently answered "the call to preach" commenced in deepest sincerity.

"Las' night it come to me in a dream thet Brother Bennett had been called from our midst to the heavenly glory which he so wondrously deserves. (I couldn't decipher whether Brother Jarrell was thinking that Grandpa "richly" deserved to die or that he had earned the opportunity to "richly" enjoy the heavenly glory.)

"What will we do when Elder Bennett is gone from amongst us? When he'll no longer be present to console us in our times of grief . . . uh . . . or wipe away our tears of sorrow . . . uh . . . nor be hyar to counsel us when our way seems so dreary . . . uh . . . an' we cain't hardly find the strength to carry on . . . uh . . . . He won't be hyar to lead us in our prayers to the Lord nor lift his mighty voice in singin' the Lord's word . . ."

Everybody was sobbing, with some weeping right out loud just as though it was the sure enough funeral for Granddaddy, who was himself wiping his eyes; probably enjoying this unusual opportunity to attend his own funeral and to witness the grief it might provoke in the hearts of the "Beloveds" at the real thing later on.

After Grandpa's eulogy and a couple more Bible-preachin' elders, everybody exited the church house for the sacrament, which would be administered by the elders for the church members, who sat in chairs in a circle under a brush arbor. Uncle Jimmie Sue and I, along with the other non-Primitive Baptist attendees, stood outside the circle and looked on over the heads of the consecrated neighbors.

The first sacrament (pronounced with a long a as in sacred) was the Lord's Supper. The bread and wine were first partaken of by the ordained preachers then passed around the circle to the seated believers.

Even though we'd all eaten our fill of the various delectables at the "dinner on the grounds" the aromas of the fresh home-baked bread and aged home-brewed wine seemed to combine into a heavenly fragrance.

Grandpa George Dowell commenced the ritual by quoting—without the assistance of a book or the actual Bible— from the Gospel of Matthew: *And as they were eating, Jesus took bread and blessed it, and brake it, and said, "Take eat; this is my body."* The bread (although leavened, not unleavened like in the scripture) was baked by one of the women in the congregation, and the wine was brewed by one of the men members; several of the men had had experience in brewing of one sort or another. Uncle Jimmie Sue told me that and he should know. The wine was in a common chalice from which everyone drank, in the same fashion that people would drink water form the same gourd dipper at the spring or out of a common dipper in the water bucket in the kitchen or on the back porch.

Before the wine was passed Grandpa again quoted without the aid of a book, *And he took the cup, and gave thanks, and gave it to them, saying, "Drink ye all of this; for this is my blood from the new testament, which is shed for many for the remission of sins."* When the wine got to one older fellow, he gulped so much of it that the cup had to be replenished. I don't recall if it had to be "blessed" again. It was Ol' Mr. Evans who was quite reluctant to relinquish the vessel of heavenly spirits. Uncle Jimmie Sue and I reckoned that the old fellow was simply desirous of obtaining an extra portion of divine grace or he could have been interpreting literally the words of Jesus, *Drink ye all of this.*

Uncle Jimmie Sue said, "He probably could have thought instead of meaning, 'All of ye drink this.' It might could've meant 'Drink up all of this wine.' An' Mr. Evans was fulfilling his Christian obligation in this important ritual.

If partaking of the spirits would have been a badge of righteousness for Uncle Jimmie Sue, he would have qualified for sainthood a long time before then. Of course, I always thought he qualified without the benefit of the consecrated Primitive Baptist wine.

When the Lord's Supper was finished, certain appointed members got out towels and wash pans filled with water, which denoted the commencing of the Footwashing sacrament. Each member had the opportunity to take the wash pan and towel—kneeling in front of another church member—and then to proceed to take off the other's shoes and wash his or her feet . . . men washing men's feet and women with women.

For this sacrament Brother Jarrell quoted from St. John, *He riseth from supper, and laid aside his garments; and took a towel, and girded himself. After that he poureth water into a basin, and began to wash the disciples' feet, and to wipe them with the towel wherewith he was girded.* The preachers had taken off their shoes and "girded" themselves with towels. They hadn't 'laid aside their garments' as was quoted from the memorized scripture.

This was a time of reconciliation with neighbors without any mention of such a term. If you'd had a "fallin' out" with someone, this would be a good time to wash that person's feet in humility and forgiveness.

Uncle Jimmie Sue and I wondered if we might suggest to politicians that they set up such a practice of footwashings for themselves.

At the end of the Association weekend service on a Sunday evening on toward milking time, the Moderator would call the Association meeting to order and ask if everyone was "in fellowship" within the Upper Snow River Primitive Baptist Association.

Sometimes there may be some contention of one sort or another—interpersonal issues or maybe even some theological concern. Someone may have strayed from the Primitive Baptist way by contributing to another denominational church. The Primitive Baptists never took up offerings or collections in the church service, but might have some monetary issue concerning maintenance of the church building or upkeep of the cemetery, but usually all that was done by church members. However, I've noticed that some church members might slip a few dollars—a kind of love offering—into Grandpa's hand as they exited the church at the end of service.

After some discussion at an Association Meeting, any matter of concerns would be taken care of by the voices and votes of the members. When those matters were cleared up one of the elders would suggest a hymn to be sung. Then he, or another elder would heist (hoist) the tune. Sometimes it might take a couple of false starts until it was in the reachable range of all of the folks present.

On the Sunday of our visit, everyone seemed to be "in fellowship"—except—that is—the dispute Mr. Otis Newman had with his son-in-law, Mr. Lloyd Dickens. Everyone was well aware, at least according to Uncle Jimmie Sue, that there was bad blood between the two men—and had been ever since Lloyd had eloped many years before with Sue Newman, the apple of her father's eye and the intended for a more upstanding and prosperous fellow. Actually, the only contention was that Mr. Dickens had run his plow across the mutual property line onto Mr. Newman's hayfield.

Granddaddy handled the situation just as though it was a matter for a justice of the peace. He was, as a matter of fact, a justice of the peace, but his position as Moderator of the Association was the appropriate place to deal with such matters between members of the same fellowship rather than taking it to the "legal law." Granddaddy, being aware of their mutual contentiousness and the subject under consideration, merely praised both men on the fine way they farmed and told Mr. Newman to plant a row of muscadine vines at the property line so his son-in-law could plainly see where to turn the plow around.

Everyone was happy with the settlement, and they all knew that it wasn't really a matter of great consequence, but it gave Mr. Newman an opportunity to air his complaint in public, an opportunity for Mr. Dickens to accept judgment in a gracious manner and an opportunity for Granddaddy to play the role of Solomon in his wisdom.

As no further matters came forth to be dealt with, Granddaddy called on Brother Hiatt to start the song by "lining", which meant to chant the first line, then everyone sang the line, hanging onto the last note while Brother Hiatt intoned the next line. It went on and on like that until the hymn was finished. Only some of the elders had songbooks, and no one but the leader would need them anyways, because by "lining" the words, everyone could join in by simply musically repeating the chanted line.

No musical instrument, such as a piano or organ, would accompany the singing, for the only musical instrument allowed in the church was the human voice in either a speaking or singing mode.

The last hymn would be one with many verses to allow sufficient time for the departing ritual to be completed. Soon after the elder would "heist" a tune, one of the preachers would embrace another, after which the embracing would expand to the other elders, who would then, while still singing, leave the platform to embrace both members and non-members. The women, without any noticeable direction, would begin embracing each other just as the men were doing.

Granddaddy George Dowell embraced several men on his way to the back pew where Uncle Jimmie Sue and I were standing and singing with everyone else. When Granddaddy got to us he momentarily stopped singing and looked at his younger brother, Uncle Jimmie Sue, directly in the eyes, as they slowly embraced while Granddaddy continued to hold onto the open songbook.

Remembering the tale about Uncle Jimmie Sue's tongue on the frozen railroad track, I wondered if these two old brothers were forgiving each other for their younger boyhood pranks. On the other hand, the pranks, even then, were probably their particular way of showing affection and brotherly love for each other. Their soft sobs were less audible than many of the others around us, and even though Granddaddy had no trouble with outward shows of emotion, particularly in a church setting, Uncle Jimmie Sue was always reluctant to demonstrate any public affection.

The whole church was filled with soft sobs of conciliation, reconciliation and joy, quite different from the weeping earlier in the service when we all got to eulogize Granddaddy during Brother Jarrell's sharing of his funereal dream.

The embracing congregants—members and non-members—bade farewell to each other and to the Lord . . . a kind of congregational benediction, "Till we meet again at Jesus' feet."

After this shared experience, Uncle Jimmie Sue and I talked a lot about religion, particularly the beliefs and practices of the old Hardshell Primitive Baptists. I even suggested that I heard that he, himself, had been "under conviction" for some time, which I realized he wouldn't then own up to.

The Hardshell Baptists were a little more strict than the Softshell Baptist group. If one of the Hardshell preachers were to stray a bit by donating a bit of money to a church bell for the local Methodist church, he may very well be read out of the Hardshell Association until the others were convinced he'd repented of his actions—not so much for giving money to the Methodists, but for contributing to a devilish instrument to be used for the service of a church. Sometimes this period of penitence may last for years to convince the Hardshells that the penitent had come to understand and accept the rigors of the Hardshells. That was probably why they were called—actually what they called themselves—Hardshells.

Uncle Jimmie Sue denied being "under conviction," but he would, in our conversation, always work the talk around to "double predestination," and I could never tell whether he was deriding that doctrine or genuinely trying to understand it. Once I mentioned to him that although Presbyterians didn't believe in double predestination, they *did* believe in predestination. "Aw," he said, "Presbyterians are just Primitive Baptists moved to town." And come to think of it, I'd noticed only a few Presbyterian churches out in the country and no Primitive Baptist churches in town, so far as I recollected.

I often wondered what their earlier life had been like for Grandpa and Uncle Jimmie Sue with the rest of their brothers and sisters and cousins . . . what other childhood pranks they might've played on one another—I mean in addition to the one he told me earlier about his tongue getting stuck on the railroad track. I'm sure they took all the younger ones on snipe hunts and watermelon stealing, as well as sure enough hunting when they'd get big enough to carry something more lethal than slingshots.

The problem is, if "problem" it was, the boyishness of Uncle Jimmie Sue was never completely expunged.

* * *

CHAPTER 4

Madeleen

Even in his old age, Uncle Jimmie Sue would still play a joke on a person or whole congregations of folks if the opportunity presented itself. When he was close to ninety, I went with Dad to visit him one Sunday afternoon, while Uncle Jimmie Sue whittled and talked about whatever came to mind—ours or his. Suddenly he asked if we'd heard about the building expansion of Mill Creek Methodist Church across the county line. Dad said that, yes, he had understood that they were adding some Sunday School rooms. "How's the work goin'?"

"Oh, they jest got the underpinnin' finished." The underpinning is what people off the mountain would call the foundation.

After a bit more whittling a little point on a nubbin of a stick, Uncle Jimmie Sue says to Dad, "John, what does this 'mind you of?"

Dad says, "It looks kinda like a shuckin' peg."

Aunt Lydie, Uncle Jimmie Sue's wife says, "Hit 'minds me of a gamblin' stick."

While giving her a disapproving look, he says, as he turns the stick around to the other whittled pointy end, "Nope, hit jest 'minds one of t'other end."

We all kinda chuckled and Aunt Lydie said, "Jimmie Sue, quit yer cuttin' up."

After an appropriately effective amount of time, Uncle Jimmie Sue reintroduced the subject of the Mill Creek Church expansion. "You know, John, what some fool done last night?"

"What some fool done what, where, last night?"

"Well, what were we talkin' 'bout?"

"I 'member us talkin' 'bout shuckin' pegs an' gamblin' sticks."

"I mean 'bout the church."

"Oh, you mean Mill Creek Church?"

"Yeah! Some fool come by thar last night an' put up all kinds of empty whiskey bottles, wine bottles an' beer cans 'roun' thet underpinnin', an' when them nice church folks come to church this mornin', they seen thet filthy stuff."

"Uncle Jimmie Sue, who in the world, do you suppose, would do a terrible, nasty trick like that?"

Uncle Jimmie Sue, while looking down at the ground, commenced whittling real fast, as he quickly replied, "I ain't got no notion in the world."

We knew by his response that although he was well past the point of discretion—perhaps to the point of indiscretion—he had stopped by the church last night and lined up those cans and bottles on his way back home from carousing over to Pierson. We also realized anew that Uncle Jimmie Sue's sense of humor was such that whenever he played a joke on someone (or a whole congregation) he wouldn't even have to be present to appreciate it when the trigger of the joke trap was tripped. His own grandson allowed as how his grandpa "would play a joke or tell a funny story on a fellow even on his own deathbed if he was able to think it up an' could bring it off."

It was told on Uncle Jimmie Sue, when he was still just a teenager, that he was sweet on Madeleen Hilton, the colored girl, whose sharecropper family had moved to the Goins' tenant farm only a few months after his fifteenth birthday. They hadn't seen very much of each other—them going to separate schools, don't you know.

After their first meeting when Great-Grandma Sue had given the Hiltons the chocolate pie, which he'd certainly begrudged, he hadn't given Madeleen much more thought.

But all sorts of things started happening that summer when she and her family swapped work to help with the tobacco priming. This required extra hands, as the work was rather labor-intensive with the need for several men and boys to be pulling off the tobacco leaves in the field and someone driving the mule from the field to the barn and back to the field.

Then several people—quite often the women and children—would hand bunches of leaves to the stringer, who'd be tying the leaves onto a four-foot-long stick to be hung on horizontal poles in the barn to be fired up later by the flues on the ground level of the barn.

To those folks not acquainted with tobacco farming, it might be helpful for them to know that there are two main ways of harvesting the crop. The air-cured way is, at the proper time, to cut the whole stalk, which is placed with several other stalks on a lath and propped up for a while in the fields. They're then brought to a large barn where they're hung for weeks to air-dry. The barn would have long vertical boards on the sides, which could be opened for the air to circulate through the barn. This method was a whole lot less labor-intensive than the flue-cured bright leaf tobacco, which needed a lot of hand work not only prior to the curing process, but also required focused attention during the firing.

It would take a couple of days and nights of constant fire-tending to complete the curing of the bright-leaf tobacco. The stringers had to be real careful in stringing the leaves, for if a leaf, while being fired, was to fall on the hot flue pipes it would catch fire and, more than likely burn down the whole barn. You'd then not only lose the barn full of tobacco but the barn, as well, which was made of flammable hand-hewn logs. This'd be a real catastrophe for the farm family where this might happen, as one barn of tobacco might be as much as ten percent of that year's whole crop.

One summer one of Mr. Nelson's barns burned and a couple of weeks later, lightning struck their packhouse, burning it down with it full of twelve firings of cured tobacco waiting to be taken off to market.

The Primitive Baptists said it was the Lord's will and "nothin' more need be said 'bout it." The holy-roller Pentecostals allowed as how Mr. Nelson's "sinful ways brung it on his ownself, an' it was a retribution from the Lord." The Methodists didn't say much but did take up a generous 'love offerin'.

It was at one of those all-night barn vigils that Wade Bowen had begun to rib Jimmie Sue about Madeleen, as he'd been seen taking particular notice of her when they were all stringing tobacco at the ridge top barn that day and talking, laughing and joshing with one another. That night, at the firing, Wade said, "You know, Jimmie Sue, they say thet Madaleen's a high-yaller gal."

Jimmie Sue headed straight for that young fellow, catching him around the waist and knocking him into the woodpile, which was being used for the firing. Rolling him over in the dirt, Jimmie Sue began pummeling him in the face with both fists, "You gonna take thet back now?" Jimmie Sue was a better fighter, so Wade took back what he'd said about Madaleen or her heritage.

Even if a person couldn't help what family he or she'd been born into, it was still an insult to be called a "high-yaller," (a scurrilous word for mulatto) because that was even a rung beneath being "colored," as far as the prejudices of that day and time went.

The Hiltons were somewhat of a mystery there in the mountains where few colored folks could be found. Well, after all, there had been no plantations requiring slave labor. It was gossiped that the Hiltons were descendants of runaway slaves before Lincoln's time and had found refuge in the mountains. Even though their lives in the hollows of the mountains were certainly hardscrabble just like all the white folks, at least they were free to do things their own way, follow their own beliefs and associate with whoever was pleased to associate with them. There was a rather flexible code of behavior between the whites and coloreds, so lots of work, music and arbor church meetings were shared.

It was also rumored that the reason the Hiltons' forbears had escaped was that one of their great-grandmas had been taken advantage of by the white boy of the plantation house, and she and her colored boyfriend had escaped to the mountains. The plantation master didn't go after them because he didn't want any scandal about him or his own family: for after all he was a respected deacon in the church. All that was just gossip, but it kind of explained how the family come to be called *high-yaller,* which would be a term white folks might use to put down some coloreds they didn't like. But the term, *White Boy,* was a term the Hiltons had carried down for several years and would use against any uppity white boy.

One day at the tobacco priming everyone, including the Hiltons and other neighbors, were pitching in to help with the labor-intensive work at the Bennetts. When the men had finished priming (pulling) the tobacco in the fields, they had come to the barn to help with the rest of the stringing and housing into the barn.

Of course, this was always a great time for talking, gossiping and generally joking around. Jimmie Sue, as usual, was kind of the center of attention while telling stories and picking on the younger kids, but still stringing more hands (handfuls) than anybody else.

He started joshing with Madeleen, the oldest Hilton girl, who was taking his bantering quite seriously. You see, she didn't know him very well yet, and she took his tomfoolery as though he really meant it.

When he got onto religion, he got a real rise out of her. She was completely serious about the Lord's will, sounding almost like the old Hardshell Primitive Baptist preachers. Jimmie Sue knew that she went with her family to the colored Pentecostal Church; and besides, the old Hardshell Baptists didn't "take in" any of the colored.

Somehow or other, Jimmie Sue and Madeleen started arguing about "livin' the rest of your life." She said, "White Boy, you don't know iffen you gonna live the rest of yoah life. Only the Lord be knowin' thet."

Jimmie Sue became a little serious by explaining, "Why, Madeleen, when you die, that's the end of your life and that's the rest of it."

She shot right back, "White Boy, you don't know if thet's supposed to be the end of yoah life. Nobody knows the 'day ner the hour.' Only the Good Lord knows, an' he ain't tellin' nobody—not even white folks."

Jimmie Sue could tell that Madaleen was so concerned about the Lord's will and knowledge that she didn't accept the logic of what *he* was saying, so he continued the teasing banter by asking Bill, the Goins middle boy, who was also handing the tobacco leaves, "Bill, do you want to live the rest of yoah life?"

Bill, picking up on the fun of the game, answered right back in a make-believe pleading voice, "Please, Jimmie Sue, will you please let me live the rest of my life?"

"Okay, Bill, I'm assurin' you here an' now that I give my permission fer you to live the rest of yoah life."

"No, White Boy," insisted Madeleen, as she jumped off the bench where she'd been handing tobacco, waving her two hands of tobacco in the air like pom-poms, and almost dancing her horror. "You can't tell Bill ner nobody else whether or not they kin live the rest of their life! Only the Lord kin tell, an' he certainly ain't been talkin' to you."

Her agitated state and determination made Jimmie Sue almost regret the polemics he'd set up for her, so he tried again to explain that when a person dies, he's lived the rest of his life, but Madeleen wasn't having anything to do with his apparent logic, as she had gone too far down (or up) the road of theological explication so that human reason no longer applied. After all, how can the finite creature explain or even understand the infinite God A'Mighty, who was her guide in all matters?

So now Madeleen went on the attack, asking Jimmie Sue if he had yet been saved. In order to avoid another debate with her—he'd begun to admire her spunk as well as her dark good looks—he lied, "Yeah, I was saved at the revival meetin' las' summer over to Pierson at the Missionary Baptist Church."

Cletus, Madeleen's, younger brother, interrupted. "Madeleen's not got the Holy Ghost, but she be tryin' to git it."

Jimmie Sue, welcoming this distraction, was rather quizzical about "tryin' to." "What you mean by 'tryin' to'?"

Madeleen saw her chance to expound on scripture and enlighten "white boy" on the ways of the Lord. "The scripture say 'Tarry ye here and watch.' It means to watch fer the Holy Ghost."

"Now how an' where do I wait fer the Holy Ghost to appear?"

"You not be waitin', you be tarryin', singin' 'Jesus, Jesus, Jesus, Jubilee, Jubilee, Jubilee' fer seven days an' seven nights."

He was truly intrigued but didn't know how to respond. His silent confusion was intercepted by his new religion teacher, as she took the inquisition a notch higher. "White Boy, how did you be gittin' the Holy Ghost?"

"You mean how did I get saved?"

"Did you go up to the pulpit an' give the preacha yoah han'?"

Appreciating the easy answer she had provided for him, he knew that was usually the way it was done, as he had seen it at the revival services when the preacher would give the altar call to "Come forward an' extend the hand of fellowship in the Lord."

He declared with a sigh of relief, "Yeah, that's what I done."

Madeleen smelled blood as she moved in for the kill, "White Boy, thet won't do atall." Jimmy Sue stopped stringing tobacco for a moment, wondering where she was headed now, as she thrust into the heart of the matter. "You can't jest walk up an' give the preacha yoah han', you gotta git down on yoah knees an' give the Lord yoah heart."

He was completely bumfuzzled, not knowing how to return an answer to that, but he did know he'd lost in this quick game of religion and wits—a rare experience for him. He was developing more than an intellectual or even a religious respect for her.

But . . . she's colored!

The second night after the tobacco priming, the leaves were "in order" (ready for the firing). Jimmie Sue, who would soon be sixteen, was put in charge of the firing, a job which he always relished. After the milking and when supper was finished he headed, with several more boys, to the barn to start the fire in the flues.

At first, he put a small pile of wood shavings and straw in the mouth of each of the two flues. He had Bill stack several pieces of split litardknot (lightwood pine knot) kindling on top of that and told Jesse to fetch a few sticks of wood the size of stove wood, which he then put on top of the smaller flammable tinder.

He could have started the fire a whole lot quicker if he'd poured some lamp oil on it, but he hadn't forgotten the lesson he received the summer before when he'd used kerosene for just such a purpose. It took a couple of months for his eyebrows to grow back and his burnt hair to quit stinking.

With a sliver of wood he'd lit from the barn lantern, he lighted each of those little piles of shavings. Soon the yellow-red flames were wrapping themselves around the stove wood. Only then, did he begin to slide the four-foot-long logs of wood into the flues.

Once the logs began to catch a little fire and sputtered to life, he assigned different jobs to each member of his task force, who might have been thought of more as conspirators. Emmett was to go get a dozen of "roasen years" (ears of corn) from ol' man Taylor's corn patch. Lige (Elijah) was to go "Git some of them little tommytoe (cherry) tomatoes from the Tedder garden patch. Walt and Roy were assigned to get two of the best watermelons from over to the Welch's. "Be sure an' thump them just right, so's you know they's good an' ripe."

Of course all of these goodies could be found on the Bennett place, but somehow or other, all the boys knew everything would taste a whole heap better if they were absconded from some other fellow's field—particularly if you didn't get caught and told on to your daddy, which would mean a dance on the end of a stiff birch tree limb.

By time it had started getting dark and all the victuals had been fetched, Jimmie Sue saw Cletus, Madeleen's younger brother, peering from around a white oak. Jimmie Sue yelled at him, "Come on out from behind that white oak, Cletus, we just beginnin' to roast up some years of corn on the flues, an' after a little while we gonna bust open these hyar two big watermelons. Surely yoah partial to some ripe watermelons. "

Cletus was a bit reluctant to join in with the white boys, for after all he was colored, an' if he was caught, his whole family would've suffered in some manner. It didn't seem to matter to the boys—either white or colored—that they had different colored skin. They all knew, whether acknowledging it or not, that they were all just farm boys, which meant that skin color wasn't nearly as important as some grownups made out it was.

It wasn't that Cletus was so shy to come on out and join the goings-on, it was that he was still thinking about that joke Jimmie Sue had played on him just the night before, when he stayed over to the Bennett place a little too long, playing mumbly-peg with jackknives on the front porch with Jimmie Sue and his brothers.

They'd been playing by the light of a barn lantern, and not paying much attention to the darkness coming on. When Cletus realized how dark it was, he jumped up and said, "Law me, hit's plumb black dark an' Mamma be tannin' my hide if I don't git on in home."

Simon, Jimmie Sue's older brother, said, "Cletus, doncha think yoah tan enough?" Jimmie Sue glowered at Simon and said, "Thar wadn't no call to say thet, Simple Simon."

Backing away from Simon's lunging fist, Jimmie jumped off the end of the porch right beside Cletus, who'd already started walking toward home. Thinking he might get a peek at Madeleen, said, "Cletus, don't you think I oughta walk over to home with ya'?'

Cletus, trying real hard to appear to be as fearless as any of the older white boys, said, "Naw, I reckon I'm big enough to go by myself, an' take keer of any haint what be down by the swamp."

Jimmie Sue, sensing the opportunity for a little fun, says, "Oh, Cletus, speaking of the haints. I hear thet the Goins' boys heard somethin' kinda skeery down there last week."

Cletus's eyes bugged out. "Whut did they hear?"

"They said it sounded like a owl...."

"I be afeared of no owls."

"They said thet hit seemed like the owl talked to them."

"Aw, a owl cain't talk."

"Hit seemed to be askin' 'em somethin'. They couldn't quite make out whut it wuz."

Cletus stretched himself up to his full five foot two inches and declared. "I be takin' keer of any ol' owl." and picked up his jackknife, folding it up and pocketing it with great deliberation, faking a big boy stance, off toward home.

In the meantime, Jimmie Sue, unbeknownst to Cletus or any of the others, had slipped around the house and into a grove of large chestnut trees right by the footpath, where Cletus would be traveling. He hid behind a mountain laurel bush and saw Cletus—no longer swaggering—coming closer. As Cletus got parallel to the laurel bush, Jimmie Sue imitated a hoot owl with a spooky, tremulous "Whooooo!" Cletus stopped abruptly; his bare feet glued to the ground.

Then another "Whooooo!"

Cletus stood his ground, not out of bravado but of sheer terror, because he'd never heard a owl quite like this. His feet felt like being tarred to the earth.

"Whooooo! . . . . Whooooooo . . . . Who are you?"

"I be Cletus Hilton!" The full impact of the question seemed to unleash his feet, as he flew in the direction of home.

Later, when Jimmie Sue owned up to Cletus that he'd played the owl spook on him, Cletus laughed a little, but acted somewhat skittish toward Jimmie Sue for a while after that. When asked if he fell in the creek on his run home, Cletus said, "Ah didn't see no creek ner rocks nuther. Ever'thin jest kinda got outta my way."

Jimmie Sue had invited Cletus, who was only twelve, over to the tobacco firing as a kind of peace offering, and also to maybe gettin' a bit closer to Madeleen. Cletus was delighted to accept the offer, but he wasn't sure how much he could trust Jimmie Sue or the other boys to not pick on him in some fashion or other. They were all somewhat older than him and besides that they were all white.

He felt assured that Jimmie Sue would protect him from the others, but was not quite so sure about Jimmie Sue, himself.

As Cletus crept from behind the white oak at the barn firing, Jimmie Sue said, "Cletus, did you come over hyar all alone?"

"Naw, Madeleen come with me."

"Well, I sure don't see her."

"Oh she be goin' on back home."

Just then Jimmie Sue saw two intense eyes of some night critter, at about the level of where a colored girl's eyes might have been, if she was peering into the secret lives of boys cavorting at the tobacco barn when they'd be pretending to be working or doing something useful.

She was rather intrigued to see that the boys were just doing everyday normal things—a couple of them playing marbles, one of them putting the roasen years on the outside end of the flue for cooking, all of them trying to learn to chew some home-twist tobacco without grimacing or retching.

The chickens, roosting in the chicken house close by had settled down and quietened for the night. The dogs—it must have been seven of them—had just come to the barn from having chased something over Maple Ridge, so they were still pantin' but lookin' for a comfortable spot in the powdery dust in front of the fire for to turn in for the night.

There was nothing particularly unusual about the scene, except the light from the two lanterns which were hanging from one of the overhang rafters. They cast spooky shadows on everything; whenever anyone would walk by the light, the shadows would shorten, then lengthen, leaning out precariously from the source of the light.

As innocent as the activities might have been, the dancing light from the lantern flames and the floating shadows could easily have been mistaken for a gathering of a coven of witches—young male witches at that.

"Well," Jimmie Sue yelled at his fellow warlocks, "I gotta go to the bushes." (Which of course meant that he was answering a call of nature.) As actual fact, he didn't care whether the boys heard him or not, but he sure wanted Madeleen to hear, because he had some scheme brewing in his brain to share with her.

As he disappeared around the far edge of the barn, Madeleen scrouged a little closer to the huge trunk of the beech tree, seemingly just another knot on the log, if a body was to see her. But she was pretty sure all the boys, and especially Jimmie Sue, thought she'd gone on back home.

When Jimmie Sue had rounded the barn he could see Madeleen plastered to the shadow side of the beech tree.

Although he was wearing his straw hat, he was still barefooted. Of course, the straw hat is an important practical item of any country boy's wardrobe—particularly to ward off the burning sun rays in the daytime and, for the tobacco farming boys, to keep the tobacco sap out of their hair when they're priming the tobacco in the field. The hat was a kind of symbol that the hat wearer was growing into manhood with all of its privileges, if not its responsibilities. So Jimmie Sue wore his straw hat most of the time—even to church; though not inside the church, itself, of course.

As Jimmie Sue was going over in his mind the events of the past couple of days, a plan fairly floated into his consciousness. He figured that if he could creep up behind Madeleen without her hearing him—after all he was barefooted, which would make it easier to accomplish his plan—he'd put his hands over her eyes and yell, "Guess who?"

This of, course, would be the first time he would have ever touched her, and as it was just an everyday kind of young folks' game, it shouldn't be considered offensive. In fact, ordinarily a person who'd have their eyes covered that way, would consider it a kind of flattery, as the prankster was paying special attention to the chosen prey.

He crept slowly across the damp ground, while thanking the good Lord that the dry fall leaves hadn't fallen yet to rustle under his feet and hoping that there weren't any bamboo briers on the ground along the path to his quarry.

Neither Madeleen nor the boys were thinking much about Jimmie Sue. They probably, all, just reckoned he was off in the bushes relieving himself.

But Madeleen was paying real close attention to how Cletus, her little brother, was being treated by the white boys. Continuing to monitor Cletus's precarious situation, she had begun to relax a little and release her grasp on the beech tree, which was seemingly being held up by her tight grip.

Ever so quietly, Jimmie Sue crept up behind Madeleen.

She thought she heard something, just as she released her hold on the tree.

Sensing that she might turn around before his plan was to work out, he clasped his hands over her eyes and yelled, "Guess . . . . ?"

He didn't have a chance to finish " . . . . who?", as she fell backward onto him while screaming like a banshee.

Cletus dropped the ear of corn he was gnawing on. Walt dropped one of the watermelons he was about to cut. Roy was poking one of the logs in the flue, but was so startled that he knocked some of the fire out of the flue onto the ground there under the tobacco barn shed, scattering burning embers out onto a pile of oily rags.

The dogs started barking, and the chickens roused up with the rooster leading a chorus of him crowing and the hens cackling.

It sounded and looked for a second there that all hell had broken loose with the beginning of a conflagration with the burning logs out on the ground smoking up the whole area; all the boys either dropping whatever it was they were doing or else standing like statues enveloped by the whirling smoke and lit up by the weird light from the lanterns. Their facial expressions bore ghoulish masks of dancing light through the swirling smoke.

If a body had walked up onto the scene they'd have been for certain in the midst of a bunch of demons or at least the haints the Goins' boys had talked about.

When Madeleen fell onto Jimmie Sue, he grabbed the closest thing that was in reach, which happened to be Madeleen. With his arms around her he stumbled backward, trying to maintain balance for the two of them.

Still shrieking and with arms flailing, she grabbed his arms, unclasping them from across her breast and turned around with eyes glaring. She took one step back to maintain her own balance. Then reaching toward Jimmie Sue she let fly a slap, missing his face but catching the brim of his hat which spun into the air like a milkweed seed being picked up by a gust of wind. It then floated down softly toward the earth, pretty close to the pile of smoldering logs and old rags.

The hat was okay, but Jimmie Sue, who'd fallen backward over a rock, was so stunned that he laid transfixed as Madeleen stood over him, fixing her piercing eyes—filled with some kind of passion—on his eyes for a good ten seconds—almost like a ten-second kiss—then twirled and ran like a deer toward home.

All the boys, including Cletus, saw the old dumb-show acted out by the two unfortunate actors, culminating in the hasty exit of the heroine. Then everybody quieted down: the boys, the dogs and even the chickens.

After all that excitement the rest of the night was fairly uneventful, after they'd put the burning log back into the flue, finished off all the victuals and curled up in various spaces and shapes, wrapped up in old worn-out quilts, to get some sleep. Of course, one of the boys would have to get up about every hour to tend the fire—poke it up and put a couple more logs on to keep the barn hot enough to cure the hanging leaves inside.

After doing this, the fireman, whichever one it might be, would go in to check the thermometer hanging down in the middle of the barn to see if the temperature was about right. Any one of the boys would relish the chance to do the temperature checking, because the tobacco smelled so good—not like the green tobacco in the field, which would sometimes give a fellow a headache from the putrid smell. Also, it was mighty welcome on a coolish night to go for a few minutes into the warm barn.

Even though barn-firing always seemed like an opportunity for the young fellows to do some things—often pranky things—outside the judgment eyes of the parents, all of them were well aware that milking time would come early the next morning and there'd be, more than likely, field work to be done all next day.

Jimmie Sue had already stashed his quilt right on the top of the cord of wood destined for the barn flues. A cord of wood is stacked four feet high and eight feet long with small (about 4 to 6 inch in diameter) four-foot-long logs, which served as the fuel for the tobacco curing.

Feeling a bit like the King of the Mountain on top of the stack of wood, Jimmie Sue looked out from his mountaintop and surveyed his realm of subjects: six unruly mountain boys, seven variously-talented hound dogs and even a chicken house full of working chickens.

Arranging the logs for his makeshift bed, he doubled the old worn-out quilt to serve as a comforting barrier between his tired body and the rough bark and knots of the logs. Within only minutes he was fast asleep, as were all the other boys and dogs . . . an' chickens.

There was no more physical activity at the barn that night—aside from checking on the barn interior temperature or the occasional call of nature. The snores of the boys, and even an occasional groan from a dog, created a harmonized chorus, joined by the regular night sounds of crickets, frogs and other sporadic sounds like those of the occasional screech owl—a real screech owl.

Jimmie Sue was a dreamer, quite often relating his dreams to the other boys. I don't mean day-dreaming, although he imbibed in quite a bit of that—but I mean night-dreaming. Maybe it was the influence of the Primitive Baptist preachers who focused much of their sermonizing on dreams—not only on the dreams recorded in the scriptures, but their own personal dreams and what they might mean.

His grandpa usually related dreams about heavenly things, but Jimmie Sue's dreams were mostly about everyday things with unusual twists and unfortunate circumstances. That night at the barn-firing was the same but different.

In his dream Jimmie Sue found himself on the lower edge of the swimming hole, all alone, which was kind of unusual, but he was ready to take a plunge into the cool water, having shucked off his overalls and brogans. However, his hat was still in place.

When he glanced up at the upper end of the swimming hole, where the water was shallow and rather marshy with cattail reeds growing at the edge, he saw a group of girls dressed like those pictures in the book he'd read, *The Arabian Nights*. One of them was commanding all of the attention, as though the others were there as her servants. He recollected that kind of scene in that book.

The main girl wore a red veil which hid the lower part of her face; a blouse which came just below her breast; a little black panty thing which covered her hips and the lower part of her torso—leaving a wide bare midriff. The pants to her panty thing were made of real thin white material, even see-through, so you could see her legs right down to her shoes which were only sandals but with curled up pointy toes. Her skin was exactly the color of brown like Madeleen's, but her hair was cut different.

There seemed to be some commotion in the marsh, as one of the girls waded into the water to retrieve something floating there in the reeds. She picked up a basket and brought it to the main girl, who carefully took a wrapped-up package out of it.

Jimmie Sue could see that it was a baby, looking to be about three months old, wrapped up in a little blue blanket. The main girl put the baby up to her shoulder, where it faced Jimmie Sue who could see that the baby saw him and smiled.

All of the brown-skinned girls started walking away with the baby, who kept looking at Jimmie Sue with his blue eyes—the baby's blue eyes. Though Jimmie Sue had blue eyes too which seemed to go just right with his red hair.

When he woke up he realized that he'd been dreaming the Moses in the bulrushes story. He had always been kind of fascinated by that Bible story and the whole slavery thing down in Egypt. In the dream he never did jump into the swimming hole. He just kept sitting there wondering what all that was about. He was pretty sure that only the baby saw him, but it wouldn't really have mattered anyways would it, if the girls had seen him naked, 'cause it was just a dream after all?

Well, the next evening, after the big barn hullabaloo the night before and that curious dream, Jimmie Sue sauntered over to the Hilton place to maybe, if possible, apologize to Madeleen—that is if she was to give him half a chance to even speak to her.

* * *

CHAPTER 5

Visit to Madeleen's

On the way over to Madeleen's, Jimmie Sue wondered what-in-all he would say to make up for what he'd done to her the night before. Though he knew it wasn't the worst thing he could've done to a girl he barely knew, he was certainly aware that it had upset her.

He didn't really have to think of the way to get over to the Hiltons', as he simply stayed on the path that went down by the swimming hole and up to the top of the next ridge. Just ambling along, he kept going over in his own mind what he might say and even had begun talking to himself as though there was someone walking beside him.

Madeleen, I'm awful sorry fer upsettin' you las' night, like I done.

For some reason that didn't seem right—too direct somehow.

Madeleen, you oughten've been aspyin' *on the boys las' night the way you done.*

That wasn't right, neither, as it seemed to be faulting her for the whole thing.

I know what I'll do, I'll just walk right up and say what comes to mind. Anyways I'm not usually short on ideas of somethin' to say.... Yep thet's just what I'll do.

By this time the path had led down by the edge of the swimming hole and not noticing what he was doing or where he was stepping he nearly stepped on a five-foot-long copperhead moccasin snake, which seemed to be appointed there to greet him.

He wouldn't have seen it even then, if it hadn't have begun rustling the dry grass a little as it started slithering out of danger's way its own self. Jimmie Sue was startled a little but not really afraid of any snakes, so he stooped down and picked up the snake by its tail. Of course it tried coiling up to bite his hand, but it was too high to bend way up there to his hand—much too high to double his length for a venomous bite.

Jimmie Sue started swinging the snake over his head like a cowboy lasso. After several circles he let it fly through the air right into the swimming hole. He thought, *I'll have some fun with the other fellers 'bout thet snake when they come down to the creek. I wonder what thet scaredy-cat Emmnet will think 'bout thet.*

As he approached the Hiltons', he saw Cletus sitting on the front porch, leaning against a porch post, and just gazing into the distance. The porch was attached to a ramshackle cabin, which'd been whitewashed real nice by Levi, Madeleen's daddy, and her brothers. Madeleen wasn't anywheres to be seen. "Lo, Cletus! You seem to be okay, after last night's doin's."

"What you mean doin's?"

"Well, weren't they a lot of doin's last night—what with the barn-firin' doin's, the vittle doin's, the jokin' doin's?"

Cletus asked, "What it be 'bout the Madeleen doin's?"

Jimmie Sue was happy that Cletus brought up the subject of Madeleen. "Yeah! How Madeleen be doin' now?"

"She not be too happy."

"She unhappy still with me?"

"I don' know. . . . It be 'bout her time, ya' know?"

"No, I don't know. What you mean, 'her time'?"

"Well, ya' know, a girl's time."

"A girl's time fer what?"

"Ya' know thet month thing."

"Oh, you talkin' 'bout that? How you know 'bout that?"

"Jimmie Sue, you don' give me credit fer knowin' nothin'."

"Well, do you know where Madeleen is right now?"

"She be behin' the house."

"What she be doin' back there?"

"She be splittin' stovewood."

"Why she doin' that? . . . I thought that wuz yoah job."

"She say she want to do somethin' vigrous-like—somethin' moah sweaty than jest warshin' the dishes."

It was then that Jimmie Sue noticed the sound for the first time of the pounding of the ax and the splitting snap of good hardwood. "Cletus, maybe I jest go back there to get a look-see at what'n all's agoin' on with Madeleen."

Not paying him much attention, Cletus responded, "Good luck!"

Jimmie Sue moseyed around the corner of the house and come up onto the sight of Madeleen heisting the ax over her head and slamming the blade in true-center of the piece of wood. She could chop wood like a full-grown man.

As he came up behind her, he wasn't about to dis-remember those doin's of last night when he slipped up and grabbed her from behind. He stopped now in mid-step, not just because of his shenanigans then, but somehow she looked different today.

She was wearing faded old frayed and patched overalls, just like Jimmie Sue and her brothers, except she did have a pretty blouse with ruffles at her wrists. Ordinarily she wouldn't be seen in public with boy's clothing. Jimmie Sue knew she could do as much work as her brothers or any of the other boys, but he could never ignore her fetching beauty.

After studying this apparition for just a second, he noticed her difference of appearance was her hair. Without considering his effect on her, who up to this point was focused on her wood-splitting job and completely unaware of his presence, he simply yelled out, "Madeleen!"

Swinging around with the ax arcing over her head, she belligerently yelled, "White Boy, don't you be slippin' up on my backside agin. With this hyar ax in my han' I ain't bein' skeered of yo' no moah."

"There be no need to be skeered of me, Madeleen. I've . . . ."

"What you mean not be skeered of you? After last night . . . ."

"I come over to 'pologize to you fer that."

Softening a bit, she countered, "To 'pologize . . . ?

"Las' night I didn't go fer to skeer you . . . . I was jest funnin' aroun'."

"Well, White Boy, I be tellin' you right now, hit shore warn't no fun fer me when you slip up behin' me, puttin' yo' greazy paws all ovuh mah face like you done."

"Oh, I know thet now . . . an' I figgered it out real quick then . . . . I reckoned since you had stayed lookin' on after you'd walked Cletus over there to the barn, thet maybe you'd wanted to talk or join in with the vittles we had."

"Thet surely were a quare way to find out 'bout thet."

"Yeah, I guess it was . . . . But I got another question fer you."

"Whut thet be?"

"What happen' to yoah hair?"

"Oh, thet!"

"Yeah . . . . it looks like somethin' I seen recen'ly."

"Seen? Seen where?"

He didn't dare divulge his dream to her so he just said, "Oh I seen hair like thet in a book sommers."

"A book? . . . What kinda book?"

"Oh, a book like the Bible with a picture of them 'Gyptians."

"You mean like thet Moses story?"

A little alarmed that she had the exact reference to his dream, he asked, "So you know thet story?"

She responded "Acourse, but I be s'prised *you* know the Bible thet good."

"Oh, hit warn't 'zactly the Bible story I be thinkin' 'bout."

"Whut be it then?"

He was really backed into a corner now. It seemed to be Madeleen's ability to best him with every encounter they had. "Oh, hit was jest somethin' thet come to mind . . . las' night."

"Las' night when you spooked me?"

"Well, no. Hit was jest kinda las' night sometime."

"You know, White Boy, you sometime seem bamfoozled or somehow bedazzled."

Bedazzled he was and increasingly so, as she stood her ground regardless of the circumstance. It was then he doubly realized how traumatic last night's event must've been for her, as she had so completely lost her usual composure.

Hoping to ingratiate himself a bit with her, he suggested, "Maybe you tell me 'bout thet Moses story."

"Well, you know 'bout little Moses bein' the grandson of Levi?"

"Oh yeah!" (He didn't have a clue about the family of Moses. It might as well have been Adam as Levi).

"An' speakin' of Levi you may 'member my Daddy's name be Levi?"

In order to become a part of this biblical exposition, Jimmie Sue contributed, "So is one of your brothers named Moses?"

"You jest be smart-alecky now. Moses was grandson of Levi—not son."

By this time Madeleen had sat on the chopping block holding the ax handle between her knees with the ax head on the wood chips on the ground pointing directly toward Jimmie Sue who had just sat hunkering (squatting) facing Madeleen. She continued with her Bible lesson. "An' you may 'member 'bout when Moses was 'dopted an' growed up an' he led the Hebrew chillun, who'd been slaves down in Egyp' lan' . . . ."

"You still ain't tole me 'bout yoah hair."

"Whut be wrong with mah hair?"

"Nothin' be wrong . . . . It jest look so diffrunt."

She stated, "You already tole me thet."

He still wanted to know. "Yeah, but why is it so diffrunt now?"

"Mamma wanted to make me feel bettah, so she sez, 'How 'bout me fix up yoah hair?' So 'I say yeah thet be fine.' So she say, 'How you want it to look?' I say maybe like thet Bible story, which you jest now 'minded me of."

This really spooked Jimmie Sue for both of them to be thinking about the same story about that Egyptian girl. Also now wanting to cut short this Bible lesson, he interrupted her. "Would you like to rest a spell an' let me split up some of them knotty pieces of stovewood fer you?" (knowing full well how tough it was to split through those hickory knots).

"White Boy, you be fergettin' somethin'."

"What would thet be?"

"I's colored!"

"Well, good godamnit, how can I ferget it when you be 'mindin' me ever' minute?"

"You come over here to make up with me fer whut you done las' night, an' now you slap me in the face."

"I ain't teched you. What you mean I slap you in the face?"

"You use the Lord's name like thet, you might as well slap me squar' in the face an' spit on me 'sides."

"Well you riled me up tellin' me to 'member you colored, when you keep 'mindin' me alla time."

"How, I be doin' thet?"

"By callin' me White Boy. My name is James, an' you know it . . . . I don't be callin' you Colored Girl, do I?"

"No, an' Ah 'preciate thet . . . Jeems."

"Might jest as well call me Jimmie Sue, like ever'body else."

"Thet be fine, . . . Jimmie Sue."

Warming up a little, he said, "Good! . . . Then thet's settled!"

Sitting there for several moments in silence, facing each other, Madeleen broke the spell. "You wanta hear more 'bout Moses?"

"Oh yeah, but hit'll have to be another time, 'cause hit's time fer me to get to home fer the milkin'."

"Yeah . . . . well I be acceptin'."

"Acceptin'? . . ."

"Yoah 'pology." She'd caught him red-faced and cornered again. "Thet is why you come ovah, weren't it?"

"Yeah . . . . oh yeah . . . . thets' why I come over today, jest specially to make up fer skeerin' you las' night, which I didn't really go fer to . . . ."

"Jimmie Sue, you already said all thet."

"Yeah, so's I did! Well now, you take keer now."

"Keer of what?"

Getting a little tired of her besting him he snapped back, "You know ver' well, what I mean."

"Yeah I do. . . . An' yo' take keer . . . of yo'self."

Although he headed toward home to do the milking, he wasn't sure what it was that had just happened.

Whenever Jimmie Sue would be over toward the Hiltons', he'd make out like he'd come to talk with Madeleen's daddy, Levi, about the crops or with her brothers, Clyde and Cletus, about their hound dogs. But eventually he'd introduce something that might touch on religion.

It was then that Madeleen, who was usually quiet up to that point, would begin to get a gleam in her eye, 'cause that was a subject she tenaciously cared about.

She could surely talk religion. Jimmie Sue didn't want to get trumped like so many times before, and he had come that time to try to apologize, but at other times he seemed to take an uncommon glee in inciting her to flail into an argument with her jaw flapping, arms waving with her whole body trembling.

Great-Grandma Sue had told Jimmie Sue that it didn't look right for him to be stopping by over to the Hiltons' so much, talking to the coloreds the way she'd heard he'd been doing.

What had kind of set her to worrying about it was one day when Jimmie Sue referred to Madeleen's mamma as Mrs. Hilton. Great-Grandma told him he should call her Lily—he'd tried to figure out if Moses' grandma was named Lily, but he couldn't find in scripture what Moses' grandma's name was. His mamma said he could even call her Aunt Lily, but it certainly wasn't right to call her Mrs. Hilton.

Jimmie Sue said, "Why, Mamma? Thet don't make no sense atall; fer in the first place she's older than you are."

She interrupted him quickly with, "Well, she's colored, an' besides . . . ."

"What color is she, Mamma?"

"Now stop thet sassin' or I'll tell Papa. What I mean to say is thet to call her Mrs. would give her a higher station in life than a colored is s'posed to have. An' although you know very well I respect her as a colored woman, she can't be called the same thing thet a white woman aroun' here might be called."

Jimmie Sue dug deeper into the matter. "I wonder what station she's s'posed to have an' what station I'm s'posed to have. It seem we all be jest 'baccer farmers. By the way, Mamma, are the Hilton's akin to us?"

She was horrified at this implication, realizing that the Hiltons were rumored to be high-yellows and with full knowledge that several of the Bennett men were outlandish philanderers. She surely wasn't about to put two and two together to get a sum of Bennett men when she answered as offhandedly as possible, "There's not a smidgen of truth to it."

"A smidgen of truth to what, Mamma?"

"I mean, acourse, they're not related to us. Whatever put that crazy notion into yoah head?"

"Well, Mamma," Jimmie Sue answered real slow-like, knowing full well that although he was flustering his mamma, which he didn't want to do, he was about to win a big one when he said, "You tol' me I should call her Aunt Lily, an' the Good Book says we're all brothers and sisters. So she must be of some a-kin to us."

While his mamma was hesitating to answer, he recalled in his own mind that Madeleen's mamma always came over with a pie or some other food whenever one of the Bennetts would be laid up with the flu or measles or something. Of course, his mamma would send one of the boys with food over to the Hiltons whenever there was some kind of illness over there, even though she realized that Aunt Lily knew all about what herbs would take care of the croup and what kind of poultice to use on skin breakouts, like boils and carbuncles. She explained that her taking things to the Hiltons was "the Christian thing to do."

He recalled in his own mind that time when Aunt Lily had come over to help when his mamma had come down with the flu. She had come over before breakfast and fixed all the meals and tended to Great-Grandma before she went back home after supper.

"Mamma, why don't we invite Mrs. . . . uh . . . Aunt Lily in to set down at the table with us when she come over with some vittles? I also notice that down to Pierson at the cafe, the coloreds can order food an' pay for it, but they're not s'posed to set down. The way I figger it is thet if we an' them stand up all the time an' never set down we won't have no problem with havin' different colored skin. What is it 'bout settin' down thet's so dangerous?"

"Now you askin' too many . . . ."

"An', Mamma, would it be the Christian thing to do to invite thet ol' colored feller in to eat with us an' spend the night when we see him roamin' aroun' in the wintertime?"

"Jimmie Sue, you know we can't do thet sort of thing."

"Why, not Mamma? You, yoahself, said in Sunday School thet Jesus tol' us to feed the hungry an' tend to the needy."

In futile exasperation, Great-Grandma Sue said, "Jimmie, honey, you jest don't understand. You're always askin' too many questions."

He knew he'd sorely tried his mamma's patience, but as he went out the door he asked yet another question.

"Mamma, how am I ever gonna understand ennythin', if I'm not allowed to ask any questions?"

* * *

CHAPTER 6

The Swimming Hole

A couple of weeks after Jimmie Sue had spooked Madeleen and then had tried to make up to her, he arranged with his brothers and the other boys to go down to the swimming hole on Saturday, after dinner. Great-Grandpa Robert never had the boys work on Saturday afternoons, unless there was some kind of emergency like a brushfire or the hogs busting out of the pen or the cow getting into the green corn.

On Friday night before the appointed swimming plans, the Bennetts went to bed with all the usual sleeping arrangements. Jimmie Sue always slept with his oldest brother, Simon. The beds were homemade of white oak, and instead of slats and springs they had ropes woven between the side rails and the head board and foot board.

The mattress was really just a coverlet made of heavy fabric and filled with goose down feathers. It was called a "feather tick." There was another lighter feather tick used in the winter time to go over the top of the sleeper and the other sheets and quilts for extra warmth, as the fires in the fireplaces downstairs would've died down long before sunup.

But it was still hot summer nights, so no covers were needed that Friday night. Both Jimmie Sue and Simon had said their required prayers. Although the whip-o-wills had finished their evening chorus, the frogs and crickets were still in full-voice.

Jimmie Sue had trouble going to sleep for he was thinking about that snake he'd thrown in the swimming hole a couple of weeks ago and wondered if it might still be there. He wasn't worried about it; he was just wondering how he might use it for a kind of ruckus with the other boys and figuring particularly how to use it on Emmett.

Simon usually fell asleep real quick, but that night he, too, was obviously awake—rolling over, back and forth. Jimmie Sue asked Simon why he'd set the alarm on the clock and hadn't blown out the oil lamp which was on his side of the bed. Simon, rather mysteriously, said, "I wanna make sure I get up at the right time."

Jimmie Sue said, "I can't see no sense in that atall, as Daddy allus makes sure we're up in time fer the milkin' an' other chores afore breakfast."

Simon said, "I reckon somethin' special might be happenin' 'roun' midnight."

Everybody knew midnight seemed to be the appointed hour for haints an' goblins an' any other spooky or witchy things.

Jimmie Sue said, "Jest 'cause thet ol' Rhode Island Red rooster crows ever' night at midnight, don't mean anything else unusual is happenin'."

Simon said, "Jest you wait!"

Jimmie Sue really couldn't fall asleep then. He kept looking over toward the clock, but drowsed off just before midnight.

Right at midnight the clock alarm went off, the Rhode Island Red rooster started crowing, and Simon jumped out of bed and went running down the stairs, yelling, "Thar's a man in the house! Thar's a man in the house!"

Everybody upstairs and downstairs had jumped out of bed and were trying to light the lamps. By the time Simon had got down the steps, Great-Grandpa had the barn lantern lit and come out of his room with his shotgun. "What's all the commotion 'bout? Where's the robber man? Did anybody see who it was?"

By this time, everybody had congregated around Simon in the kitchen.

Great-Grandpa again yelled at Simon. "Who'd you see? What man is it thet you seen in the house?"

With a big grin on his face, Simon said, "I'm the man. I hope yawl didn't fergit thet today is my twenty-first birthday, an' I'm a man today."

Great-Grandpa said, "If I'd a used this gun on you, you'd uv been a dead man. In fact, I've a notion not to let this buckshot go to waste."

Everybody got to laughing and punching at Simon for pulling such a silly trick. When Jimmie Sue and Simon went back up to bed, Simon this time did blow out the lamp.

Before rolling over to face the wall, Jimmie Sue said, "No wonder Mamma named you Simple Simon."

"Mamma didn't name me Simple. She jest named me Simon."

"But Simple goes real good with Simon, don't it? I mean particularly in yoah case! Simple Simon met a pie man, goin' to the fair, Sez Simple Simon to the pie man, 'Let me taste yoah ware. Sez the pie man to Simple Simon, 'Well I have aplenty.' Sez Simon to the pie man, 'I'm now one and twenty.'"

Simon said, "You might've thought that was cute an' funny, but there weren't a clever thing 'bout it."

Jimmie Sue answered right back, "Simple is as simple does and as far as factual goes yoah simply Simon."

Their voices had risen quite a bit in volume and in tone, and before Simon had a chance to punch Jimmie Sue for his sassiness, Great-Grandpa yelled from downstairs. "You boys get quiet up there. We already had too much foolishness tonight an' tomorrow's sun will soon be gettin' you up fer sure."

They both answered together, "All right, Papa."

The next day was Saturday, and they were all up early for the milking. Jimmie Sue was particularly anxious to get the breakfast and chores finished, so as they could get out to the cornfield for the last cultivating run with the single-wing plow to get the corn laid-by.

Laying-by meant the last plowing for weeds in the balks (spaces between the corn rows) and at the same time pushing extra dirt up against the corn stalks to prevent the roots from drying out so much.

Actually, it wasn't that Jimmie Sue loved the field work that much, but he had arranged—as it was Saturday—for the other boys to meet him down at the swimming hole after dinner, 'cause none of the neighborhood daddies would make the boys work on Saturday afternoon, and that Saturday was perfect for a swimming hole.

He'd already made sure that George Dowell, his next oldest brother, was going, but when he asked Simon, Simon said, "Ain't you fergettin' somethin'?"

Jimmie Sue said, "What am I fergettin'?"

"Whatta you think all the squawkin' las' night was about?"

"You mean cause yore twenny-one today?"

"What else? In the Bible it says, 'When ye become a man ye put away childish things'."

Jimmie Sue says, "Why that's the very thing. You come down to the swimmin' hole with us an' then me an' the others'll make sure you get baptized good an' proper into yore new manhood—a baptism which should last fer 'time and eternity'."

Simon thought about it for a minute and realized how foolish it was to miss out on going to the swimming hole, just because he was a *man* now.

On the other hand, he reckoned that since he had made such a big deal of the whole thing and even now reminding Jimmie Sue about it, that the boys would be sure to gang up on him, even though he was the oldest. So he said, "Naw, I figure I oughtta stay an' help Papa with fixin' the fence where the cow broke through yestiddy."

"Well," Jimmie Sue said, "suit yoahself."

After dinner, and just as Jimmie Sue and George Dowell was about to bolt from the table for the swimming hole, their mamma said, "Now, don't go in the deep water until a hour after you've finished eatin'."

George Dowell said, "We know thet ol' caution, Mamma."

"Well, jest do as I say, an' by the way don't you be takin' any of my new clothespins. I found out what'd been happenin' to them."

Jimmie Sue piped up. "Oh, we don't need them no more to cover our noses to keep us from drownin'. But thet little spring on that thar clothespin would hold our nose closed, until the clothespin would fall off an' warsh down the creek. We know now how to hold our breaths our own selves without extra outside help from clothespins. Lige learnt to do thet from his uncle what learnt it when he went off to Richmon'."

"You jest pay 'tention to my word, cause you 'member you nearly got a whuppin' from Papa when he learnt you'd been losin' my store-boughten clothespins in the creek. You know we don' get to the store ever' day to get such supplies."

"Yeah, Mamma," answered both Jimmie Sue an' George Dowell together, as they flew out the door.

By time they'd got to the swimming hole, they'd shucked their shirts. They weren't wearing any shoes.

Emmett and Bill were already there and dressed appropriately, by being undressed, for the swimming hole. Walt and Roy were coming from behind George Dowell and Jimmie Sue. Lige was walking up from down creek.

While the others were taking off their work clothes, Jimmie Sue started talking with Bill, who was one of his best buddies. Emmett, Bill's brother, was standing on the diving rock as though he was about to jump into the water, when he saw Cletus come out of the bushes on the far side of the creek. "What the hell's thet niggah doin' down here at our swimmin' hole? I'll make sousemeat outta thet black son-uv-a . . . ."

He didn't get a chance to finish his pronouncement. Jimmie Sue, still with his overalls on, headed straight for Emmett, knocking him down on the rock.

Emmett, who was somewhat bigger then Jimmie Sue, swung back, hitting Jimmie Sue in the right eye. Jimmie Sue staggered back just as Emmett grabbed him around the waist, lifting him up off the rock, but Jimmie Sue clasped his legs together around Emmett's waist as they both collapsed onto the rock. Jimmie Sue was able to roll onto the top, as the both of them, in their squirming, started sliding off the rock into the water. Of course, Emmett, being on the bottom and naked, felt every bump and ridge and cutting edge of that rock.

When they landed in the water, they both let go, of course. Otherwise they would've drowned as neither one of them was a very good swimmer. When they came to the surface of the water, there appeared a red streak floating down the creek from where Emmett was treading water.

About that time that copperhead moccasin snake swum out from in under the diving rock, right straight toward Emmett and all that blood.

Emmett, scrambling toward Jimmie Sue, yelled, "Jimmie Sue's tried to kill me on thet rock, an' now the devil's sendin' a water mockerson snake to finish me off." Jimmie Sue's hope for the snake and Emmett was materializing.

George Dowell, who, even though still a teenager, already had Primitive Baptist leanings, intoned, "What is to be, will be!"

Jimmie Sue had already made his way to the far bank with his water-drenched overall pockets full of water, and weighing him down so that he had a hard time climbing up onto the bank. But seeing that snake swimming in the stream of red blood, jumped back in, catching the snake by the tail again. Swinging it over his head he seemed to speak to it, "Now go back to the devil from whence you came." as he threw it back into the opening under the diving rock, perhaps to hope for another encounter before the summer was over.

Lige said, "Hit'll come right back, fer sure."

Roy said, "Thet don't differ . . . right now, anyways."

All the rest of the boys had, by this time, jumped into the water—some naked and some still with their clothes on. They swam over to Emmett and asked what all that red blood was about. "It's about my butt." he painfully answered.

Gradually, Bill and Walt helped Emmett up onto the bank beside Jimmie Sue, where they could all examine the damage, which was rather massive: a lot of bruises and scratches all over his right buttock and down his right thigh. But the most impressive hurt was a deep gash, nearly ten inches long, starting near his tailbone and running slantwise down toward his right leg. When he reached back and felt the blood, he started moaning.

"My Gawd," said George Dowell, nearly fainting backward into the creek. "We gotta do somethin' quick, afore he bleeds to death."

By this time Emmett wasn't feeling so big and mighty and had lowered his moaning to a whimper, "You s'pose I'm gonna die?"

Jimmie Sue, not very sympathetic and still a little miffed at Emmett, said, "Yeah . . . we all gotta go sometime."

Lige said, "Stop yer foolin' now, Jimmie Sue. This is serious bizness. We gotta stop this bleedin', somehow."

"If we was to home, I'd get some soot an' salt an' rub thet in, an' hit'd stop right up," Roy offered.

Bill said, "Why in the world would you do thet, Roy?"

"Thet's what I do fer my fightin' game roosters when I cut their combs off afore I put 'em in a pit fight. You don't want the other rooster to get aholt of the comb when they be fightin', so's you cut their comb off with a razorblade an' stop the blood with soot an' salt."

Someone said, "Thet sounds awful painful."

"The roosters ain't never complained 'bout thet."

"Quit foolin' around now," Lige said. "We ain't got no soot an' no salt, an' this ain't no rooster's head comb. It's Emmett's rear bottom."

Cletus, who had been standing to one side and had said nothing, suggested, "If you want me to help, I kin fetch some pokeberries to stop the bleedin'."

"How you know 'bout thet?" Roy asked.

"Mamma tol' me."

Everybody all of a sudden remembered rumors about Aunt Lily, Cletus's mamma, being a conjure woman.

"Ain't they pizziness?" asked Walt.

Bill answered timidly, "He ain't gonna eat 'em . . . is he?"

So they told Cletus to hurry up with the pokeberries. He quickly picked a couple of bunches and made a kind of salve of the berries on a hollowed-out rock and applied it like an expert to the guy who had, just a few minutes earlier, made light of Cletus being colored.

Emmett again protested about a "colored" boy actually touching him—"An' my backside at that."

Walt suggested, "Should we jest let you bleed to death then?"

"Naw, go ahead an' finish, Cletus," begged Emmett.

Cletus held the poultice of pokeberry salve in place with the shirt Jimmie Sue had contributed to the cause.

Emmett said, "Mamma's gonna kill me fer sure when she see this big cut on my rear end."

"You gonna show yo' mamma yo' rear end?" Jimmie Sue asked.

"Well she told me I wadn't to go swimmin' today. She thinks I'm hoein' in the tater patch down behin' the barn."

Lige said, "Jest don't tell 'er."

"How'm I gonna 'splain why I can't set down an' have to eat my supper off the fireboard (fireplace mantle) standin' up?"

Cletus piped up, after having already inserted himself into the gang of white boys by playing the role of a nurse, "Mamma be knowin' how to poultice bad cuts an bruises like thet to keep it from goin' bad."

Roy added to the drama by saying, "Yeah, afore the blowflys get in thar an' lay them little maggot eggs."

Emmett began yelling even louder. All the boys were really enjoying this experience with Emmett, who tended to be the bully of the bunch, even when they'd be at school.

George Dowell says, "Why thet's the very thang. We'll haul Emmett over to the Hiltons' an' let Aunt Lily dose him with one of her pow'ful potions." George Dowell was only half serious as he was enjoying the irony of the situation.

Emmett objected furiously, "I ain't gonna go over to no nig . . . to let thet colored woman . . . ."

Cletus interrupted quietly, "She jest be my mamma."

Jimmie Sue said, "Yeah, she yoah mamma, Cletus, an' I hear tell she have real strong medicine from yerbs an' roots an' thangs,"

Emmett reckoned that if he wanted some help he'd better shut up, so he didn't say another word . . . right then anyway.

Roy said, "Cletus you bring his overhauls an' you, Jimmie Sue, kin wrap yoah wet shirt 'round his butt."

The boys, who'd been naked, started putting their clothes on, except Emmett who'd only been swathed with Jimmie Sue's shirt.

Walt said, "We can't carry him by crossin' our arms together like a make-believe chair, 'cause with thet gash, he can't set down."

Lige grabbed Emmet from behind and clasped his hands together across Emmett's chest and yelled at Roy to get one leg and Walt the other. They'd have to carry him feet first.

Emmett couldn't get away but protested, "At least let me get mah overhauls."

Jimmie Sue said, "Why my shirt is already coverin' yore privates jest like a didie. An' besides if you have on yoah overhauls, nobody can doctor yoah hurt. Jest don't go messin' in my shirt on the way up the ridge."

Cletus ran to get Emmett's overalls to carry alongside, while the rest of the boys finished putting on their clothes—all except Jimmie Sue who still was wearing his overalls, completely soaked with creek water.

The Hiltons' place wasn't too far up the next ridge. There was a great deal of talking, yelling and some cussing all the way up the steep incline. Emmett emitted an occasional moan or yelp, when his special diaper rubbed across his injured part, and especially when Roy and Walt didn't lift him high enough over a rock or log.

Cletus, of course, led the way because he knew the best way back home. Anyone looking on from the outside would've sworn that he was the "leader of the band'—*a colored boy heading up a bunch of mountain white boys.*

* * *

CHAPTER 7

The Healing

Cletus took the shortcut up to home out of consideration for the ailing Emmet. However, even though it was the shortest . . . as the crow flies . . . Cletus had not taken into consideration the many steep slopes and rock outcroppings.

Because Emmett was a pretty hefty boy, Lige asked George Dowell to help with the other shoulder while Walt and Roy were carrying the legs. It took only a few steps to discover that George Dowell and Lige couldn't walk backward up the side of the ridge, so they turned the whole arrangement around with Walt and Roy hauling Emmett's legs to follow first in close behind Cletus and, of course, George Dowell and Lige now on the rear end—or rather the head end—of Emmett.

Jimmie Sue said, "Sometimes it don't seem to matter whether you be dealin' with Emmett's head end or rear end—he don't allus seem to know the difference his own self." Following close behind the rag-tag string of boys, hauling the fallen warrior, Jimmie Sue was seemingly serving as the caboose of that strange train that'd somehow jumped the tracks.

This arrangement didn't last long. The first big rock outcropping was no real challenge for Cletus, as he scrambled right up over it, but it was a major obstacle for Emmett for he was revictimized when his carriers failed to raise his rump high enough to clear the boulder. Emmett let out another yell, calling on the Lord to do some outlandish things to his buddies.

It was then they abandoned the idea of carrying him all the way up the mountain. Emmett declared that with a little help on each side, he could manage his own legs. Thus they continued their life-saving mission with Emmett's arms across the shoulders of Jimmie Sue and Walt who had spelled Roy and Lige. Of course then they had to hide his nakedness by draping Jimmie Sue's shirt around his backside and tying it between his legs like a sure-enough diaper. This obviously miffed him even more.

When they finally got to the top of the ridge, and in sight of the Hiltons' cabin, Cletus seemed to come more alive and confident. He was, of course, in more familiar territory, both ground-wise and people-wise. Carrying out his role in the healing campaign, he went running and yelling toward home, "Mamma, Mamma, we need help!"

As the troupe approached the Hiltons', the first one to appear out the front door onto the porch was Madeleen. Jimmie Sue's step got a little livelier and his burden of Emmett seemed to get a tad lighter.

When they approached the porch, Madeleen leaned—ever so casually—against the porch post and silently met Jimmie Sue's eyes. Jimmie Sue stopped abruptly like a statue, returning her gaze.

This mutual sharing of stares didn't go unnoticed by the rest of the entourage, as they punched each other in the ribs, laughing and grinning like 'possums.

Emmett yelled, "What the hell's the mattah? Is my bottom gonna get some 'tention or what?"

The first person to answer was Madeleen with another question, as she diverted her eyes from Jimmie Sue. "You got bottom problems?"

He asked her, "Where the hell's yoah mamma?"

When Emmett cussed at Madeleen thetaway, Jimmie Sue let go of Emmett's shoulder. He nearly fell as Walt steadied him and said, "Emmett, I wouldn't be fergettin' what started this whole mess, if'n I was you."

By that time, Aunt Lily had come out onto the porch. "Howdy, Jimmie Sue. How's yoah mamma?" Looking closely at the strange entourage, she asked, "What're you boys up to? Have you got yoahselves inta some kinda mess?"

Jimmie Sue said, "Mamma's fine. She sends her hello. Me an' Emmett got into a little scuffle, an' Emmet got scratched on a rock."

George Dowell said, "We thought you might could help. Cletus said you're real good at that sort of thing. We'd be much obliged."

Aunt Lily said, "Where he get hurt?"

Cletus answered, "Down by the swimmin' hole."

His mamma became more specific. "Cletus, don't be sassy. I mean where on his body be the hurt."

"Hit be on his backside."

As Emmett moaned, Lige contributed, "Yeah, his rearend, an' real bad."

"Well, we gotta take off what he got wropped 'round him."

Emmett continued to yell and complain, as the others explained to Aunt Lily that Cletus had made a poultice of pokeberries.

"I be mighty proud of you, Cletus, to be a doctorin' thisaway. So them pokeberries an' the boy's blood must've colored up his dydie like this."

Emmett shot back, "This ain't no dydie. Hit's only Jimmie Sue's shirt whut he lent me."

"Well we kin leave the dydie on till we get him inside an' onto a bed."

"I don' aim to go into the house."

The eyes of Aunt Lily and those of Emmett glowered at each other for a few seconds—quite different from the looks Jimmie Sue and Madeleen had directed toward each other only a few seconds earlier.

Aunt Lily straightened herself up and took charge, almost as though she just recalled her own calling of being a medicine woman. She had not only birthed many babies on the ridges and in the hollows, she had also been available for other healing occasions—for her own people as well as for the white folks. "We won't need to go inta the house. We be usin' the banch right here on the poach. Come on ovah here, White Boy, an' lay yo' frontside on the banch."

Emmett dutifully did what he was told.

"Now you gotta undo yo' diapah."

"I done tole you this ain't no diapah. It's Jimmie Sue's shirt."

"Why don' you then jest real careful-like take Jimmie Sue's shirt off 'n yoah bottom an' han' it back to Jimmie Sue? Be sure an' thank him fer the loan of his shirt." She was clearly in charge now, as she began washing her hands in the wash pan Cletus had already fetched. She made sure that her hands were good and lathered up with some good strong lye soap, which she had made at hog-killing time, last fall.

Emmett objected. "I don' wanna 'xpose myself."

Aunt Lily answered, "I be seein' 'nough baby bottoms in my time. As far as I keer, yoah bottom's jest another injured rear end. Now how'm I gonna tend to yoah hurt, iffen I can't even see it?" Then turning toward Cletus and the other boys, "Cletus take all them boys off an' show 'em yo' chickens or somethin'."

Cletus headed out toward the barn with the other boys in tow.

Madeleen was still standing on the porch—of course, watching the boys, especially Jimmie Sue.

"Now, Madeleen, you first run an' get a clean white sheet to cover this boy's nekkidness, an' han' the sheet out the door to me. You ain't got no call to be lookin' at a white boy's bottom. Nur a colored one's nuther—not jest yet, anyways."

Madeleen hurried into the house and quickly returned with the sheet, discreetly holding it out the door for her mamma to reach.

Aunt Lily was shocked when she unwrapped Jimmie Sue's shirt from Emmett's bottom. "My Lawd, this hyar is a real bad cut, with so many bruises an scratches."

She yelled back in the house to Madeleen. "Madeleen you gotta get my medicines fer me to fix up this boy. Run an' get a cup of lard, an' see if I have any mo' ches'nut leaves in the cubbard. An' run out to the grapevine fer some grape leaves fer to stew up some tea fer the boy to drink, an' some hawthorn leaves fer the boy to chew up, whilst I be doctorin' on him...."

"Oh, an' take this bloody shirt back to Jimmie Sue. An' tell Cletus to run an' break off some nightshade vine fer to hang 'roun' the boy's neck."

Madeleen was thankful for an excuse to run after the boys. When she walked behind her mamma's chair and across the porch she reached for the shirt with her right hand, trying to avoid looking at Emmett's injuries, but curiosity got the better of her, as she glanced over her mamma's shoulder. All she could see was a bloody lump of white boy flesh, which nearly made her throw up. She was really grateful now to have a chance to run after the other boys.

Aunt Lily asked, "You say you be E-mman-u-el?"

"No, I be.... My name is Emmett Goins."

She corrected him. "Yoah name may've been Emmett Goins befoah, but it now gonna be E-mman-u-el."

"I don't aim to change my name."

She continued, "You ain't changin' yoah name, an I ain't changin' yo' name. Hit be changed in the book."

"What book? I don't know nothin' 'bout my name bein' in no book."

"Nevah you min'. You jest pay 'tention to what I'm asayin'. I seen yo' name in the book of light which the Lawd has writ down all the things thet *was* an' *is* to be."

Emmett wasn't used to this kind of talk. "Aunt Lily, thet skeers me more'n my cut. Hit jest sounds awful Bible-like ta me."

"Oh yeah, it be scripture awright. In 'Zkiel hit say, 'But he was wounded for our transgressions, he was bruised for our iniquities.' Thet now be yoah workin' orders. Emmanuel has to help his people jest like down in Egypt land."

Madeleen stuck her hand out the front door with her eyes turned toward the edge of the woods—whether to avoid lookin' at Emmett's bloody rear or to keep a watch on Jimmie Sue, she probably couldn't say. "Here, Mamma's yoah cup a lard an' ches'nut leaves. I awready scrunched up the leaves a little to mix with the lard, an' I got the grape leaves in the kettle fer some tea. You might want some too."

"Yeah, thet'd be real nice to have some tea while I'm adoctorin'. But where be the hawthorn leaves?"

"They right hyar," as she hands the hawthorn leaves out with her other hand. If a stranger might have been standing across the yard, he'd have thought it mighty queer for a beautiful colored girl to be standing in a doorway, while looking over to her left with both hands extended to her right holding leaves and a cup of lard.

"Did you 'mind Cletus to get them nightshade vines?"

"Yeah, I tol' 'im, but hit's gonna take—."

"I won't need that fer a little while yet. You be sure now an' give Jimmie Sue his shirt, but offer to warsh hit fer 'im."

Madeleen bridled at this suggestion. "I not be Jimmie Sue's washerwoman."

"No, honey, you ain't, but we can still be neighborly."

While Aunt Lily commenced applying the poultice of lard and chestnut leaves to Emmett's injury, Madeleen took out after the boys again. She was waving the bloody shirt like a flag and calling for Jimmie Sue when they nearly ran into each other round the corner of the house. "Here be yoah shirt, Jimmie Sue."

As Jimmie Sue examined it, "Hit sure is a mess, ain't it?"

She answered, "Yeah, but it's got some mighty purty colors."

"Yeah, thet purple pokeberry juice mixed with Emmett's backside blood looks almost purty."

They spread the shirt on the ground to admire the mixed-up colors on Jimmie Sue's blue shirt. Spread out that way, they could see patterns of the colors. They began to wonder what the figures were—like trying to figure out the shape of clouds. The middle back of the shirt must have been directly over Emmett's wound. There seemed to be a large winged creature painted there.

Jimmie Sue said, "Is thet a dark butterfly?

"No . . . it be a angel."

"Why do you allus hafta—?" Jimmie Sue wanted to chide Madeleen by always thinking of Bible things, but he checked himself just in time to avoid another misunderstanding with Madeleen. "Yeah, maybe you right. A beautiful black angel."

"Hit ain't black!"

"Well, a kinda dark, reddish, purplish, bluish angel."

Madeleen thought for a second, then suggested, "A colored angel!"

Jimmie Sue welcomed this assessment of the figure. "Yeah, a beautiful colored angel."

"I be warshin' the shirt fer you if you like," offered Madeleen.

"Oh no, I don' think I'll warsh this shirt."

"You won't hafta. *Ah* offered to do it fer you."

"I'm gonna keep it jest like this."

"What fer?"

"I'll jest hang it up to 'mind me."

"'Mind you of what?"

"Today!"

"Today?"

"An' the goin's on today . . . an', a course, all the people today," as he stole a glance toward her, who met his eyes with a questioning intensity.

Madeleen and Jimmie Sue and the rest of the boys got back to the porch just as Aunt Lily was finishing up with her doctoring. Cletus was coming from behind the house with the nightshade vines.

Ruthie, Madeleen's little sister came out of the house and announced, "Jimmie Sue, did Madeleen tell you thet Queenie found puppies?"

"No, Ruthie, she didn't tell me. I didn't know they was lost."

"Huh?"

Madeleen scolded him. "Jimmie Sue, you quit teasin' Ruthie."

"I'm sorry, Ruthie. Where did she find them?"

"Under the poach."

"Who's thar daddy?"

Madeleen glowered at Jimmie Sue. Ruthie looked puzzled. "They don't have a daddy. She found 'em."

Aunt Lily turned from her healin' work and reproached Jimmie Sue. "Jimmie Sue, I think I'd be payin' 'tention to whatevah warnin' you might get from Madeleen."

Jimmie Sue apologized and in a more friendly, less teasin' tone said, "Ruthie. Did you pick out a favorite?"

"Yeah, it be a baby dog girl, an' I name her Rosie."

He was touched that Ruthie was honoring his little sister by naming a pup after her. "I'll tell Rosie 'bout thet. She'll be tickled pink."

He wasn't aware until he'd said it that the Hiltons might be offended by him using a word like "pink" to refer to a person's color. He glanced furtively toward Madeleen and then Aunt Lily. It was almost as though they hadn't heard the word or at least it hadn't registered on their defensive gauge.

Aunt Lily had continued her "angel of mercy" mission.

"Hyar, now E-mman-u-el, while you be finishin' up chewin' them hawthorn leaves, I'll jest wrop a piece of this sheet 'round yo' hurt here, an' you kin put on yoah overhauls. Cletus, han' me the nightshade now." Aunt Lily tied the nightshade in a circle like a wreath and put it around Emmett's neck.

Emmett objected, "Nightshade is pizzinous. Hit kin kill a body."

"This nightshade be fer curin', not fer killin'. Jest don't eat it, an' wear it fer one week, an' you'll have no mo' hurt. Oh, I almost fergot myself. Go down by the swimmin' hole whar you got yo' hurt and knock off a chunk of thet rock 'bout whar hit cut ya. Put thet little chunk on the fireboard at home. Then thar'll be no infection set in."

"What if someone asks me why I'm wearin' this nightshade?"

"Jest tell 'em thet you are Emmanuel now, an' this be yoah sign."

Emmett figured he'd be wise to drop the subject.

As Aunt Lily looked at Jimmie Sue and Madeleen standing awfully close to each other, she said, "Come over hyar, Jimmie Sue." Madeleen jumped like a jack-in-the-box to one side. Aunt Lily continued, "Let me take a look at thet thar eye."

Jimmie Sue walked sheepishly over to Aunt Lily, who called to Madeleen, "Madeleen, go git me one uv them new-dug arsh taters [Irish potatoes] an' bring it hyar along with a peelin' knife."

He asked, "What you gonna do, Aunt Lily?"

"I be peelin' the tater an then scrapin' it to get scrapin's to put in a clean white cloth to hold ovah yoah eye. Them scrapin's'll take the swellin' an' blackin' right out. Tell yoah mamma to do the same thing 'morrow mornin', an then hit'll be all well again. I allus do this thang fer my chillren, an' I sure it work fer you."

After the doctoring was finished on Jimmie Sue's black eye and Emmett had finished dressing, the boys thanked Aunt Lily, said goodbye to Cletus and Madeleen, and started off to home with Lige now leading the pack.

Madeleen said, "I be walkin' you as far as the fence gate."

Jimmie Sue asked, "No farther than thet?"

"Nope . . . not now anyways."

Madeleen walked in front of the white boys all the way to the fence gate, but then stopped so abruptly that Jimmie Sue ran into her—another mistake he made of touching her, even though completely accidentally, but certainly not incidentally.

"Can't you watch whar you be goin', White Boy?"

By this time it had become clear to Jimmie Sue that whenever Madeleen got riled at him for whatever reason, she'd call him, "White Boy," even though by then she was well acquainted with his Christian name, James Lafayette Bennett, as well as his everyday name, which everybody called him, "Jimmie Sue."

He apologized to her again, "I'm sorry, Madeleen. I musta been payin' 'tention to Emmett, 'stead watchin' whar I'm goin'."

She asked, "Whut's wrong with Emmett now?"

"Nothin' new. He jest don' seem natchel."

"I'spose."

Emmett spoke up. "Did you hear what thet conjure woman call me? . . . She call me

E-mann-u-el."

Madeleen replied, "Yeah, Mamma be knowin' the direction, generally, where a body be goin'."

"Jest 'cause mah las' name be Goins?"

"Naw, she don' go by thet. She somehow see whut be in a person's eyes or soul or, I think mabe in the stars. But she don't really make much of it . . . I mean of her bein' able to tell things thetaway. Hit jest seem natchel to her like the book scholars kin jest natcherlly read a thang from a book without puttin' much thought in it. She jest say hit be thar fer abody to read, who's learnt awready to read."

Lige asked, "She read thet stuff in a book?"

"Oh no! She be reading the soul through the book pages of the eyes."

Jimmie Sue, not wanting to appear skeptical, but not understanding, simply noted, "Ever'body read with they eyes."

"Don' be smart-alecky, White Boy. She read with her eyes . . . into an' through somebody else's eyes . . . right all the way down to the soul in they heart. An' then she tell the body whut she read there in they heart."

Jimmie Sue said, "You mean she can jest look inta my eyes and tell me what she read there in my heart?"

"If you stan's still long 'nough."

By this time all the boys but Jimmie Sue were through the gate, leaving Madeleen standing there leaning against the gatepost.

Jimmie Sue had lagged behind, wondering how things stood between him and Madeleen. It had seemed by her last remarks that she was getting a little contentious toward him.

She'd been holding the gate open for the other boys, and when Jimmie Sue got there he started to hold the gate open for himself, but instead of putting his hand on the top of the gate, his hand landed surreptitiously right on top of her hand.

Pulling her hand away, quickly she asked—not with rancor—"White Boy, whut you be doin' now?"

"Oh, 'scuse me again, Madeleen, I guess I jest weren't lookin'. I meant to hold the gate open fer my own self."

She said, "Jimmie Sue, it seem you be 'scusin' yoahself a lot, but it be okay. A touch nevah hurt nobody. An' you know, I didn't mind openin' the gate fer the other boys . . . . There comes times when it might be very nice to have somebody hold the gate open fer you."

"Don' you reckon thet depends on what thet gate be opening up to?"

Madeleen was suddenly impressed by this little bit of sarcastic wisdom from Jimmie Sue, even though it had one-upped her.

For a moment they stood facing each other—their eyes seeming to read into each other's soul just like Aunt Lily's heart literacy.

Directly Jimmie Sue said, "Much obliged to yoah mamma fer her help. You tell her. Okay?"

"I tell her."

Without another word, and daring not to wave to her, Jimmie Sue turned and joined the boys, heading down the mountain.

* * *

CHAPTER 8

Down the Mountain

Jimmie Sue, just before disappearing into the mountain laurel brake, took one last look at Madeleen who was still standing by the gate, as though she might be the permanent gatepost attachment. Like being drawn by some unknown force, he took several steps back toward her, but stopped abruptly before saying, "Madeleen? . . ."

Not hearing anything further, Madeleen answered, "Yes?" . . . Then in a whisper almost to herself, "Jimmie Sue . . ."

She probably hadn't intended for him to hear her voice his name, but he did hear and reassured himself. "She didn't call me White Boy, even when she barely mentioned my name."

Nothing more was said by either of them. They simply exchanged enigmatic smiles before Jimmie Sue joined the rest of the boys, who were by then clamoring for him to come on to join them on the return trip toward home . . . their respective homes. "An' leave thet colored girl alone."

The rag-tag line of boys heading down the mountain could easily have been mistaken for a disgruntled band of gypsies.

All the way across the ridge and down the slope to the swimming hole, the boys didn't say much. They were all a little weary from the excitement of the day and also worrying about getting in home in time enough for the evening chores.

Emmett was quieter than the rest of them. He was still limping a little, almost as though he was carrying a heavy load; perhaps it was the new burden on his mind about the name, Emmanuel, Aunt Lily assigned to him. Of course the injury to his backside was still bothering him more than a little.

Jimmie Sue said to Emmett, "You better be rememberin' whut Aunt Lily warned you you was s'posed to do."

"Whut was thet?"

Jimmie Sue answered, "Whut'd she tell you to do oncet we got back down hyar to the swimmin' hole?"

"Oh, yeah! She tol' me I was to take a chunk off the rock, right where I'd been cut an' take it home with me."

"Whut're you s'posed to do with it then?"

"She said I was to put it up on the fireboard an' leave it there. Why do s'pose she'd have me do thet?"

"She said it was to keep you from gettin' an infection."

Having heard his fill of the conjure woman's superstitions, Emmet said, "Well it don't make no sense atall to me."

"At least," Jimmie Sue said, "If you break off thet little sharp edge what cut you, at least it won't be cuttin' nobody else."

"Yeah, I guess you right 'bout thet."

All the boys went over to inspect the diving-off rock and saw blood splotched all over the moss and lichens that were growing there. Of course it didn't take them long to locate the offending sharp edge.

Feeling a bit guilty about the whole episode, Jimmie Sue volunteered to break off the part that Emmett was supposed to take home and put on the fireplace mantel. It could very well serve as a memento for years to come.

After breaking off the escarpment with a smaller rock, Jimmie Sue handed it to Emmett and said, "I'd be happy to 'pologize fer ever' thing thet happened today, if you was to promise to 'pologize to Cletus nex' time we see him."

Emmett pondered on the proposition for just a minute before he answered, "Yeah I think I oughtta do thet."

After that they all split up and went their separate ways. Jimmie Sue, walking around the swimming hole in front of George Dowell, carried the bloodied-pokeberry-juiced shirt on the end of a stick like a victory flag after a difficult military encounter.

George Dowell confronted him about carrying the shirt that way. "You act jest like you'd won somethin'."

"I won a whole lot."

"Like what?"

Jimmie Sue couldn't really confide what he felt he'd actually won, because he wasn't exactly sure what that was, but he sure felt better than he had that morning, so he just said, "I kinda won my self-respect."

"How much of thet kin you take to the bank?"

Jimmie Sue answered, "I can take it all to the bank an' to the barn an' to the church meetin' tomorry."

"You plum' daffy."

"I druther be daffy than ignernt."

"Who you sayin's ignernt?"

About that time they were crawling back over the jumping-off rock, and Jimmie Sue said, "Better not be fergettin' the last feller who argued with me on this hyar rock."

George Dowell was somewhat taken aback with Jimmie Sue's new confidence. "Jimmie Sue, don't be fergettin' who's older and bigger than you, so you better quit yakkin' an' tail it on in home, 'cause I reckin hit's yore time to do the milkin' this evenin'."

It didn't take them long to get on in home. The chores were finished in a hurry, an' supper was even faster than usual, because everyone had in mind the big doin's at their church the next morning.

Breakfast and the morning chores proved just as hurried as the evening before.

Great-Grandpa and the boys got the team of mules hooked up to the buckboard while Great-Grandma and Jimmie Sue's sister, Thelma Lou, finished the breakfast dishes and loaded the picnic basket for "dinner on the grounds."

Jimmie Sue could never figure out why they called it "dinner on the grounds," because they always put the food on the long wooden tables under the red oak trees. He supposed a fellow could sit on the ground if he had a mind to. He'd asked his mamma that morning if she'd baked a chocolate pie, his favorite, for the picnic.

"No, 'cause the peaches has come in, an' you know I wanna use as many of them as possible, afore they start goin' bad. I kin always fix chocolate pie, fer there's no p'tickular time fer thet. I thought you was silly 'bout peach pie."

"Oh, I dote on peach pie, but fer some reason, I wuz kinda countin' on chocolate this mornin'."

It was a custom in the mountains that even though there were lots of little churches with different beliefs and doctrines, on special celebrational days, folks from other churches would be invited, particularly for the *dinner on the grounds.*

All the neighborhood churches would have a mourner's bench where folks would sit—folks with some problem or other (money, sickness, family, some wrongdoing, etc.) and would ask the preacher to pray for some special dispensation on their behalf. Quite often the bench would be occupied by a poor soul under religious conviction—quite often a few weeks, but maybe months, before they'd seek baptism. This bench would be up in front where the mourners and the preachers could be in close proximity to each other.

On the other side of the center church aisle was another front pew, where the shouters and ameners sat, which was the basis of its name, the "amen corner."

The back pew seemed to be reserved for all the bachelor boys—the age of fourteen and above. It wasn't deliberately arranged that way, but Jimmie Sue and the other boys somehow seemed to have laid claim to this little piece of church real estate.

That particular morning was a little different, as the boys noticed that Emmett hadn't joined them on their bench, but then they recalled that Emmett didn't come to church often anyways.

But as this was a special Homecoming Sunday with lots of singing and good eats and pretty girls, they had thought that Emmett would be there. Walt noticed that Emmett was sitting up close to the front, not on the mourner's bench nor in the amen corner, but awfully close to both of them. This worried the boys a little, but George Dowell, who seemed predestined later to become one of the preachers himself, cautioned the boys to "not make too much of Emmett settin' up closter to the serious end of the church. He may be under conviction in one way or 'nother."

The boys kind of forgot about Emmett when they noticed Walt making a little valentine on the back of the pew, just in front of them, with his penknife. That was the usual place where the boys would put their initials with those of their (hoped for) girlfriends. While the preacher was droning on and on, Walt continued boring little holes, indicating the edge of a heart.

The boys, of course, were paying a whole lot more attention to what he was doing than what the preacher was saying, and they even sat there when everyone was standing, singing one of their favorite songs, "On Jordan's Stormy Banks I Stand."

They were anxious to learn what girl's initials Walt might carve beneath his initials and the plus sign.

It soon became obvious that he wasn't about to reveal his true love, particularly after he failed to whittle his initials, W.B., but instead whittled

J.S.B. Jimmie Sue knew it wasn't his real initials, J.L.B., but he figured, and rightly so, that those initials were for Jimmie Sue Bennett. As they all watched with rapt attention, Walt cut in a fancy M and then very carefully a real flowery H.

Of course, everyone, even Jimmie Sue, realized that the newly crafted valentine was meant for Jimmie Sue and Madeleen.

At about this time the preacher was benedicting and inviting everyone to the feast to be shared in the church yard.

As Jimmie Sue looked around, he noticed that the Hiltons had come into the back of the church and were standing next to the back wall. They had already gone to their church, which let out early in order to visit the white folks' church for their special homecoming day.

It was a good thing that there weren't any empty spaces on the church benches, as it saved both the coloreds and the whites from having to deal with the code of not sitting down together. As long as everyone could stand, there'd be no problem for anyone, which Jimmie Sue had earlier noted and had pointed out to his mamma.

Now, Jimmie Sue was afraid Madeleen had seen what Walt had carved on the pew back, so instead of trying to get to Walt—who'd slipped out the end of the pew—he sidled down to stand between the new art work and Madeleen. He'd "howdyed" to Cletus and Aunt Lily, but Madeleen was deliberately looking in the other direction, and he couldn't tell whether she'd seen him yet or not.

He waited for them to leave until he could move away from standing in front of the valentine heart.

While he had been positioning himself in that defensive pose, Roy, unbeknownst to Jimmie Sue—but egged on by the other boys—had gone into the pew in front of Jimmie Sue and, slipping under the seat, had tied the ends of Jimmie Sue's shoelaces to each other.

When Jimmie Sue saw the Hiltons starting to leave, he began his own exit, but the tied-up condition of his brogans abruptly halted his intentions. As he was in such a hurry to try to catch up with Madeleen, his forward motion catapulted him forward when his right foot reached the end of his left foot shoelaces. This, of course, was the end of his rope, so to speak, as he went crashing down onto the back of the forward pew, onto the seat of his pew and all the way to the floor.

The intense racket of the boy's arms and knees and head thumping on various solid hardwood surfaces produced astonishing sounds, even though not exactly melodic.

Now, Madeleen couldn't avoid looking at him, and he caught her eye for a second on his way down to the floor. When she heard the clatter of boy parts thudding against the pew boards, she turned quickly, instinctively reaching for Jimmie Sue's flailing arm, as though to prevent a fallen sinner in the Church of the Lord from final damnation.

Of course, that wasn't in the mind of either Madeleen nor Jimmie Sue, but the good church folk standing close by felt her gesture was a christian thing to do. It hadn't entered their consciousness at all that there might be a boy-girl thing going on, for after all they were of different colors.

The shared looks of horror of both Jimmie Sue and Madeleen, included unacknowledged feelings between them, but the depth and nuances of those messages were yet to be fully determined.

* * *

CHAPTER 9

Dinner on the Grounds

Jimmie Sue's falling in the church pew caused a great deal of laughter from all of the boys, even from Lige who was concerned about the ultimate ramifications of his actions; some real concern from the adults, who were trying to figure what had caused the fall; and sheer wonder from Madeleen, who was a little worried that he might be hurt.

Madeleen didn't dare go to Jimmie Sue's aid, but she did stand in the doorway until she saw that he was fine and looking around for whoever had played the prank on him.

Everyone outside was bustling around getting together all the *fixin's* for the shared "dinner on the grounds." The womenfolk were unloading baskets and lard cans and apple crates—any kind of container holding the contents of the anticipated meal.

Around the oak trees the little ones were chasing each other, relieved to be out-of-doors, off the hard wooden benches and away from the thunderous preachers' voices. Older girls and boys were assisting a bit with their mammas putting the food out, but mostly just eying each other.

Menfolk were making sure the horses and mules had some water and feed.

The preachers, even the colored ones, were assembling themselves at the head of the long wooden table, preparing for another go at "calling upon the Lord," and probably also to be first in line for the victuals. The exhorters of course wouldn't be paid for their religious duties, except for a few dollars occasionally slipped to them, but they did feel that a chicken dinner or dibs on the shared church dinners was appropriate recompense.

Madeleen, glancing at the preachers arranging themselves in that manner, caused her to recall the scripture—something to the effect that "the first shall be last and the last shall be first." She concluded that that wouldn't happen right away, not, anyways for today's neighborly *dinner on the grounds* which she'd been looking forward to ever since the colored preachers had announced that the colored church members were also invited.

Of course, they couldn't set in to eating until there had been another song and a few more words from at least one of the preachers and the blessing of the food.

Someone chose the song, *Victory,* which was quite appropriate, as neither hymnbooks nor pianos were needed and, as everyone from all of the churches represented there would know the tune and the words.

This selection particularly pleased Madeleen, and when a songleader heisted the song in the right key and register, everyone could hear Madeleen's clear sweet voice, seemingly wafting through the overhanging tree branches, as though emanating from heaven itself.

> *"When we all get to heav'n*
> *What a day of rejoicin' that will be.*
> *When we all see Jesus,*
> *We'll sing and shout the victory."*

Jimmie Sue, instead of singing himself, listened intently to Madeleen's angelic voice, and when she got to the word "heaven", it was almost as though she was ready to start her "day of rejoicing." But even more puzzling to him was when the singers sang the last word, he distinctly heard her sing "Jubilee" instead of "victory."

He wondered what that was all about. *Surely Madeleen hadn't forgot the right words fer a church song.* It seemed as though to Madeleen the celebration of a *Jubilee* was of greater importance than any mere *victory.*

Then the host preacher, Elder Hiatt, called on Brother Peeples, the visiting colored preacher, to bless the assembly and the food.

Brother Peeples began in a deep bass, sonorous voice, "We thank Thee, O Lord, for this occasion of brotherhood and for all the good folks who worship Thee and love Jesus. And we ask thee to bless . . ."

His voice had begun to rise in fervor, but was interrupted by the shrill scream of hunger by the Spencers' two-month-old baby boy.

All of the women immediately understood the young mother's situation, so they began to focus on her and her baby, who had had the croup of late. The women, closest to Mrs. Spencer, appeared to be dancers, as they moved slowly and deliberately around the feeding mother to form a protective circular wall, so that she could daintily unlace her dress front, maintaining her modesty as she attended to the hunger needs of her newborn.

Brother Peeples was already a little uneasy, as he was well aware that even though this was the Lord's church, it was currently maintained and occupied by white folks, and the magic of his voice was already broken by the baby's crying, plus the sounds of the animals as well as the continual rasping sounds of that year's invasion of the 17-year locusts. It was obvious that he had lost the attention of the ladies and he was quite aware that youngsters were anxious to start the feast. Everyone was already enjoying the pungent smells of the various dishes the ladies had prepared.

So he concluded. "We ask Thee to bless all those assembled here, and may our lives be now touched by Thy grace and nurtured fully by the provisions of the good yearth pervided by Thy benevolence and lovin'ly prepared by the good sisters of these congregations, under the canopy of my voice. In the name of Jesus, our Lord, we ask these blessings. Amen."

Echoing amens from various spaces in the oak grove could be heard. Some were voiced by people in the crowd, while others seemed to be sounded directly off the trunks of the mighty oaks or wafting from the very tree branches.

There was hardly a pause between Brother Peeples' *Amen* and a hullabaloo of noise from the youngsters, and their mammas' forbidding them from starting with the desserts. The sounds of pot-lids being lifted, mixed with the clanking of silverware against porcelain and tin plates and the pouring of gurgling lemonade into glasses were countered by the gossip and explanations of the attending cooks what the ingredients of each dish contained and how it was prepared and why her particular offering was a favorite dish in her family.

Jimmie Sue, although quite skinny in those days, loved trying a little of everything on the table. He wasn't sure he could accomplish that that day, because the spread was larger than the usual "dinner on the grounds." All of the women in his church were aware of his gustatory ability, so each of them would try to make sure he'd try what they had brought.

This predilection of his was a distraction from his recently acquired interest in Madeleen, but he attempted to balance these two priorities in his young life.

Madeleen, in the meantime, had laid out a little blanket next to the tallest oak tree, and after filling her plate had sat down and leaned against the tree. She also had a covered pie tin, which she hadn't yet put on the table.

She knew very well that local custom didn't call for whites and coloreds to sit down together to eat but she figured *I reckin hit don't make no never mind if I be settin' on the groun'. Thet prob'ly don't count as settin' down together. After all, the good yearth is the dwelling of the Lord where all folks would be welcome.*

She continued to monitor Jimmie Sue's whereabouts, but didn't openly exhibit any real interest.

He had nearly filled his belly with beans, cole slaw, mashed potatoes, country cured ham, cornbread and ponebread and corn on the cob. That was before he sampled the souse meat from last winter's hog butchering, Mrs. Wilkins's pickled pigs' feet and Mrs. Bowman's watermelon rind preserves. He had become so proficient at this kind of gorging that he seemed to be able to do this without looking at what he was eating.

It could have been that his sense of smell was more important to accomplish the feat than his sense of sight. This ability also provided him the luxury of keeping his vision, even if only slantwise, on Madeleen, and especially as she was no longer moving around but had anchored herself to the granddaddy oak tree.

Of course, Jimmie Sue's cronies were well aware of his attention toward Madeleen. It was almost like the weakening of Samson when Delilah cut off his hair. Madeleen hadn't cut off Jimmie Sue's hair, but the boys certainly noticed that he wasn't on top of things in his life as he ordinarily would be.

So when he was trying to eat without looking at what he was putting into his mouth and watching Madeleen without being noticed, Walt Bowen slipped a hot pepper on his plate unbeknownst to him.

Jimmie Sue absentmindedly picked up the pepper, stuffing all of it into his mouth before chomping vigorously down on it. One chomp was enough to provide the full flavor and temperature of the tidbit. He sputtered the whole thing out, as he went running to the lemonade jug.

Only the boys knew for sure what was happening. The other folks thought that Jimmie Sue was becoming a real klutz. They usually saw him as self-confident, if not a little cocky at times.

After the fall in the church and his running around spitting something out of his mouth made them wonder what had happened to him. *Was he maybe getting' some kin of ailment like the St. Vitus Dance?*

When Jimmie Sue finished washing out his mouth, he went and stood next to his mamma, who was standing right in front of his daddy. It wasn't that he'd ordinarily stand that close to his folks at any gathering what might be attended by his cronies, but Madeleen's perch on the ground was only a few feet away.

In fact, when Jimmie Sue stood next to Great-Grandma Sue, he was only about five feet from Madeleen.

He had noticed that Madeleen had uncovered a pie, which she was holding there in her lap. He couldn't tell if it was chocolate or not, as it was topped high with a luscious-looking brown-tipped meringue.

When everyone's stomachs were full, the noise subsided a bit, except for an occasional belch provided by one of the boys for the entertainment of the other boys everyone else. The children had quieted down with some having fallen asleep; the grownups seemed to have run out of local news to exchange before clearing things away; and some of the young folks had paired off, somewhat hidden behind some tree trunk.

Elder Hiatt took all this as his cue to "say a few words."

"Brothers an' Sisters, it's good to see so many of you here today to share in Christian fellowship and the yields of our fields. For some reason or other the thought comes to me of Emmanuel, which name means that God is with us."

When he said "Emmanuel", Emmett, who had been leaning against a tree, looked as though he'd been struck by lightning. He glanced over toward the Hiltons, where Aunt Lily was standing next to Levi, but watching Emmett. Emmett's eyes, sparkling with fear, met Aunt Lily's smiling eyes of understanding and reassurance.

Brother Hiatt went on. "Hit's so good to see the Methodists here and the Presbyterians, an' even some folks from outta town. As I've said so many times before, that when we do get to heaven, the Good Lord's not gonna separate us an' put the Baptists hyar an' the Methodists thar an' the Presbyterian ovah yondah, jest 'cause we go to different churches hyar on th' yearth. No, my friends we'll all share thet mansion with Jesus, as he said, 'In my Father's house are many mansions.' An hit's my belief thet he's not building differnt pigpens to keep us apart."

This caused some laughter and some awkward glances toward the coloreds, as some folks were a little uncomfortable with this thought of celestial togetherness.

Jimmie Sue simply muttered under his breath, "Will he have different cowpens to keep the Black Angus heifer 'way from the Whiteface Hereford bull?"

He hadn't thought anyone could hear him, but his mamma did hear him and swung 'round to slap him in the face for such sacrilege. Seeing her right hand coming, he stepped back but his heel hit a rock, causing him to lose his balance, falling on his backside. His beloved hat fell to one side, as his head went all the way down into a cushion-like softness.

Madeleen looked down onto her lap, where Jimmie Sue's head had landed right plop in the middle of her meringue-topped chocolate pie. She tittered slightly, then asked sternly, "White Boy, why yoah head be in my lap squishin' my chocolate pie? Ya' know ya' ruint mah pie, whut I cooked las' night afta you boys lef' our place! An' whether you reelize it or not, you be techin' me agin." This wasn't nearly as serious as it sounded. She seemed to enjoy seeing Jimmie Sue, every once in awhile being brought down a peg or two.

It wasn't so much the touch as the proximity of the eyes that then intimidated Madeleen. Perhaps she was beginning to develop the conjuring abilities of her mamma to look into and through a person's eyes all the way deep into their soul.

Jimmie Sue apologized as well as he could, as he stood up in the midst of the merriment of amused onlookers. The boys thought this accident of Jimmie Sue's was even better than any of the pranks they could have planned.

Walt said, "You like chocolate so good, you got plenny uv it now." as he looked toward the chocolate girl.

Someone, Jimmie Sue couldn't tell who, yelled from the crowd, "You always got sech a waggin' tongue, let's see now whether yoah tongue be long 'nuff to lick all thet good chocolate an' meringue off the top of yoah head."

Roy, who was standing close by, whispered in Jimmie Sue's ear, "You like it better with the white on top uv the chocolate or the chocolate on top uv the white?"

Jimmie Sue, knowing full well what Roy was meaning, jumped up and took off after him, leaving Madeleen sitting on the ground with a ruined pie amidst a crowd of people who had thoroughly enjoyed the show, after they realized that no one was really hurt.

A sideshow, hardly noticed by anyone but the participants, happened concurrently with Jimmie Sue's crashing onto Madeleen's lap. When

Great-Grandma tried to slap Jimmie Sue for his disrespectful sassiness toward Preacher Hiatt's assessment of the togetherness of heaven, her miss threw off her equilibrium.

And, as Jimmie Sue was literally falling for and toward Madeleen, Great-Grandma Sue stumbled awkwardly sideways into Great-Grandpa's arms, when he tried to prevent her from falling all the way to the ground. It was a new physical situation for the both of them—at least a renewed situation of closeness—in a way that had long been forgotten. They held the embrace for a few moments until Jimmie Sue's cataclysm drew their attention in his direction.

When Jimmie Sue returned to the "scene of the crime," he saw Madeleen still sitting on the quilt pallet, holding the battered pie in her lap. Her full attention was on her destroyed work of art. Jimmie Sue wanted so much to make amends, but he knew of no strategy except to apologize again. "Madeleen, I'm jest as sorry as I kin be. I didn't go to a'fend you agin."

Without taking her gaze off the pie, Madeleen stuck her finger in the remains, which she brought slowly and deliberately to her mouth to taste her masterpiece, before breaking the awkward silence. "Jimmie, I heered you's partial to chocolate pie, so my cookin' it was kinda special."

"You baked it yoahself? I really be 'pologizin' all ovah agin."

"Ya know, I nevah heered abody 'pologize so much. Maybe I be callin' you Sorry Sue, 'stead of Jimmie Sue."

Jimmie Sue was uncharacteristically at a complete loss for words.

"Naw, Jimmie Sue, now I be sorry, fer thar be no call to be namin' you nasty names. Hit's nice to know a person kin try to make up fer his shortcomin's, an' I nevah seen no white boy be so cordial to a colored girl.... I 'preciate thet."

Not knowing what else to do, Jimmie Sue stuck his forefinger into the demolished pie, headed it toward his anxious mouth, but stopping in mid-air, he cautiously pointed the luscious chocolate-tipped finger toward Madeleen's full red lips.

"No, White Boy, we ain't goin' thet far. You go 'head an' taste what deliciousness you *coulda* had. Maybe the Good Lord be standin' in the way."

Jimmie Sue blurted back, "Have ya evah thought hit might be the devil what stand in the way?"

The mention of the devil alerted Madeleen's flashing eyes.

He didn't want to rile her again so he accepted her lack of approval and stuck his finger in his mouth with the most delicious chocolate and meringue pie he'd ever tasted—even that of his mamma's—as he gazed back at the colored girl.

Her hypnotic eyes, compounded by the heavenly chocolate on the end of his forefinger, caused him to forget the circumstances surrounding them. He stood there transfixed with his finger in his mouth like a toddler who hadn't given up thumb-sucking. Becoming aware of the boys standing around them, he quickly popped out his finger, causing all of them to laugh uncontrollably, slapping each other on the back and pointing to their troubled friend.

Madeleen didn't laugh. She continued to look—even with a bit of sympathy.

After their few moments of shared silence—filled with their own questions, fantasies, regrets— they quietly turned away to join their respective families, cleaning up and clearing out to head to home and the evening chores.

* * *

CHAPTER 10

Grounded

Jimmie Sue was uncharacteristically quiet all the way home in the buckboard, causing his siblings to wonder if he had some kind of ailment. His folks figured they knew what his problem was, but neither of them knew how to help him except to leave him alone with his own thoughts and contemplations.

He was wondering what Madeleen might be thinking about on her way home with her family.

As a matter of fact, she was unusually talkative—not about what had happened between her and Jimmie Sue at the dinner on the grounds, but the church service itself, and how the white folks had treated the Hiltons so neighborly. "Maybe," she said, "we be heedin' the voice of Jesus, when he say, in the Good Book, 'Love one another.'"

Cletus agreed, "Especially don't you mean when it come to the lovin' of Jimmie Sue."

This abrupt challenge to her meditation caused her to say, "Hesh yo' mouth, Cletus. Hit got nothin' to do with Jimmie Sue."

"Oh yeah? You know he ain't been saved. You 'member thet time when you chastised him when you said 'hit won't do to give the preachah yo' han', you gotta go to the altar rail an' give the Lord yoah heart'?"

She then corrected Cletus, "An' you have no idee whether or not he's give his heart to the Lord. 'Ye shall seek him in secret'."

There was a pause before Clyde, her older brother, replied hesitantly. *And He shall reward thee openly.*

Madeleen, being the scripture authority in the family, glowered at him, not because he misquoted scripture, but because he quoted it exactly, taking the argument in a direction she didn't want to go.

Clyde then defensively responded to her accusative stare, "Well, hit says somethin' like thet, an' we ain't seen no 'openly' God reward diffrence in Jimmie Sue of late, 'cept him fallin' down so much at the church today. Thet don't really seem natchel fer him."

Cletus came up with a great suggestion. "Why don't you . . . why don't we invite Jimmie Sue to go to our revival services, whut be comin' up after corn-shuckin' time?"

Madeleen thought for awhile about Cletus's suggestion then agreed that she thought that was a good idea.

Their conversation was accompanied by the sounds the of the clanking of the iron wagon tires on the road gravel and the clopping of the mule's shoes on the hard-pan surface of the road.

The little sister, Ruthie, who was called "Sistah", was curled up in a blanket and asleep on the wagon bed floor next to Madeleen.

Their daddy, Levi, hadn't said a word after he hitched the mule to the wagon, and their mamma, Lily, was also rather quiet—but paying real close attention to everything her children had been talking about.

Madeleen thought it was strange that what was done and said and sung and prayed at the white church wasn't that much different from that in their own colored church. She said to her mamma, "It seemed kinda normal an' natcheral to me, an' ever'one, even those boys what're friends of Jimmie Sue's acted real decent to me an' Cletus."

Cletus said, "I think they learnt somethin' when they come to our house yesterday."

Clyde said, "Emmett sure was a whole heap different from what I usually see him bein'."

When Aunt Lily determined that they had ended their conversation, she smiled knowingly and looked up the country road ahead, while wondering what the *family* road ahead might be. *She'd have to set her conjurin' min' on lookin' ahead down thet road.*

When Jimmie Sue and family got home, everyone went about their usual evening chores and activities. After the milking and feeding were done, they all sat down—rather tired from the full day they'd had—to the supper Great-Grandma Sue had warmed over from the leftover dinner on the grounds.

They all gradually began discussing the events of the day: the church service, the abilities and styles of the various preachers, who was there and who wasn't.

What seemed to occupy most of the attention was the presence of the Hiltons, the only colored family there, aside from the colored preacher and his family, who had actually accepted the open invitation that had been extended to all the churches in the surrounding vicinity.

"Well, they had a right to be there, didn't they?" blurted out Jimmie Sue.

"Yes, honey, they did," answered his mamma, "but hit jest felt un . . ."

"Un*natchel?*" asked Jimmie Sue.

"No, . . . jest un*usual,*" answered his mamma.

George Dowell piped up, "Why wuz you fallin' all ovah the place so many times today, Jimmie Sue? Surely you don't have the palsy at yoah age, do you?"

Jimmie Sue just bit his tongue and didn't attempt to answer.

Rosie, the youngest of the Bennetts, broke the awkwardness when she said, "Whut I liked most was gettin' to play with Ruthie."

Simon yelled, "You mean thet little colored Hilton girl?"

"Yeah!"

Simon continued, "What I found to be the funniest . . ."

Great-Grandpa Robert said, "I don't think the day was s'posed to be funny."

Jimmie Sue didn't say anything out loud, but under his breath said, *Why don't you keep yoah fat mouth shut, Simple Simon?*

Thelma Lou, Jimmie Sue's older sister, said, "Well hit sure *was* funny to see Jimmie Sue land his head in that chocolate pie in the lap of thet chocolate girl. Thet white meringue with thet chocolate fillin' on top of all thet red hair was sure 'nuff colorful enough fer a circus, even if it wadn't s'posed to be funny."

"Hesh up!" cautioned Great-Grandma.

Thelma Lou wasn't about to quit, now that she had the floor. "I think thet not only did Jimmy Sue fall *in* her lap, but he be fallin' *fer* her . . . Madeleen . . . a colored girl."

Jimmie Sue had had about all he was going to take. The day's events were humiliating enough without the family now compounding his embarrassment.

It was time to take action with more than words, so he loaded a blob of mashed potatoes onto the tines of his fork, then holding the handle in his right hand he held the other end of the loaded fork with his left hand, putting a lot of backward pressure on it until he deliberately let it slip from under his left hand—thus sending a projectile of squishy potatoes across the table aimed directly at Thelma Lou.

The potato cannonball hit its mark, right on the bridge of Thelma Lou's nose and splattering over both her eyes. She started yelling, calling Jimmie Sue names that certainly weren't heard at church.

Great-Grandma stood up and hurriedly walked behind Thelma Lou, and shook her shoulder vigorously. "You know better then to use them kinda words at the suppah table or anywhere else in this house."

Wiping the goo from her face, she retorted, "But Jimmie Sue . . ."

Great-Grandpa said, "I'll take keer of Jimmie Sue, but you pay 'tention to yo' mamma an' leave the table."

"Whut you gonna do to Jimmie Sue?"

"Nevah you nevah min'."

Everyone waited . . . *im*patiently . . . for Great-Grandpa to deliver his verdict on Jimmie Sue. Quite calmly, almost like any other evening when he might be outlining the next day's jobs, he said, "Jimmie Sue, I need you to sucker the north field 'baccer t'morrow. An' when thet's done you can muck out the cow's stall."

This was a punishment worse than being sent to the chain-gang. "But we wuz goin' to Frank Fulp's livestock barn t'morrow to take a look at them Missouri mules he brung in on the train las' week. You promised."

Frank Fulp was noted, far and wide, for having the best livestock barn within three counties. He occasionally had a milkcow or a bull and sometimes a goat—billy or nanny—even a hound dog every now and then. Other folks might bring in all sorts of animals and chickens to swap in the livestock yard.

The whole event was almost like the county fair, without the cooking contests.

But Frank's horses, and more especially his Missouri mules, were the talk of all the farmers for miles around. It was a special treat just to go and inspect all the livestock, even if a body had no notion of buying anything. The Bennett men seemed to enjoy that more than even the traveling circus or going fishing.

"We *will* be goin'—me an' Simon an' George Dowell."

"But why . . ."

"Thet'll be yo' punishment fer throwin' yoah taters at Thelma Lou."

"But she . . ."

"Don't make it no worse, son. An' while you be thinkin' 'bout it, why don't you jest 'pologize to her, an' she'll 'pologize to you."

Thelma Lou was indignant. "I don't see why . . ."

"Thelma Lou, you wanna help Jimmie Sue sucker the 'baccer t'morrow? I'm sure he'd 'preciate a little help."

She reconsidered her situation with any further ramifications of her sharp tongue. "I be sorry Jimmie Sue fer throwin' off on ya an' Madeleen thetaway."

After a slight pause; "I didn't go t'hurt ya, Thelma Lou."

"Jest hurt m'feelin's."

Their daddy interrupted their little friendly exchange, "Jimmy Sue, you ain't 'pologized to 'er yet."

"I 'pologize, Thelma Lou . . . but, I hope you won't badmouth the Hiltons no moah."

"Naw, they seem to be good folks, even if they are colored."

Her mamma said, "Let's have no more colored talk tonight."

Jimmie Sue welcomed his mamma's admonition for no more colored talk. It eased some of the pressure of the day's activities and the absolute puzzlement unleashed by his feelings, which he was still attempting to sort out.

Even though there was to be no more out-loud colored talk, the cautious warning ran again through his head,

But, she's colored.

* * *

CHAPTER 11

Water Encounter

    Jimmie Sue hadn't slept well that night after his daddy had told him he wouldn't get to go to Ralph Fulp's livestock sales barn the next day. Great-Grandpa said that Jimmie Sue was probably too old to thrash. He told Great-Grandma, "He might be 'bout the right age to sucker a patch uv 'baccer right by hisself."

It wasn't so much the punishment that kept Jimmie Sue awake, as it was all the happenings and feelings the day before at the homecoming meeting at the church and the *dinner on the grounds* afterwards.

The next morning he was so all-fired mad about having to do all that work by himself, but especially missing seeing those new Missouri mules at the livestock barn. He'd even been thinking he'd try to convince his daddy to bid on one of them.

It was Simon's turn to do the milking, but after Jimmie Sue had slopped the hogs, eaten his breakfast of country ham and gravy with a dollop of molasses on his biscuit, he headed off to the field to take his punishment.

He would sometimes stand up to his daddy, but not this time. Maybe he was welcoming the opportunity to spend some time alone without so many people—grown-ups and kids alike—all around him.

He knew it was going to be a hot day, as dog days were still in full force, and it hadn't rained in—what seemed to be—weeks. He reckoned if he got the job done quickly, he'd be able to take a dip in the swimming hole, which was also the baptizing hole for all the churches, including Madeleen's colored church.

Leaving the house for the suckering job in such a hurry, and worrying about the heat, he didn't wear anything except his overalls. Even his pant legs were rolled up to this knees. And, of course, he was barefoot. He even forget his straw hat. It was most unusual for Jimmie Sue to step out of the house without his straw hat.

I might explain about suckering tobacco. In order for the leaves to grow as large as possible, the top of the plant must be topped at about four to five feet high. If this weren't done, the plant would grow much taller with spindly leaves all the way up and down. This also prevented it from going to seed at the top, which would sap all the plant's energy and would nurture the seeds instead of the leaves.

A few sturdy plants were left to go to seed for next year's crop. But after it was topped, little suckers would grow at the base of each leaf where it joined the stalk, and they would have to be snapped off by hand. The hot messy job of suckering had to be done at least twice each summer in all the fields.

Jimmie Sue was so angry and flustered about his punishment that he finished the suckering in record time, although he was lucky that no one was checking on him and on how good a job he might've been doing.

It should be mentioned that having on so few clothes would be a problem because of the tar on the green tobacco, which would deposit itself on anything that touched it, seemingly, particularly any part of the human body that had any hair on it. The tarry substance would cover every part not covered by clothing, particularly hair bristles, which included those on the arms as well as on the head. So by time he'd finished suckering, his red hair looked black from the tar and his arms looked like those of a colored boy.

He finished the job so quick that he got to the house nearly two hours before dinnertime. But when he got to the house Great-Grandma looked at him in that fix and said, "Law me, Jimmie, what was you thinkin' 'bout goin' off to the 'baccer field without bein' covered?"

"I reckin I wadn't thinkin' 'bout much."

"I should say you wadn't. Jest look at yoahself. You a sight in this world. You look like you belong to the Hilton family."

"Maybe I do."

"James Lafayette Bennett, don't you be asassin' yoah mamma thetaway. You wouldn't want me to be tellin' yoah daddy now, would you?"

"No, ma'am."

"Well, we'll ferget 'bout tellin' Papa, but yoah certainly not comin' inta the houses lookin' like thet. You got plenny uv time to go down to the creek an' get warshed up. Dinnah ain't gonna be ready fer quite a spell ennyway."

"Okay, Mamma. I was kinda aimin' to go down thar to the swimmin' hole."

"Is thet thar swimmin' hole whut we all use fer baptizin's?"

"Yeah!"

"Hit don't seem right to be usin' the baptizin' place fer a swimmin' hole where all kinds athings prob'ly be goin' on."

"Ain't nothin' goin' on but swimmin an' playin' 'roun a little."

"Hit's the 'playin' 'round a little' what seem troublesome."

"Yes'm!"

"An' don't you ferget the soap—the strong lye soap, 'cause you know thet storeboughten stuff won't get all thet tar off."

"Yes ma'am," he answered, as he picked up a bar of his mamma's homemade lye soap off the back porch shelf next to the washpan, and then sauntered off toward the creek.

"An' don't ferget yoah hat, even though yoah head already be filthed up with all thet black tar. A body can't even tell thet you got red hair."

He answered her only by picking his hat off the peg on the porch post, plopping it on his head and hastening his steps down the hill toward the water for a hoped-for refreshing dip in the swimming hole for some private swimming.

He knew no one else would be there, as they would either be in the fields or over to Pierson at Frank Fulp's livestock barn.

Once he got within the protective screening of the bushes at the edge of the woods, but before he was even within eyesight of the creek, he'd already shucked his overalls, which, of course, was all he had on—except his hat which was still perched on top of his tarred-over red shock of hair. The outline of his overalls' bib silhouetted on his chest and the white outlines of the galluses crossed his shoulders, criss-crossing over his back.

While standing there in his birthday suit with his overalls flung across his shoulder and only his hat on his head, he drank in the quiet of the scene. He could hear the burbling from the downstream side of the waterhole where there was a little kind of a waterfall. Chirping of all sorts of birds could be heard, as well as the crickets fiddling with their hind legs.

Everything seemed so peaceful that he was about to forget what he'd been so upset about, and he certainly was looking forward to jumping into that cool swimming hole, even though this time it was supposed to be for washing off all that black gunk.

Then, all of a sudden, he heard an unusual sound, seemingly coming from underneath the rock overhang which he and the other boys would use as a jumping-off place. But his cronies wouldn't be to the swimming hole until next Saturday when the bosses—their daddies—would give them a work-break from the fields.

The sound was slight, barely audible, splashing sounds of water. He heard, harmonizing with the water sound, a girl's voice softly singing, "Shall we gather at the river, Where bright angel feet have trod; With the crystal tide forever, Flowing by the throne of God?"

By the time he heard the answer "Yes, we'll gather at the river . . ." he knew that it was assuredly Madeleen's voice, but what would she be doing down here at the creek? The Hiltons were never known to come down here except for their baptizings, and everyone would know when those times would be appointed.

Wanting to check out for sure what was going on, he sneaked up close where he could peek through a thick wild azalea bush right above the diving-off rock. Apparently the source of the singing was beneath the overhang, but as he continued to watch he saw a dark brown figure start toward the opposite, north creek bank. Patches of sunlight, beaming through the tree branches, glistened on the wet black curly hair of Madeleen and glowed on her brown tawny shoulders.

This situation was indeed an obstacle to his washing up for dinner—but the predicament was much more than that, as he was mesmerized by the vision of this dark angel, even though he didn't know where the "bright angel feet (might) have trod."

He realized that being a bit of a trickster himself, that every curve in the road or bend in the river presents a new opportunity, so he made up his mind right then and there to take advantage of this chance to encounter Madeleen in a new, although tricky, situation. It didn't take him long to devise a plan.

Pretending that he didn't know whether there was a soul within a mile, he went running down the slope toward the diving rock, wearing nothing but his hat. He leapt high into the air off the rock, gathering his knees up to his chest. He splashed an impressive cannonball into the swimming hole, sounding like the thud of a huge rock being dropped into deep water. As his balled-up body went hurtling through the air, his hat hovered in the air above him.

Madeleen was startled out of her wits and, turning abruptly toward the sound, she saw only a straw hat floating on the top of bobbing waves.

She hurriedly waded to deeper water where only her head and shoulders were visible. She was holding in her right hand a knobby stick, which she was using to help maintain her balance and to ward off any threatening snake, which would likely put the fear of God in her. She was well aware of the Garden of Eden story about Eve and the conniving snake, which she often dreamed about but hoped never to meet.

Now here was a completely unexpected encounter in her precious baptizing pool, which was a sacred site to her.

Emerging from his audacious water spout, Jimmie Sue's head came up right under his floating straw hat, about fifteen feet from Madeleen.

For several seconds, which seemed like an eternity to each of them, they stood transfixed with a rainbow of emotions, both realizing the compromising situation they were in.

Jimmie Sue broke the silence. "If this creek wadn't so nice an' cool, I'd say we wuz in some mighty hot watah." His feet sank into the miry sand with each step as he started wading over closer to her.

Madeleen wasted no time in pulling her stick out of the water, raising it above her head and warning, "White Boy, you come one step closter an' I be makin' souse meat outta yoah punkin-head—noggin." She lowered the stick until it rested on top of the water with one end in her hand and the other pointing right at Jimmie Sue's bare chest.

Somewhat imitating Madeleen's and her family's mode of speech, he said, "Why you be callin' me 'White Boy' agin?"

"'cause you be actin' like White Boy."

"Oh! an' whut do White Boy be actin' like?" By this time he had taken a hold of his end of the pole forming the barrier between the two of them.

"White Boy always acts like he can get whatever he wants, whenever he wants it, from whoever he wants it from. But nothin' can be happenin' atween us, 'cause there already be too much high-yaller in our fambly."

"There ain't nothin' wrong with a touch."

"I know what be happenin' if we be atouchin'. If we's someplace else an we be somebody else, things'd be different, maybe, but we ain't someplace else an' we ain't somebody else 'cept our ownselves. I gotta live with my fambly, an' you gotta live with yoah folks an' neighbors an' church members."

"Thet ain't no call to be namin' me 'White Boy'."

"We be a talkin' too much. White Boy."

"Maybe I ain't bein' no white boy. Maybe I be colored like Mamma said."

"Whut you mean?"

"Mamma said with all the 'baccer gum all ovah me thet I look like I belong to yoah family."

"Why yoah mamma be throwin' off on my fambly thetaway? Thet don't sound like Mrs. Bennett atall."

"She didn't mean nothin' bad 'bout whut she said."

"Well, I tell you right now, I seen lotsa things in mah time, but I ain't never seed no colored boy nor white boy nor high-yallered boy with the colorin' you got, what with them black arms an' head, speckeldy spots on yoah face an' streakedy stripes down yoah back. Yo look mo' like a Dominecker chicken than a boy of any color . . . . Yo'd look even mo' like a Dominecker rooster iffen I could see some of yo' red rooster comb through thet black gum on yoah chicken head."

Jimmie Sue really enjoyed her spunk and her sense of humor. "You think you be the Black Cornish pullet?"

"White Boy, don't you be belittlin' me an' don't you be fergettin' thet me an' you both be nekkid 'neath the top of this hyar watah, though I can't really see you an' you can't really see me. But we both see 'nuff to know we can get inta a heap of trouble."

"You right 'bout both of us be nekkid undah the watah, but the same thing be true with our clothes on."

"What you mean?"

"Neath our clothes we jest nekkid as a jaybird."

"Don't be afoolin'. Jest don't be fergettin'."

"Believe you me, I ain't fergettin' nothin', p'tickular *'bout faith is fer things hoped fer, the evidence of things not seen.*"

"I didn't know you was no han' fer quotin' scripture . . . . You musta been readin the Bible of late."

"Yeah . . . a little . . . especially fer askin' the Lord for things hoped fer but seem right nigh impossible"

"This ain't no time fer quotin' scripture to me standin' hyar in the deepest watah I evah been in in mah life. An' as hit sez in the book of Proverbs, *as in watah face answereth to face,* but this hyar face gonna quit answerin' to yoah face."

Jimmie Sue was stunned by her quick retort and amazing insight into the reality of the situation. They had both been schooled in lots of Bible verse, which could be useful in times of peril or even embarrassing when someone else was quoting.

He changed the subject. "Don't you know thet this is where us boys come swimmin'? . . . An' you know we don't wear no clothes in hyar?"

"Yeah!"

He asked, "Why you come down hyar this mawnin'?"

"I knowed all the boys'd be workin' in the fields this mawnin' or ovah to Frank Fulp's livestock barn. Thet's whar Daddy an' Cletus an' Clyde be today. So they all gone, so I hadda sucker the 'baccer. I come down to warsh off my 'baccer tar.

"But why you be hyar; why not you be ovah to Frank Fulp's sales barn?"

Jimmie Sue started laughing so hard it caused ripples across the surface of the swimming hole. "Thet's 'zactly, why I be hyar. I hadda sucker 'baccer too. I come down to warsh off all that black 'baccer gum. Looka hyar, I'm jest as black as you now."

Madeleen couldn't help from laughing her ownself, as she loosened her grip on her end of the barricading stick. Jimmie Sue jiggled the stick a little as a kind of pretend tug-of-war. She immediately joined in the game, pulling it back toward her. Jimmie Sue applied more power, almost pulling her off her feet and up toward the surface of the water. The next time, she pulled with such energy that Jimmie Sue deliberately released the stick, causing her to fall backwards into the water, completely immersing herself like being immersed in this very spot if she was to come to the Lord at their next revival meeting. Maybe this was a different kind of baptism—not the usual churchy baptism. The whole thing was certainly a new reality for her.

He rushed toward her, not knowing his own self whether it was to take advantage of her or to save her from drowning.

Before he got to her, she resurfaced, spitting and sputtering, and, seeing him so dangerously close, her frightened eyes looked deeply into his perplexed blue eyes.

He was so completely mesmerized that he could neither move nor speak, but saw in the bewildered black pools of her eyes a different stream of water flowing over her high cheekbones and down her face, dripping off the edge of her jaw . . . not the obvious creek water, but the overflowing spring of her innocent soul.

She had by now dropped her protective pole, as it hadn't really helped anyway to keep him at arm's length.

Usually in control of any situation in which she found herself, she attempted to terminate this awkward situation as judiciously as possible. "I done warshed off all my 'baccer tar; now you go 'head an' warsh off yoah blackness. My black skin ain't nevah gonna warsh away, no mattah how long I be in this watah hole an' no mattah how much lye soap I scrub with. You go ahead an' warsh yoahself off."

Jimmie Sue was feeling terrible about putting Madeleen into this compromising spot, but he couldn't go to her—that'd just make matters worse. He couldn't very well turn away and leave her—that would seem like a complete rejection.

It was then he saw his snake friend, swimming out from under the diving rock straight toward Madeleen. He yelled, "Watch out Madeleen! A snake is swimmin' right twarge you."

"I be plum' sick an' tired uv yoah foolishness, White Boy. Thet ain't nothin' but my stick I wuz usin' to keep you 'way from me."

"No! Look!"

She turned and saw over her right shoulder the snake about halfway between her and the far bank, slithering languorously in her direction.

She screamed, jumping up out of the water away from the impending danger, which caused the devil snake to reverse course and head downstream.

The damage had already been done. She had turned around to see the snake and in her fright had fallen backward into Jimmie Sue's arms. He couldn't avoid her, even if he had tried to—even if he had wanted to.

The last time this had happened, they had clothes on, which kept skin from skin.

This time was different—the water provided no real barricade.

If he had earlier thought he was in hot water, he was now in a sizzling stew.

Madeleen's attention changed abruptly from the retreating snake to Jimmie Sue, as she pulled away immediately, although the density of the water prevented her from retreating quickly.

Jimmie Sue, attempting to make light of the whole thing, said, "This time *you* teched me."

Realizing she was in deep water in more ways than one, rebounded, "Whatever be teching you, you be teching."

"Whut good be techin', if they ain't no holdin'?

Madeleen was a safe distance away from him by then. "Holdin' *on* is like holdin' *up*. Thar gotta be somethin' thar to hold *up*. An' to hold *on* thar gotta be somethin' to *hold on to*. An' you know as good as me thet we can't be holdin' onto nothin.'"

Jimmie Sue thought, *Sometimes cain't a person jest hold, without it bein' holdin' up or holdin' on?* He didn't dare say it, as this didn't seem the right time to get to arguin' with Madeleen about anything.

Instead, he retrieved his hat, perched it precariously on the back of his head, and said, "Maybe I better be finishin' dressin' after I get this 'baccer tar off."

Anxious to get out of the water and the difficult situation, Madeleen answered, "While you be finishin' yoah bathin', I be gettin' outta the watah, an' dressin' mah own self."

"Yeah! All right."

"But you be scrubbin' yoahself lookin' up the creek, so's you not be lookin' at me in mah sinful nekkedness."

"There's nothin' sinful 'bout nekkedness."

"Hit be sinful now if you be lookin'."

"All right," he said as he turned upstream and started scrubbing, although he'd left the lye soap in his overalls pocket up behind the azalea bush. Instead of the soap he picked up some of the coarse sand from the creek bed. Although it was like emery on his skin, it was quite effective in getting rid of the tobacco tar.

He could hear, over the sound of the gurgling creek, Madeleen beginning to hum. He stopped washing, trying to make out what church tune it might be.

Then she started putting the words to it. "Yield not to temptation, for yielding is sin."

As he was assuredly tempted to look, he thought, *How does she always seem to know whut I'm thinkin'?*

It took him quite a while to rid himself of the tobacco gunk with the creek bottom sand. When he'd finished scraping off all the gum encasing so much of his body, still looking upstream, he yelled, "You dressed now?"

"Yeah!"

"Well I bettah get out an' get dressed."

"Yeah!"

"You gonna stay hyar?

"Yeah!"

"But when I get out to go up the bank to get mah clothes, I'll be nekked."

"Yeah! . . . You got yoah hat."

This really flustered him, as he wasn't sure whether to hold his hat over his behind or just wear it like normal on top of his head. "You turn yoah head now?"

"Yeah! . . . But which way?"

"You look twarge yoah home, while I be clim'in' up twarge my home."

"Yeah!"

He scrambled as quickly as possible up the south bank over the diving rock and retrieved his overalls. After putting them on he peered back toward Madeleen and saw her sitting on the north bank, looking straight at him.

He didn't know if she had just then turned around or had been looking the whole time—but then, it didn't differ one way or the other with him. If she'd wanted to look, he thought, *She kin look anytime she's a mind to.*

He walked back down and sat on the jumping-off rock. She was sitting on a stump on the opposite bank. They sat there for a while looking at each other, as though in deep meditation with the baptizing hole between them. They were as though contemplating each other as some strange creature looking back from across a vast expanse of water. It might have been the Red Sea so far as each of them may have known. No doubt they were both mulling over in their minds what had just happened and what it all meant then—or in the days still to come.

Finally, she broke the silence by yelling across the creek.. "We be havin' revival meetin's at our church the first week in October."

Jimmie Sue didn't answer. He just let her finish her thought or announcement or whatever it was she was intending to say to him.

"I be thinkin' you might like to . . . Cletus say we might invite you to our church for the revival . . . . That is if yoah innerested."

Another moment of silence!

"Brothah Hiatt be so nice as to invite us to yoah church homecomin' meetin' an' dinner on the grounds."

Jimmie Sue started to say something, but she continued.

"You like to visit our church fer revival meetin'?"

"Maybe."

After a bit more individual contemplation in silence, she began humming again. This time it wasn't *Yield Not to Temptation* but instead it was *Shall We Gather at the River.*

Saying their goodbyes, they headed off in different directions—he, up the south ridge and she up the north ridge –

To their respective homes in opposite directions, but each harboring similar thoughts.

Maybe—just maybe—there'll be more GATHERIN'S AT THE RIVER.

* * *

CHAPTER 12

Bringing in the Sheaves

As Dog Days had ended and it was getting on toward the end of August, reaping and haying time was fast approaching. Reaping would be the order of the day that particular day, and the last of the haying would be the following week.

Jimmie Sue knew that the Hiltons would be coming over for their swapping-work agreement, but he reckoned that only Uncle Levi and the boys would be coming. Although Jimmie Sue knew Madeleen could handle men's work like chopping wood and plowing, he was fairly sure that she'd be assigned that day only to help with the kitchen work.

Still, he was a little jubous (dubious) 'cause he hadn't seen her since their running into each other—literally—down at the swimming/baptizing hole a couple of weeks earlier. He'd reflected a lot about that incident, but had no idea what Madeleen might have thought about it.

Was she angry about how things had happened? or *Was she a little bewitched about what might could have happened?* or *Is she gonna avoid ever havin' anything to do with me again?* or *Maybe she thought the whole thing wadn't happenstance at all but was just a put-up thing deliberately conjured up by my own muddled brain.*

He had to admit to himself that indeed his brain was a little muddled up about his feelings and how things might have turned out either disastrously or more contentious on one hand or even more exciting on the other. He was pleased that overall they had left the crime scene fairly unscathed with either scandal or sin.

He had gone his way, and she had gone hers, even though they both had known that somehow things would never be quite as innocent for them as before.

He didn't have long to think about the situation when he saw the Hiltons coming over in their hay wagon. Madeleen was standing right in the middle of the wagon, leaning on her daddy for balance and scanning the view ahead. She saw Jimmie Sue at the exact moment that he saw her.

Even though the mule and wagon and Hilton family continued to move ahead, for a few moments, time stood still for both Madeleen and Jimmie Sue. When she was able to divert her eyes, she went to the back of the wagon and sat beside Ruthie with her legs dangling over the coupling pole, which extended a couple of feet behind the wagon bed. Cletus was riding the coupling pole and Clyde was walking with the dogs alongside of the Hilton parade. Aunt Lily was sitting by her husband on the wagon seat.

Some folks may not know what a coupling pole might be. It's a two-by-four hardwood beam, usually oak, that connects the front axle of the wagon to the back axle. The length of the wagon bed can be changed by moving the back axle forward or backward on the coupling pole, which normally extends at least a couple of feet past the end of the wagon bed. The boys might get into a fight over who was going to get to ride the coupling pole, which would give the lucky rider a jouncy ride even over fairly even ground.

Madeleen's action, so far, wasn't at all reassuring to Jimmie Sue, but he figured that maybe she had been looking ahead to see if he might be in sight, and when she saw him, she simply went and sat down, satisfied that he would be working in the field that day with her family.

Yeah, he told himself, *thet's 'zactly how it happened. She wanted to make sure thet I'm on hand, even if we be only workin' an' not havin' no chance really to be atalkin'.*

Great-Grandpa Robert and Uncle Levi decided how the work was going to be divided up for the grain reaping.

Using the sickle for cutting the hay was a whole lot easier than cutting the wheat and rye at harvesting time. Of course this was a long time before mowing machines had come in, so everything was done by hand . . . and with the proper tools of course.

Jimmie Sue hadn't yet been assigned the job of cutting the grain crops; that was still left up to Uncle Levi and Great-Grandpa Robert, because the cradle was mighty heavy and required a great deal of dexterity. Previous experience was also helpful.

The scythe that was used on the grain was called a cradle, since you might just think of it as cradling the stalks and grain heads when they were cut, leaving behind only the cut stubble. At the lower end of the cradle's curved handle—about five feet long—the arced blade projected out at an oblique angle. Right above the blade were four wooden fingers—the same length as the blade (four-foot) and curved the same as the blade. They were also fastened to the handle by a right-angled extension bar.

The mower or reaper would swing the blade only a few inches above the ground in an arcing motion, and the cut stalks would fall into the cradle or wooden tines. The force of the swing would also move all the stalks toward the vortex or point closest to the reaper.

He would then let go of the handle with his left hand and picking up the handful of grain stalks from the wooden tines, he would lay them down on the ground for the fellow following close behind to bunch up the handfuls and then to tie them with a few other cut stalks into a sheaf.

It was a marvel to watch the reaper as he had to step forward with his right foot as he swung the grain cradle back toward the right. Then as he stepped forward with his left foot he would swing the grain cradle to the left cutting the grain stalks. It was like an elegant dance by the stalwart reaper.

They would work themselves clockwise around the grain field with this harvesting dance, as the unharvested area grew smaller and smaller. Breaking (plowing) the field in the spring always proceeded counter-clockwise, but the reaping went in the opposite direction.

Jimmie Sue and Simon were assigned to binding the sheaves and then laying them down for the next fellow—usually George Dowell—who would stack the sheaves in a little teepee-like affair with one sheaf spread out on top as a kind of roof so that if it was to rain before they'd bring in the sheaves the top sheaf would serve to shed the water. The reason the sheaves were left for a few days in the field was to give them time to dry out before packing them into the barn. Otherwise, if they would be packed while still damp, they could develop mold or else start a fire by internal combustion.

It looked somewhat like a thatched roof so that drops of rain running down the grain stalk, just the way water would be shed by the thatched roofs in the old country, like in the pictures they'd seen. These little hut-like stacks were left in the field for three or four days for the grain to get properly dried.

But on that day, Madeleen volunteered to help George Dowell with stacking the sheaves. Jimmie Sue said to himself, *Now why would she offer to work aside of George Dowell? Is she jest tryin' to get my goat by doin' thet or does she like perticular to build them little sheaf tepees afore we have to bring them in to the barn shed.?*

Oh, speaking of bringing in the sheaves there was a church song about sheaves which George Dowell always liked singing, and it nearly drove Jimmie Sue and everyone else crazy at reaping time by him continually singing it—over and over again:

> *Sowing in the morning, sowing seeds of kindness,*
> *Sowing in the noontide and the dewy eve;*
> *Waiting for the harvest and the time of reaping,*
> *We shall come rejoicing, bringing in the sheaves.*
> *Bringing in the sheaves, Bringing in the sheaves, We shall come rejoicing,*
> *Bringing in the sheaves, Bringing in the sheaves, Bringing in the sheaves,*
> *We shall come rejoicing, Bringing in the sheaves.*

George Dowell would keep on singing that song and even making up new verses, just unnerving everybody within hearing range, particularly Jimmie Sue.

Not only was Madeleen lending a hand to stacking up the sheaves, she was doing a much better job of it than George Dowell at topping the teepee of sheaves with the conical straw roof.

And what had begun really to irk Jimmie Sue—much more than George Dowell's singing—was the fact that his brother was working so close to Madeleen and that she seemed to be thoroughly enjoying joining in the stacking, as well as adding her melodic voice to his singing.

Jimmie Sue had heard her sing before, but not like this. He was truly amazed all over again at the clarity and sweetness of her voice. Adding insult to injury, when she began to take the lead part in the singing, George Dowell would start harmonizing.

The other workers would even stop occasionally to listen. It seemed almost as though those two voices were meant to go together. *Was this what George Dowell had begun to talk about as double-predestination? Was it pre-ordained that George Dowell and Madeleen would be harmonizin' through life?*

Jimmie Sue wasn't quite sure how he felt about the whole thing. It wasn't that he was outlandishly jealous; it was just that he felt completely left out of the music and perhaps left out of even more ever since that day he had encountered Madeleen in the baptizing hole.

After the morning reaping and sheaf-stacking were completed, everyone went to the Bennett house for dinner—the grown-ups eating in the kitchen and all the kids out on the front porch. After Madeleen filled her plate, she sat down right between Ruthie and the center porch post. Rosie was already sitting on the other side of Ruthie, who was swinging her little chubby legs which couldn't quite reach the ground.

Jimmie Sue was ahead of George Dowell in filling his plate, so he took advantage of sitting as close as possible to Madeleen, even though there was a post between the two of them.

Madeleen broke the awkward silence between them. "Jimmie Sue, you don't seem to have much to say today. I ain't heard you utter a single word, 'cept when you yelled at George Dowell to 'cut off thet infernal caterwaulin'."

"Well thet racket was getting' on my nerves."

"You didn't like my singin'?"

"Oh, nauw, it warn't thet. Yoah singin' was beaut . . . . it was purtier then a meadow . . . . it sounded right good." He cautioned himself about being too effusive with his assessment of her voice.

I don't know how she'll take it if I lay it on too much 'bout her purty singin'. 'sides, we ain't spoke a word since the swimmin' hole till right now.

She countered his awkwardness. "Thank ya!"

"'bout what?"

"'bout likin' my singin'."

"Oh yeah! I did like thet. But George Dowell'd been singin' thet song all mornin' afore you folks even got here. I s'pose he thought he was bein' right bright to sing *Bringin' in the Sheaves,* the very day we would be doin' thet very thing."

Madeleen said, "You know I was hummin' thet very same song on our way ovah here this mornin'."

"You did . . . I mean you wuz?"

They both chuckled a little before indulging themselves with eating, which helped to avoid further awkwardness of trying to find something uncompromising to say. After Jimmie Sue gulped the last of his glass of buttermilk he intoned, "Well there seems always to be somethin' thet comes atween us."

She asked, "Atween you an' me, you mean?"

"Yeah!"

"Like this porch post, ya' mean?"

He retorted "Dang the dad-blamed porch post! There be other things beside porch posts . . . ."

Her quick answer was, "Like what?" Receiving no answer, she continued, "Maybe, it's the Lord's will . . . ."

He didn't give her enough time to finish her pat response. "To hel . . . ."

Neither his—nor her—truncated statement was a considered thought. Both Jimmie Sue and Madeleen had just kind of blurted out a thoughtless response, and each of them would have regretted finishing the full sentence, knowing full well the other one would have felt wounded.

Realizing that her interrupted statement was just a too-hasty response to lots of life's mysteries, Madeleen also understood that Jimmie Sue almost swore at her.

They had both cleaned their plates, and Jimmie Sue stood up, turning toward the kitchen to return his plate. Sensing that Madeleen was awfully quiet, he stopped and turned to look at her. She sat as though stunned by images running through her mind or some catastrophe having almost happened.

He reached for her plate, which she continued to hold tightly. Without diverting her eyes from the blank stare over the mountain ridge, she said. "You don't need to. I can . . . ."

Tugging a little more insistently on her empty plate, Jimmie Sue replied, "And so can I."

She released the plate, which would have ordinarily been her responsibility to take to the kitchen to wash.

That afternoon everyone resumed their forenoon jobs. By time they'd got the rhythm of the reaping going, George Dowell had started the song all over again. Well it seems that Madeleen didn't join in. George Dowell started the last verse which starts with

Going forth with weeping, sowing for the master . . .

Madeleen would normally sing the sad, weeping songs and especially anything about the Master, but she was concerned that *Jimmie Sue seems to be bothered by my singin' . . . or is it just my singin' alongside George Dowell? MaybeI jest listen to George Dowell fer a while.*

George Dowell sang a bit more of *Bringing in the Sheaves* before he switched to another working song.

Work, for the night is coming, Work through the morning hours.

He looked over toward Madeleen, who still didn't join in the singing. He figured that maybe Madeleen didn't know that hymn in the colored church, so he just kept on singing right by himself. He was used to that anyways.

When he got to the last part of the last verse,

Work till the last beam fadeth, Fadeth to shine no more;
Work while the night is dark'ning, When man's work is o'er.

Madeleen felt compelled to join in then; again harmonizing her sweet angelic voice with George Dowell's.

George Dowell then commenced "Amazing Grace," knowing full well that that was one of Madeleen's favorite hymns, but after the *work* song, her singing seemed to be finished for the day.

Jimmie Sue noticed that during the last few times that George Dowell and Madeleen were constructing the wheat sheaf tepees, their hands would occasionally touch when she was topping the stack with the conical roof. Jimmie Sue began to watch much more closely until Simon yelled at him, "Jimmie Sue, you bettah hurry up! Yoah beginnin' to lag behind."

While trying to catch up with his work, Jimmie Sue tried to look as often as possible to see what was going on between the two stackers. He was sure that his brother was deliberately making sure his hand touched hers.

Jimmie Sue thought to himself, *Though she be makin' a play of keepin' away from him, she don't 'pear to be serious 'bout stayin' completely away from him. She prob'ly already fergot what I said thet there seems always to be somethin' what comes atween us, an' in this case it ain't jest some <u>thing</u>; it's some <u>body</u> an' thet somebody be my religious brother.*

When the day's work was finished, George Dowell thought it only fitting to sing the last of the work song:

Work while the night is dark'ning, When man's work is o'er.

Jimmie Sue reminded George Dowell, "You better not be fergettin' yoah work ain't over today till you get the milkin' done tonight. It's yoah turn tonight, don't you know?"

As the Hiltons clambered onto their wagon to head home for their chores and supper, Ruthie tried to claim the coupling pole, but Cletus reminded her that her legs were too short to reach the ground, "Sistah when you rides the couplin' pole you gotta be able to ride and walk at the same time or the bouncin' couplin' pole will throw you jest like a buckin' horse."

Cletus took his place on the coupling pole after he lifted Ruthie up onto the back of the wagon next to Madeleen.

Jimmie Sue stood at the corner of the barn, wondering whether he ought to say goodbye or not. Neither he nor Madeleen said anything, but she did wave in his direction.

As George Dowell was standing there too, it wasn't clear which one she was waving to or to the whole Bennett family or simply waving goodbye to the day, itself, with all that'd been shared.

That evening at supper, Jimmie Sue was almost remorseful and unusually docile. George Dowell seemed to be all wound up and still occasionally humming a line or two of "Bringing in the Sheaves". Jimmie Sue had almost had enough of the song, of George Dowell and of the image of Madeleen singing so sweetly with him.

Their mamma had heated up some of the garden vegetables and country ham they'd had at dinner that day. Thelma Lou had even gone out and picked enough blackberries for a cobbler.

The cobbler with a couple of tablespoons of fresh cream had mollified Jimmie Sue for a spell, until George Dowell started in again—this time not humming, but singing right out, knowing full well that Jimmie Sue was at his rope's end.

Slapping his hand on the top of the table hard enough to make the milk glasses dance and quiver, Jimmie Sue said, "Ain't we already had enough of thet infernal squally noise in the wheat field today?"

Great-Grandma said, "Why, Jimmie Sue, I'm real surprised at you not likin' George Dowell's singin'. Why I think he sing real purty."

Jimmie Sue retorted, "Yeah! Real purty when he be singin' with Madeleen—*thet colored girl.*"

George Dowell retorted, "So thet's what's eatin' at yoah craw—me singin' with Madeleen. Are yoah britches bunched up an' twisted 'cause I be singin' with a colored girl—or jest 'cause *thet* colored girl be the Hilton girl? Ever'body knows you been sweet on . . . ." George Dowell wasn't able to finish what he'd set out to say and what he'd been intending to tease Jimmie Sue about.

As Jimmie Sue was sitting across the table from George Dowell, he'd started to throw a forkful of mashed potatoes at his brother, but recalling what had happened the last time he'd done that to Thelma Lou, he simply threw his chair backwards and headed around the table to get to George Dowell, just rousting for a fight.

However, he hadn't taken into consideration that he had to run around his daddy, who caught him by his wrist and twisting it violently forced Jimmie Sue all the way to the floor to his knees.

"Now, Jimmie Sue, you know I don't tolerate no fightin' at the table—nor away from the table nuther."

"Well, he started—."

"Started what?"

"Started . . . the trouble."

"Started what trouble?"

"He started in singin' just to start thet thing he already been ribbin' me 'bout."

While everyone else was deafeningly silent, Great-Grandma added, "You mean 'bout Madeleen?"

"Yes'm."

She continued, "I thought we'd already talked all thet out."

"Yeah we did, but thet weren't no call fer him to start up all over . . . ."

Rosie, who'd been so startled by all the racket, climbed down from her highchair to intervene in Jimmie Sue's punishment which up to that moment had only been to force him into a kneeling position by his daddy's chair.

Trotting over to her daddy, she leaned against his knee and with her eyes brimming full with little sisterly love she said, "Daddy, could you let Jimmie Sue git up ? I know he be a good boy now."

She gave her daddy a little kiss on the cheek.

When his daddy relinquished and let go of Jimmie Sue's wrist, Rosie took his hand in hers and rubbing his released hand, she said, "Jimmie Sue, do you got a oweey-ouchy?"

"No, Rosie, my oweey jest got cured."

That seemed to settle the matter for the time being. Even though Rosie couldn't understand the complexities of grown-ups or even her older siblings, she had a way of simplifying everything by a tear or a kiss.

That evening the tear *and* the kiss were sufficient to calm down any brotherly misgivings, family differences or Jimmie Sue's personal perplexity.

* * *

CHAPTER 13

Haying

The week after the grain crops had been taken in, Great-Grandpa told the boys that the last of the haying would need to be finished, as they had already seen the Corn Moon . . . the full moon in September. "But first, we'll have to go help the Hiltons, 'cause in our work-swappin agreement they were ovah to our place last with the wheat-reapin'." The Hilton and Bennett menfolk had already agreed on that arrangement.

It had been a good year for all the crops on both farms, so the Hiltons' barn loft was practically full, except for room enough for moving around to throw hay down the hay mow into the cow and mule stalls. On all the neighbor farms the hay loft would be filled before any haystacks needed to be considered. But it was apparent that new haystacks would need to be built at the Hiltons'.

After their morning chores and breakfast were finished, Uncle Levi and the Hilton boys completed putting up the haystack pole where they'd be stacking the last of the hay crop. The night before, they'd used the post-hole diggers to dig the hole for the twelve-foot pole, which would be the center of the haystack to stabilize it against any rough weather.

Uncle Levi cautioned, "Now you boys make sure you tamp thet dirt down real good 'round thet pole so's it don't shift none with nary big winds."

Clyde said, "You might oughter throw some rocks in there too. Then it won't take so long to get it done." He was always eager to take a shortcut.

Everybody looked at Clyde as Uncle Levi spoke up again. "The rocks won't do no good iffen you don't tamp the dirt down real tight. But go ahead an' throw in a few smaller rocks. They certainly won't hurt nothin'."

At about that time the Bennetts could be seen with the whole family on board the buckboard. The grown-ups were sitting on the seat up front. Thelma Lou, George Dowell and Simon were sitting on the floorboard. Jimmie Sue was riding the coupling pole and holding Rosie so she could get the thrill of riding the coupling pole.

When the wagon came to a stop Great-Grandma Sue and Thelma Lou headed toward the kitchen but were met by Aunt Lily on the porch. Rosie went running to find Ruthie.

Once Jimmie Sue let Rosie loose, he got off the coupling pole and started looking for Madeleen, while he was wondering why she wasn't seen with Aunt Lily on the porch.

Is she gonna help in the kitchen work today or is she gonna try agin to work with the boys as another field hand?

The reason that it was so important for him was because the week before when they were harvesting the grain, Madeleen had seemed to pay more attention to George Dowell than to him.

Actually, that stood to reason, as Madeleen and George Dowell were doing the same kind of work then, stacking the sheaves for drying. And besides that they both knew how to sing and enjoyed singing together. Jimmie Sue thought, *I had no call to feel bad 'bout thet. I got no holt on Madeleen nor her on me.*

But then he countered his own contemplation, *Well George Dowell acted so persnickedy 'bout the whole dad-blamed matter, it was enough to gag a mule. Hit don't differ none atall to me whether she works in the kitchen or in the hay field.* Then he knew he was kidding himself about that. He knew he'd be terribly disappointed if she didn't work with the men and boys, which she was certainly capable of doing.

There was no point in further conjecture, as he saw her come out of the house, walk past Aunt Lily on the porch and head out toward the menfolks.

Jimmie Sue wondered again if Madeleen was going to go back into the house for womanly duties or would maybe go again like last week to work in the fields. His confusion continued as he saw her rush over to the hay wagon which her daddy had already hitched up.

It sure looked as if Madeleen was getting ready to go work with the haying crew. Jimmie Sue was anxious to say something to Madeleen . . .

but not anything really significant . . . so he just said, "Yoah helpin' today with the hayin'?"

"Yeah!"

"You not workin' in the kitchen?"

"Nope!"

"You rakin' or you pitchin'?"

What he was referring to was the raking job that would require a person with a big pitchfork to rake the mown dried hay into small mounds that could be managed by someone else to pitch the mound up onto the wagon..

"I ain't rakin' nor pitchin'."

"You jest gonna be ridin'?"

"I be trompin'."

He then understood that she'd be working on the wagon with a smaller pitchfork than the others on the ground. She, of course, would have an important but less strenuous job than the raking or pitching. She would have to place the hay as flat as possible and tramp it into place. This really was a crucial job, because if the tramper didn't do a good job, the whole hay load could shift and slip off the wagon on the hillside or while going over any bumps.

What concerned him was not so much the work she would need to do nor her ability to do it. But she wasn't wearing overalls, which was an outfit he knew she'd consider not womanly enough, although he had seen her at the Hiltons' wearing overalls while chopping wood.

Instead of overalls today, away from the safety and comfort in her own house, she was wearing her usual ankle-length work dress. He wondered about her being up on the wagon and him and the other men pitching hay and looking up at her . . . *an' what if a big wind comes along an' blows her dress up?*

Madeleen saw him ogling her dress, so she addressed the issue. "You be worried 'bout me wearin' a dress way up on thet wagon load of hay thetaway?"

"Nauw, I ain't worried 'bout thet . . . ."

She knew he was lying just to keep from being embarrassed or from embarrassing her. "Well, I'll jest fix thet." Right in front of him while he was still staring at her work clothes, she bent down and, taking a handful of the front of her dress hem and another at the back, she tied the handfuls into a square knot just below and between her knees. Her outfit then looked like a pair of pantaloons.

Jimmie Sue was amazed at her ingenuity and even more so at her daredevil attitude. She really seemed to be much less guarded now toward him.

The Bennetts' wagon was going to bring in the first hayload, and it became obvious that there must have been something about the coupling pole that enticed Madeleen. It was a sight to see her step up onto the wagon coupling pole with her left foot in such a way that she used it to spring all the way up onto the wagon bed with her right foot.

Jimmie Sue was paying particular attention to where Madeleen was going to sit in the wagon on the way to the hayfield. *Is she gonna go up front there an' set by George Dowell or is she gonna stay near the couplin' pole?*

He'd already plopped himself on the coupling pole, for he figured that she might would sit close by and maybe on it with him. Although some time people would ride the coupling pole facing backwards, Jimmie Sue had sat facing forward to check on where Madeleen was going to place herself.

Actually he didn't have much time to ponder, as George Dowell, not paying attention to anyone, clucked the mules to start. When the wagon jerked forward, Madeleen, who hadn't yet decided on where she was going to sit, fell backward onto her rump on the back edge of the wagon bed. She continued to fall, tumbling toward the coupling pole.

Screaming like a banshee, she lost not only her balance but her composure which she had so studiously maintained that morning up to that crucial moment. Now she was in a free fall right toward Jimmie Sue who'd perched himself all alone on the coupling pole.

Her scream caught everyone's attention who was within earshot, as they turned to see what in tarnation the commotion was all about, only to see Jimmie Sue sitting on the coupling pole with Madeleen having fallen awkwardly on top of him with her feet and calves of her legs still up on the wagon bed.

There was little he could do but to clasp his arms around her breast to prevent her from falling all the way to the ground. However, the springy coupling pole now bearing their combined weight, began bouncing up and down, as Jimmie Sue delightfully welcomed Madeleen to share his riding position. To the onlookers it surely looked like the "coupling pole" was aptly named.

Great-Grandpa yelled, "Jimmie Sue, what's goin' on ovah there?"

Madeleen didn't give Jimmie Sue a chance to answer. "Mr. Bennett, this weren't Jimmie Sue's fault atall. I was a-standin' on the wagon bed when George Dowell clucked the mules to start, an' I fell backwards, an' if it hadn't been for Jimmie Sue I'd of landed on the ground fer sure, prob'ly right on the top of my cotton-pickin' head."

By that time the bouncing of the coupling pole had slowed down, but roars of laughter had started with everyone, even Jimmie Sue and Madeleen, joining in.

Well, George Dowell looked a little grim from having been so unreliable in his wagon-driving responsibility.

Madeleen looked at Jimmie Sue and said with a grin, "Hit sure was a bless-ed thing."

Jimmie Sue thought, *It surely was a bless-ed thing,* but only replied, "What was a bless-ed thing?'

"Hit was a bless-ed thing I fixed my dress."

He noticed that the pantalooned dress had remained intact and had not impacted Madeleen's modesty in the least. Her position of having landed in Jimmie Sue's arms was a bit compromising, but she shrugged it off as though it was nothing.

It was more than nothing for Jimmie Sue. Her warm, pulsating body enclosed in his arms would be sufficient for several nights of dreams.

Dismounting the coupling pole, the two youngsters set themselves on the back edge of the wagon, and George Dowell yelled the mules ahead again—after he'd carefully looked around to make sure all the passengers were safely seated this time.

Great-Grandpa and Uncle Levi sat up next to George Dowell. Cletus was driving the Hiltons' wagon where Simon and Clyde were already on board.

Uncle Levi and his boys had already finished the mowing two days earlier. That was necessary to do in advance for the mown hay to lie out in the air and sunshine to dry. Otherwise, if the hay were put into the barn while still wet or even a little damp, it could start a fire.

The hay scythe was different from the grain cradle, not having the wooden tines, so the mower could just let the hay fall scattered on the ground for the drying out. No one came behind to bundle into sheaves like the cradled grain stalks.

The day of the hay hauling, itself, required several field hands. Great-Granddaddy said that Clyde and Simon would use their pitchforks to rake the dried hay into little mounds, which could be picked up easily by the pitchforks of the loaders for pitching up onto the wagon. Great-Granddaddy and Uncle Levi would pitch the hay onto the wagons.

Cletus was assigned to drive the Hilton mules pulling their wagon, while Madeleen would secure the hay on that wagon, and George Dowell would drive the Bennett mules with Jimmie Sue on top.

Jimmie Sue was grateful that the work assignments were different this time than the week before when George Dowell and Madeleen had worked so closely together. He wondered, *Did Daddy change things 'round today, 'cause I pitched a fuss las' week 'bout George Dowell and Madeleen workin' so nigh one another in the wheat field?*

Pitching the hay onto the wagon wasn't so difficult at the beginning of the load, but as the load got higher and higher the reach to the top took a bit of extra effort.

Likewise, the job of securing the hay became increasingly problematic with the height of the load, as the hay could more easily topple over. But you'd want to get as much hay as possible with each trip to keep the number of trips at a minimum.

The loading and hauling was rather uneventful. Nothing really to report except Jimmie Sue got switched in the face by a low hanging tree branch. He made George Dowell stop the mules, so Jimmie Sue could cut off the limb, so it wouldn't slap Madeleen in the face, whose wagon was right behind. Actually they'd piled the hay much too high in both the wagons, but then they wouldn't have to fetch another wagonload after the two they were hauling.

However, Madeleen's load was so high that it started shifting when one wheel rut got a little deeper than the other one. Uncle Levi yelled at Simon and Clyde to prop the lower side with their pitchforks, and walk beside that way until the road leveled out. That seemed to do the trick.

It was a good thing Madeleen knew how to tromp or she'd have had a ride off the side of the wagon. She had spread out each pitchfork load so evenly that the hay stalks kind of grabbed a hold on each other to keep the whole load from shifting, when the wagon got tipsy.

Of course, Simon and Clyde helped a bit with their strength and pitchforks.

As the hay loads continued on toward the destination of the haystack pole, Great-Grandpa and Uncle Levi lingered awhile down by the creek to discuss some business about some timber, but not before Uncle Levi warned the workers that a thunderstorm was likely to come up.

Jimmie Sue, nor any of the others had seen any sign of a thunderstorm, so he asked Madeleen's daddy why he'd made such a pronouncement.

Uncle Levi replied, "'cause Lily said this mawnin' right after breakfast that the sign was right for some rain . . . . She didn't say how much."

Even though he knew Madeleen believed in the signs—a little—Jimmie Sue claimed he "just didn't put much in store for any unseen signs." And there certainly weren't any obvious signs that he'd seen, as there wasn't a cloud in sight—except a few wisps of cloud over towards Pierson.

His daddy hadn't seen any sky signs for rain either, but he had come to respect Aunt Lily's ability to know these things, so he said "Ever'body's gotta work real fast so's the hay don't get wet before it's stacked and completely thatched."

When the wagons arrived at the haystack pole, they were greeted by two excited little girls. Rosie and Ruthie were talking a mile a minute but walking so slowly as though something was terribly wrong with their feet or clothing.

Madeleen yelled down from atop of her hay load. "What's wrong with you girls?"

They were jabbering so fast that no one could understand a word they were saying, while they were both holding their little aprons out in front of them.

Cletus said, "What you girls holdin' in yoah aperns?"

Rosie slowed her words down a bit and said, "We found a guinea hen's nest."

Everyone was aware that the guinea hens would never lay their eggs in a regular chicken house nest. They'd hide their nest away from possible human intervention, and finding a guinea hen's nest was always a sort of celebration.

George Dowell wanted to know, "Where'd ya' find the nest?"

Rosie said, "Under the back side of thet ol' haystack." At the bottom of a haystack was a favorite spot for guinea nests.

Madeleen yelled down to Ruthie, "Sistah, how many eggs did you get outta there?"

Sorrowfully, Ruthie looked up at her, as a big tear began to appear in her dark eyes, "Madeleen, I can't count thet high yet." The boys began to snicker at the comic scene of the naïve little girls walking awkwardly that way with their egg treasure fetched in their aprons, until Madeleen gave all the boys a stern look.

The drama of the girls and their discovery temporarily interrupted the task at hand, which then was to pitch the hay off the wagons and stack the hay around the stack pole.

There seemed still to be the need for more information about the egg hunt. Jimmie Sue said, "Rosie how did you take the eggs outta the nest."

She proudly replied, "I jest stuck my arm in an' started handin' out guinea eggs to Sistah."

George Dowell said, "Rosie, don't you understan' thet a snake coulda been in there under the haystack. Thet's a favorite spot fer blacksnakes."

The thought of a snake really started to panic Rosie, as though she were reaching under the haystack right then and there.

Jimmie Sue continued to pursue the method the girls had used in retrieving the eggs. "Rosie, don't you know thet you don't nevah stick yoah hand in a guinea hen's nest."

"Yeah what George Dowell jest said 'bout snakes . . . ."

Jimmie Sue said, a little more harshly than judgmental, "The blacksnakes be danged. They kill the rats anyways. What I mean is you oughtta know thet the guinea hens won't nevah go back to the nest if they smell where a human's hand's been. I'm sure Mama's told you to get the guinea eggs outta the nest with a wooden spoon, so the guineas won't smell you afterwards."

"Jimmie Sue, we didn't have time—" She interrupted herself with intense sobbing from having been scolded by her favorite brother.

Ruthie was still quietly crying from being so embarrassed about not being able to count the eggs. She and Rosie grabbed each other to protect themselves from their siblings and the whole misunderstanding grown-up world.

By this time, Madeleen had slid down off the wagonload of hay and hurried to console the two small farm girls.

The two daddys had come up by that time and witnessed the next little scene of Madeleen's own drama.

After comforting and shushing her sister and friend, she took charge of the whole situation, including her commands to the rest of the work crew. "Now the rest of you might as well unhitch the mules fer some hay an' water. We can do the stackin' after dinnah."

Everyone was so startled with her assertiveness that they simply gaped and started following orders. Great-Grandpa had never experienced a girl, and especially a colored girl, taking control of a work situation like that. He couldn't have said that he wasn't impressed, particularly how all the boys immediately obeyed.

As soon as she realized she was not going to get any opposition to her plan, Madeleen took hold of the little girls' hands and, while glowering daggers at the boys, she said, "Us girls will take ourselves into the house, an' warsh up fer dinnah. You boys can do what you gotta do an' what you may be capable of doin'."

Knowing that he'd been too harsh with Rosie, Jimmie Sue was positive that Madeleen's hateful look and reprimanding words were meant especially for him.

He mused to himself, *Hit sure looks like I've done cluttered up things agin with Madeleen, an' it looks like this time I'm the one what put somethin' atween us.*

It was then that he noticed the growing scuds of clouds were darkening over the west ridge.

* * *

CHAPTER 14

The Rain Cometh

After a scrumptious summer dinner, including new sweet potatoes, everyone pushed their chairs back in preparation for their different jobs that afternoon. All the men-folk, still smacking their lips and wiping any pot-liquor off their mouths with the back of their hands, put on their hats and headed out the door. The two little girls trotted right on behind them, because it was a whole lot more exciting in the barnyard than in the kitchen—especially with the actual haystacking that would be taking place down by the barn.

Jimmie Sue had noticed that Madeleen had untied her dress hem just before dinner, so he figured she'd be staying in the house to help with the clean-up. "So, yoah stayin' in the house to help with the dishes?"

"Nauw, why would I wanna do thet? 'cause it's womenfolks' job to clean up after ever'body?"

"Oh, nauw. Hit weren't thet. I jest thought 'cause you already—"

"Fixed my dress?"

"Well, *un*-fixed it, really." As he quietly chuckled at his own precision of vocabulary.

"We'll jest fix thet *unfix* right now." She repeated her earlier morning action of transforming her farm skirt into exotic pantaloons. "Did you think I *oughter* stay to the house to do the dishes?"

"Well. not thet you oughter . . . . It's jest thet it gets awful hot out there, even though it be September, already."

Madeleen replied, "If you've ever cooked a big dinner ovah the hot cookstove in the middle o' dog days, you'd know what *hot* is. I can keep up with you boys any time of day or night."

"Like thet night at the 'baccer barn firin'?"

She warned him, "I thought we might'n not talk 'bout thet agin."

Jimmie Sue just pulled down his hat a little farther over his forehead without answering her about bygone problem situations.

By the time they'd got to the edge of the porch the two little girls were waiting for them. Ruthie said to her older sister, "Madeleen, kin I hold yoah hand on the way to the haystack?"

Madeleen wondered what that was all about. "Acourse, Sistah, but what for? We just headed down to the barn."

Ruthie answered, "I be skeered."

This further puzzled Ruthie's big sister. "Of what? Thet blacksnake George Dowell tole 'bout?"

"Nauw, the guinea hen Jimmie Sue tole 'bout. I be skeered of thet ol' guinea hen. She might could smell me an' chase me down an' peck my eyes out, for robbin' her nest of all her eggs."

Madeleen shot a dirty look at Jimmie Sue who defended himself. "Now I didn't say a thing 'bout guinea hens chasin' a person down . . . ."

Madeleen said, "Don't pay no never-mind to Jimmie Sue, Sistah. He has a way of allus sayin' the wrong thing at the wrong time."

Rosie said, "Jimmie Sue, if Ruthie gets to hold Madeleen's hand, kin I get to ride on yoah shoulders?"

This seemed to present a perfect occasion for Jimmie Sue to begin, hopefully, to ingratiate himself with all three of the girls, but especially Madeleen, who needed a new sign from Jimmie Sue.

"Shur! Why not?" With that he hoisted his little sister over his head and onto his shoulders, but by that time they were only a few steps from the hay wagons parked on opposite sides of the stack pole—about sixteen feet from each other; just in the right positions for unloading the hay for beginning the building of the haystack.

The two daddies announced that they were going again back down to the edge of the woodlot to talk a little more about the timber prospects there. They both reckoned that the youngsters could do the haystacking right, as they'd done such a good job of haying that morning.

Great-Grandaddy Robert, recalling to himself Madeleen's taking command of the awkward situation just before dinner, said, "Madeleen, do you think you kin strawboss this gang of rogues?" *Strawboss* of course meant the boss of a particular job and not the big boss, itself.

She answered, while looking over the miffed crew of under-appreciated boys, "I think I might could."

Jimmie Sue mumbled under his breath, but still so all the rest of the boys could hear it, "Thet ain't bein' no straw boss. I figger they oughtta be callin' her to be the hay boss."

The other boys started snickerin'.

Madeleen quickly took charge. "Are you gonna stan' 'round gigglin' like guinea hens (This prompted Ruthie and Rosie to start giggling.) or are we gonna finish this hyar job of work?"

She didn't wait for an answer. "Cletus, you run to the spring with the watah bucket an' bring some watah for us. Oh, an' you take Ruthie an' Rosie, so's they don't get in the way or maybe havin' one of these yahoos drop a pitchfork of hay on them.

"Clyde, you an' Jimmie Sue can pitch off our wagon an' Simon catch pitch off his'n. But George Dowell, afore any pitchin' gets started you must need cut some tree branches to put undah the bottom of the hay."

This of course was necessary to keep the hay off the damp ground and provide some ventilation for the bottom of the haystack to stay dry. The stack pole would serve as a kind of chimney with the bit of air around it, and that way the air rising up from the ground would also keep the inner core of the haystack dry and prevent any molding of the hay.

Jimmie Sue said, "An, whatta you gonna do?"

"I'm gonna tromp again."

The tramping on the haystack, itself, was to pack it tightly to keep the rain from seeping in.

Clyde said, "You think you kin keep up the trompin with us pitchin' from both wagons?"

She said, "Don't you worry 'bout thet, you just keep up yoah end of the job."

Jimmie Sue said, "An' don't you worry 'bout us, 'cause we know what we gotta do." His wink at the other hay pitchers was fully understood by them as to mean they'd make sure she'd have a tough time keeping up with them.

George Dowell whined, "An', whatta I do aftah I cut the bresh?"

"You gonna help me by thatchin'."

Thatching was somewhat like building a thatched roof with grass or straw. As the haystack would get higher, the thatcher would continue to rake down the sides, so that the stalks of the hay would be vertical and thus serve as a conduit for the water to run down the outside of the stack — further protection against the inner part of the stack from rotting with too much moisture in a similar fashion as the wheat sheaves.

Jimmie Sue thought to himself, *Thar they go agin . . . she fixin' it so's they kin be workin' together.*

"Well," Madeleen said, "what yawl waitin' for—the night train?" She was already standing on the brush pile with her right arm around the stack pole . . . just waiting for the onslaught of pitchforks of hay.

Her taunting was all the direction or inspiration needed, as pitchforks of hay started flying from both wagons. Within only a few minutes Madeleen was almost completely covered with hay — only her head showing. Even with just a slight wind breeze, the fast pace of the hay flying through the air had hay chaff flying everywhere, settling on any exposed body parts and down open-necked shirts.

Madeleen severely chastised them for pitching the hay so vigorously. "You boys not givin' me 'nuff time to tromp, an you know Daddy be real upset if we get this haystack wrong."

Jimmie Sue asked, "Who he be upset with?"

She retorted, "I just bet Jimmie Sue Bennett thet this was a put-up thing for you boys to get even with me for me bestin' you with yoah papa. I b'lieve you be plumb wicked sometimes."

He just grinned and didn't deny the charge.

Some of the flying hay had landed on the tops of the boys' hats, but hatless Madeleen had chaff completely covering the kerchief that she had over her head almost like an actually real hat, itself.

Simon said, "This hay chaff undah my shirt collar is most oncomfortable." With that pronouncement, he began taking off his shirt. Greatly appreciating the expected relief from the heat and the itchy hay, the other boys copied Simon's action, and looking at Madeleen to see what her reaction might be.

By that time, Madeleen had crawled up out of her hay entombment, and upon seeing the boys taking off their shirts, she reached for the top button of her blouse. Slowly she unbuttoned the top button and then the next one, while looking at Jimmie Sue out of the corner of her eye.

Jimmie Sue thought, *I know she thinks she kin keep up with us boys, but surely she ain't gonna take off her shirt.*

Simply fanning her throat and face with her hands, she untied the knot holding the head scarf in place before running her fingers through her hair to brush out the hay chaff. Watching Jimmie Sue closely to catch his reaction, she didn't do any more undressing but said, "Maybe, Jimmie Sue, you can help me tromp, 'cause Clyde don't need no extra help with pitchin' the hay offen our wagon."

Jimmie Sue said, "You mean you might could need some help with somethin'?"

She quietly warned, "Jimmie Sue, this ain't no time to be gettin' sarcastic."

He didn't say another word, but just jumped from the Hilton wagon onto the haystack. Grabbing onto the stack pole for balance, he realized that his hand was clasped tightly right over Madeleen's. However, she didn't appear to be in a hurry to retract her hand from the pole and from underneath his. Of course the hay trampers had to hold onto the hay pole for fear of sliding off to the ground.

After a slight pause, with everyone staring at everyone else, the hay-pitching began again—a bit more seriously, as then the dark thundercloud was moving rather ominously toward the little haying crew.

Madeleen and Jimmie Sue continued tramping, going in circles following each other around the hay pole, as the haystack got higher and higher. No one seemed to notice that quite often Jimmie Sue's hand would land on top of Madeleen's. And more then once her hand landed on top of his on the hay pole. She didn't seem to take any notice of it and Jimmie Sue was just going to enjoy silently the soft touch of her hand.

George Dowell tried to keep up with the thatching process. As soon as Clyde had finished pitching all the hay off his wagon and Simon had finished with his, they both jumped down and commenced helping George Dowell with the thatching.

By this time Madeleen and Jimmie Sue were perched rather high up on the top of the haystack.

As they were high enough to reach the top of the pole, Madeleen took off her headscarf from around her neck and tied it to the tip-top of the pole.

Jimmie Sue asked incredulously, "Why'd you do thet?"

"I don't know . . . . Kind of a sign I s'pose."

"What kinda sign?"

"Mebbe jest a sign we be finished."

Worrying, he asked, "Finished with what?"

"Why, finished with the haystackin', silly."

"Oh, yeah! Silly me!"

Just as the thatching was finished, the rain began to drizzle, and in only a few minutes it had begun to really pelt them. George Dowell, Clyde and Simon headed for the house. Cletus and the little girls were nowhere to be seen.

Madeleen proclaimed, "The rain cometh," as she and Jimmie Sue plopped down on the top of the haystack, using the side surfaces of the hay to slide all the way to the ground.

As the rain was coming down in such torrents, they headed for the nearest shelter, which was the barn shed.

By the time they were under roof, their clothes were wringing wet. Of course, as Jimmie Sue was shirtless, his young skin glistened with the rainwater, still dripping from his hair and shoulders.

Madeleen's white skirt/pantaloons and blouse were luminous and almost transparent.

They both looked at each other in a renewed amazement, until Madeleen started laughing.

Jimmie Sue asked, "What you laughin' 'bout?"

She answered, "The watah drippin' off yoah nose make out like you got a real bad cold with a runny nose."

He wondered but didn't say out loud, *How can she allus puncture my bubble, jest when I begin thinkin' things?*

They were both barefoot and, having run through the muddy barnyard, their feet were encased in red mud. That combined with their wet matted clothing produced a completely disheveled appearance, not conducive to anything but laughter.

However, Madeleen did interject a note of seriousness, almost like quoting from scripture: "The rain cometh."

Jimmie Sue, looking back toward the haystack, said, "An' the rain droopeth yoah hangin' flag sign on the top of the stack pole."

"Waal now it jest be a saggy sign of finishin'. Wondah what thet means."

"Maybe it means there's gotta be a dryin' out time?"

* * *

CHAPTER 15

The Barn Loft

Madeleen and Jimmie Sue gazed for a few moments at Madeleen's wet red kerchief, dangling at the top of the haystack, transforming the stack pole into a flag pole with what she had said was a sign of finishing something or other.

Madeleen suddenly wondered, "Where do you s'pose Cletus an' our little sistahs might be?"

Jimmie Sue said, "Cletus brung the bucket of watah up from the spring an' put it undah our wagon when you was buried under all thet hay."

She said, "You wanna 'splain to me how all thet happened with me bein' covered with thet hay like thet?"

"Nauw, I don't wanna 'splain thet."

"Well," she said, "I still be worried 'bout those teensy girls in this rainstorm."

He answered, "I seen Cletus run off toward the house when we all seen the thundercloud comin'."

"But the little girls?"

"I couldn't see good from where I was standin', but I figgered they went runnin' to the house too, 'specially since they both allus seem so skeered o' things."

Still with a furrowed brow, she said, "Yeah, I s'pose yoah right."

Noticing that Madeleen was a bit more relaxed, but still somewhat uneasy, himself, about what to talk about, Jimmie Sue said, "Well, it shur looks like the rain ain't gonna let up no time soon."

She replied, "I guess yoah right, but we can't jest stand hyar under the barn shed fer the rest of the day."

He suggested, "Well, we could allus climb up inta the barn loft. We kin set down up there. In our barn loft I go up there all the time. Thet's where I stash my readin' books."

She looked at him suspiciously, but after a couple of minutes nodded that that was okay with her.

While he was climbing the ladder to the loft, from down below she yelled up, "Could you mebbe share some of yoah books with me so's I can do my own readin'?"

He answered, as she was climbing the ladder, "Yeah, I reckon I could."

He began digging around in the hay for a hen's nest, but only halfheartedly, as he was more interested in seeing that she got up there.

Just before she stepped onto the loft floor off the ladder, Jimmie Sue tried to take her hand to help her up.

She refused his help by saying, "Don't fergit, Jimmie Sue, thet I kin do most anything you boys kin do, an' bedads I surely don't need no help to git up inta no barn loft, perticularly our own."

He was surprised that she almost swore by using that word *bedads*.

"Yeah," he said, as he settled himself back into a half-supine position on the slope of the hay.

Madeleen settled herself on the hay across from Jimmie Sue, who said, "I'd think thet knot in yoah skirt thetway might be a mite oncomfortable, when you go to set down sommers up hyar."

"Thanks," she replied as she looked at him suspiciously then reached down and untied the knot in the hem of her skirt. Settling back onto the hay, she affirmed, "Yeah, you right, Jimmie Sue, this feels a whole lot more bettah."

Jimmie Sue could hardly believe she'd take any suggestion from him, particularly about her clothing, which reminded all over again as several times every day about the time when neither of them had on any clothes.

Noticing that he was looking at her rather funny, she said, "Did you tell anybody?"

"Tell anybody 'bout what?"

A bit slowly, she continued, "'Bout thet time in the baptizin' hole."

Picking up on the topic he said, "Oh, yeah, you mean that day down in the swimmin' hole. Nauw, I didn't tell anyone. How 'bout you?"

She quickly answered, "Nauw, I didn't tell a livin' soul, 'cause I be too shamed."

"You mean 'cause we both be naked there in the watah?"

He crawled over toward her and lay down beside her on the hay without any kind of objection from her. She simply responded to his last question with a little admonishment, "Don't be usin thet word."

"What word? . . . You mean the word naked?"

"Yeah, it sounds like a naughty word."

He replied. "Nothin' naughty 'bout it. We come into this world naked, an' I bet you get nekkid some time ever' day."

"But not in no watah with no boy!"

He was beginning to enjoy the sound of the word and the images it brought to his teenage boy's mind . . . . naked . . . naked . . . naked."

"Some times you use the wrong word or at least a word at the wrong time."

This intrigued him even further. "Does this be the wrong time to talk 'bout nakedness?"

"Why do you keep usin' thet word?"

"I sometimes say things afore . . . ."

"You think!"

"Yeah!"

"You do thet kinda usual, doncha?"

Jimmie Sue hesitated. "Well, yes . . . sometimes . . . but right now, I'm takin' the time to do some extra special thinkin'," as he rolled closer to her on the hay, facing her.

Suspiciously, she asked, "Thinkin'? 'bout what?"

He had no ready answer, so simply said, "Of this an' thet . . . an' the rain."

Picking up his cue about the rain, she replied, "The rain cometh down and watereth the earth."

Hoping to cultivate some harmless conversation, Jimmie Sue said, "Is thet writ down sommers?"

"Yeah!"

"Where?"

"In the Bible.

"Where in the Bible?"

"I don't know 'zactly. In the Old Testament sommers, I think."

Jimmie Sue asked, "When it reads 'the rain cometh' does thet mean thet the rain is a good thing?"

"Well, whatta you think?"

After a lengthy pause, he answered her query, "Yeah, sometime when it watahs the fields and fills the spring with drinkin' watah, but at other times, like right now, it kin be a pain in the butt . . . ."

Before Madeleen could yell at him about his language again, they heard laughter from atop the hay up next to the roof, and then a small voice, attempting a whisper, "Ruthie, did you hear Jimmie Sue, say 'butt'?" This was followed by a lot of giggling.

Madeleen started to crawl up the stack of hay toward the voices, until she realized that her dress then was an inappropriate encumbrance, particularly with Jimmie Sue sitting down at the floor level and her dress then being untied.

"Hyar," he said, "I'll fetch those little imps."

As he got to the top of the hay he saw two small faces peering at him from just under the roof. "What you two young'uns doin', way up hyar?"

Ruthie said, "Rosie told me when it was 'bout to start rainin' thet we oughtta climb up hyar in the barn loft to hear the raindrops doin' music on the roof."

Rosie corroborated, "An' it was true too. The rain at first was real nice till the big rain come. An' when the thunder come it skeered us might nigh to death."

Taking their hands and pulling them over the top of the hay, Jimmie Sue said, "Well, both of you slide on down hyar with me an' Madeleen."

As the little girls settled down with their older siblings, Madeleen took advantage of the pause to scold Jimmie Sue. "Jimmie Sue, I'd be plumb 'shamed of myself."

"Fer what?"

"Fer usin' thet nasty word where yoah little sistah an' my little sistah could hear it."

Knowing full well what she was referring to, he said, "BUTT, I don't know what word you talkin' 'bout." He interrupted her glare. "An' 'sides, I didn't even know they was hyar."

"You shouldn't of used language like thet anyways."

Defensively, he retorted, "I'm jest gettin' dad-blamed sick an' tired of bein' caught in somethin', when I ain't been tol' what the circumstances might be. I wouldn't never say somethin' harmful nor dirty in the hearin' of Rosie . . . nor little Ruthie neither. Like I wouldn't either in the presence of Mamma or Aunt Lily."

"But you would in front of me?"

"Thet's diffrunt."

"What's diffrunt? Ain't I a girl?"

He didn't need someone to remind him that Madeleen was a girl. "Yeah! You some girl, all right."

"Now what you mean by thet?"

"I mean yoah . . . a grown-up girl . . . a girl nigh my own age."

She retorted, "An' grown-up girls don't need be shown no respect! Is thet it?"

"Nauw, now what I meant . . . ."

"An' what 'bout colored girls. They *really* don't need no . . . ."

Rosie came to Jimmie Sue's defense. "Oh, Jimmie Sue like girls."

Madeleen jumped at this opportunity. "Oh, what kinda girls does Jimmie Sue like?"

Rosie added, "He like all kinda girls. I think he like thet Susie Goins girl a whole lot."

Jimmie Sue let out an audible moan. His little sister continued, "Jimmie Sue, you ailin'?"

Madeleen suggested, "I think he might could have a big ailment."

Before Jimmie Sue had a chance to answer either one of them, Rosie said, "Jimmie Sue, could you tell me an' Ruthie thet Bible story 'bout the feller who had a wheat field and let a girl pick up extra wheat, an' then he jest up an' married her? An' didn't you say she was a colored girl?"

Madeleen quickly asked, "What color was she, Jimmie Sue?"

"I don't think I said she was colored. I think I jest said she was darker than the man, who was a whole lot whiter, an' the folks didn't think they oughter marry, but they jest married up anyways, regardless of what other people thought."

Madeleen asked him, "Is thet the way you see thet story of Boaz an' Ruth?"

"That's the way I think 'bout it an' how it might be like thet sometime in this day an' time."

She hesitantly asked, "Mebbe like you an' me?"

"Hit might could be."

Their excursion into a more personal conversation was interrupted abruptly by a streak of lightning that shone through the cracks between the barn logs, and a thunderous crack that could be heard from just outside the barn.

They all quickly took the couple of steps to the barn wall and could see that lightning had struck the haystack pole and split it down all the way into the haystack, itself. The flag was still tied to one of the split ends bending over to one side.

Ordinarily when lightning would strike something like a haystack, a tree or even a barn, it would start a fire. And that was no exception then, as they all watched in amazement as smoke started coming out the chimney effect of the stack pole.

They were so stunned they didn't know what to say, and as the rain was still coming down like buckets and the lightning flashing, they didn't dare do anything except to stare through the cracks between the barn logs. Jimmie Sue, expecting a conflagration, yelled, "Good Lord!"

This prompted an immediate response from Madeleen. "Thou shalt not take the name of the Lord thy God in vain."

Jimmie Sue answered, "It weren't in vain. I meant ever' word of it. An' I'm sure you use them same words an' call on the Good Lord in yoah church all the time an particularly in times of trouble.'"

"But you wadn't callin' on the Lord for mercy. You was aswearin'."

"Madeleen, you don't allus know how I'm usin' my words. An' I kin call on the Lord jest as good as any preacher kin, at any time I want, 'specially at a lightnin' strike."

Looking again at the haystack, they were sure they'd see flames shooting out the top at any moment, but while they were still watching, the smoke merged and transformed into steam. Apparently the downpour of water had put out the fire.

The worst seemed to be over, but the excitement still stirred up a lot of talk. Rosie said, "Madeleen, this log crack hyar ireminds me of the time when Jimmie Sue got his head stuck in a crack beween the logs in our barn.."

Madeleen was amused, to Jimmie Sue's dismay, at this little bit of humorous news. "Rosie, how did thet happen?"

"Jimmie Sue kin tell you."

A slight pause while the three girls looked at Jimmie Sue. Madeleen probed deeper: "Well, Jimmie Sue, how did it happen?"

Reluctantly and certainly awkwardly, Jimmie Sue answered. "Well me an' Simon was up in the barn loft pitchin' down some hay, an' fer some reason there was lottsa folks out in front of the barn. So me and Simon started cuttin' up here in front of the hay mow door fer the folks down there jest to get some laughs, an' Simon stuck his head out atween two logs like these hyar."

Madeleen said, "An' then what?"

"Well, Simon got a big laugh so I figgered if Simon could do it an' get a laugh, I surely could do it too. So I done it, an' I did get a laugh, but when I tried to pull my head back in, it was stuck. They was afraid they'd have to jack up the top log fer me to get my head out."

Rosie said, "Thet's when Jimmie Sue got a real big laugh."

He replied, "Well, it surely wadn't thet funny . . . not to me leastwise."

Ruthie said, "Jimmie Sue, why couldn't you get yoah head out?"

Rosie answered for him, "'cause his ears was too big."

That, of course, got another huge laugh from Madeleen, who inquired further into the matter, "Well, how could Simon get his head out?"

Jimmie Sue, disgusted with the whole story, said, " 'cause Simple Simon's a pinhead, an' his ears ain't big enough to get stuck in nothin'."

Suddenly the rain was accompanied by a surge of hailstones, making such a racket on the tin roof of the barn, that no one could hear what anyone else was saying.

The hail was hitting so hard that it sounded as though the hailstones were going to cut right through the roof, even though it was metal. This, of course, really scared the small girls, who began wailing, and of course Madeleen started praying. "Dear Lord . . . ."

She was interrupted by Jimmie Sue saying, "Thet was 'zactly what I was sayin' fer what you chastised *me* . . . ."

His self-defense wasn't completed before there was a deafening lightning hit on the corner of the barn roof. This set up a renewed caterwauling and praying with a new verbal response from Jimmie Sue, "Holeeey shiii . . . ."

He didn't get to finish his sentiment this time. Madeleen slapped him right square across his mouth and for a minute he couldn't say anything, but finally said, "What'd you do thet fer?"

"Jimmie Sue Bennett, I already warned you 'bout cussin' an' usin' foul language. An' in front of our little sistahs."

"I didn't mean to . . . ."

"Don't you tell me what you *didn't*. I'm tellin' you what you *did*. An' I'm puttin' you on notice right now, if you can't clean up yoah language there won't be no moah language atween the two of us." She took hold of the little girls' hands and headed toward the ladder. "Come on little ones, we be headin' toward the house."

Jimmie Sue said, "But the rain an' lightnin'."

"The rain has let up a little an' the lightnin' seems finished."

He said, "Kin I help youall down the . . . ."

Madeleen answered with determined finality, "No, you can't help with nothin' fer us right now."

Jimmie Sue heard the three girls scoot down the ladder and watched them run toward the house through the rain, which had slacked to a soft drizzle.

He stayed up in the barn loft trying to sort out things, but it was time for the whole Bennett family to head on toward home, as it would soon be milking time.

One the way home he remembered that it was his turn to do the milking. As the rain had stopped completely by the time they got back, he walked meditatively across the barnyard to the back porch to fetch the milk bucket, which was hanging upside down on a peg on the porch post.

After feeding some hay and feed chop to Bossie, the milk cow, he put down his three-legged milk stool just in front of her right hind leg.

Earlier the rain had stopped but was beginning slowly again—rather leisurely this time, making tiny pings on the barn tin roof. Of course the first streams of milk also would make little pinging noises on the bottom of the metal bucket.

That evening there was an extra ping heard in the cow stall. As he leaned his head into the hollow of the old cow's side, his tears of sorrow and remorse pinged on the bottom of the bucket. The reverberating sounds, emanating from different sources, merged in a percussive melody of tones: the raindrops on the tin roof of the barn and the streams of milk, as well as his own tears of sadness, on the bottom of the galvanized milk bucket.

Upbraiding himself, while squeezing out the milk and weeping into the bucket, he thought to himself, *Surely Madeleen will come ovah hyar with her folks to the corn shuckin' we'll be havin' next week. . . . But what if she don't come?*

Why do I keer anyways?

* * *

CHAPTER 16

Corn Shucking

After the haystacking and the unfortunate, compromising encounter with Madeleen in the barn loft, Jimmie Sue thought back further to the incident at the swimming/baptizing hole. As exciting as that was, that incident hadn't ended very happily for Jimmie Sue either.

But he was surely hoping that he'd see her at the corn shucking, which was always such fun. He couldn't quite figure out why it was so important for him to see her, as it seemed always to lead to some misunderstanding between them.

He recalled to himself the scripture he'd quoted to her at their encounter at the swimming hole. *Faith is for things hoped for; the evidence of things not seen.* After that watery meeting there, he'd gone back often to see if she might be there as he had kept on *hoping for* but *not seeing*.

Seeing and working with her at the sheaving and haystacking times was nice, except at the end, when she was so upset about his language. *I wonder if she really meant it when she said she wadn't never ever gonna speak to me agin if I didn't clean up my language. But how will she know if I've cleaned up my language or not unless she talks to me—at least a little bit.*

Surely he'd find that out at the corn shucking which was coming up in just a couple of days. She could then find out how much his language had improved.

There had already been a couple of shuckings over to the Goins' and the Taylors'. Great-Grandpa put out the word that the Bennetts would be having a shucking on the second Friday night in October.

Jimmie Sue had hoped that the Hiltons might come, as they were usually included in such things as tobacco primings and threshing days. A lot of hands were needed to keep those operations in gear with so many different kinds of things needing to be done to keep it all working smoothly.

But at the corn shuckings, everyone doing the shucking would be engaged in similar tasks—one person or twenty would simply be doing the same thing; shucking the ears of corn, throwing the ears in a nearby basket and piling the shucks up to be used for livestock bedding. The shucked corn, of course, would be stored in the corn crib for feed for the livestock, except for the best ears that were saved for the gristmill to be ground up in cornmeal for cooking. Although a big crew wasn't necessary for the shucking, it was certainly much nicer to have a lot of folks sharing in the work.

In fact, it was almost like a party. Adding to the festive feeling, was the usual practice of the host farmer putting a jug of hard cider or corn squeezings somewhere in the piled-up unshucked corn, as a kind of treasure hunt. The lucky man finding the spirits would be expected to share with all the other men, which, of course, would add to the general merriment of the evening.

Occasionally, the corn crop might have a few ears of red kernels. No one would know for sure where they might be, as they would still be hidden under the husks of the ears. It would be a great disappointment if there weren't any red ears.

Actually, I believe that the complete absence of a red ear meant something rather dire for the farmer with the crop with no red corn. It was accepted practice that any boy who found a red ear would be able to kiss the girl of his choice, and no one—not even the girl nor her mamma—could prevent the kiss.

At the Bowens' corn shucking, Lige had found a red ear. He partially shucked it, but upon seeing the red grains at the end of the ear, he held it proudly over his head and started yelling, "Thelma Lou, Thelma Lou! I getta kiss my Thelma Lou."

That was Jimmie Sue's sister, who was standing close by and, of course, started running, which was kind of expected of the girl. She wasn't supposed to be too anxious for the kiss, even though she would have been hoping that she'd be the one chosen by the red ear finder. He didn't have to chase her too far before he caught and kissed her, much to the delight of everyone, especially Jimmie Sue and all his cronies.

However, in the excitement of Lige getting his kiss, he had tossed the ear to one side and paid no more attention to it. Jimmie Sue picked it up, pulled the shuck back up over the grain and stuck it in his overalls pocket, as a kind of investment for future shuckings, where there might not be a red ear or where he may not be the one to find it.

The Hiltons didn't usually go to the shuckings with the white folks the way they would to the tobacco primings and wheat threshings, probably because it was too much like a party, which would make everyone, white and colored, a little uneasy.

They hadn't been to the Goins' or the Bowens', but Jimmie Sue had urged his daddy to invite Uncle Levi and his family to the Bennetts' shucking whenever he would see him down to the feed store.

As the various families were gathering, Jimmie Sue saw the Hiltons' mule pulling the wagon with only Uncle Levi and Aunt Lily sitting on the plank seat. Other folks stopped whatever it was they were doing, wondering what this meant for coloreds to be at a play-party like a corn shucking.

Great-Grandpa eased the tension when he said, "Levi, I sure 'preciate you comin' like I said. I'll need a hand with gettin' all these shucks into the barn stalls. An' hit's awful good of you, Lily, to come and help Sue and Thelma Lou with the fixin's fer a little after-work snack."

The Hilton children weren't along, and it was obvious to everyone that the party part of the evening was going to be for the white folks, which made them feel a little less queasy about it.

Jimmie Sue had the opposite reaction, as he didn't like and didn't understand why Cletus and Clyde and Ruthie and Madeleen couldn't have come also. He reached into his overalls pocket to make sure the red ear of corn was secure—*but secure for what—an investment without a payoff?*

While the shuckers were busy shucking and gossiping, one of the older men saw a tattered and battered kerchief flapping on the top of the haystack pole. He yelled at Simon, "Hey, Simon, whut's thet flag doin' at the top of the haystack? Whut's it for?"

Simon said, "Don't ask me. Ask Jimmie Sue. He put it up there, 'cause there was a similar one put on the Hiltons' haystack by Madeleen. I reckon Jimmie Sue just wanted to keep up with the Hiltons."

Mr. Goins asked, "Ain't Madeleen thet colored girl . . . the oldest Hilton Girl?"

Everyone looked at Jimmie Sue, who simply answered, "Yeah!"

His daddy came to his defense by saying, "Thet's just part of our swapping-off work with the Hiltons." He eased the tension a little more by asking Jimmie Sue, "Yeah, Jimmie Sue, whut's thet little flag 'bout?"

Trying to be vague, because even he didn't understand why Madeleen had tied it up on their haystack pole, Jimmie Sue answered, "Oh, it's jest a sign."

Mr. Taylor asked, "A sign for whut?"

"It was a sign thet we finished the haystack."

Mr. Taylor then said, "Well thet stands to reason, but I reckon a body would know the haystack was finished when you finally slid offen the top."

Everyone laughed at Jimmie Sue's expense.

Walt Bowen said, "I saw the haystack pole at the Hiltons an' it sure looked like somebody split the top of the pole, with the flag hangin' off to one side."

"Yeah," Jimmie Sue answered. "Lightnin' hit it right after we all had finished stackin' an' we had go to the barn loft to get outta the rain."

That, of course, started several new conversations. The boys were anxious to find out what happened in the barn loft.

The older folks had all kinds of lightning stories: of cows getting struck, of how lightning struck a tree which then landed on a house, a barn getting burned down and even how ol' man Gillespie when still a young man had been struck dumb by lightning even though he lived after that unfortunate experience to a ripe old age.

During the evening, Emmett found the jar of moonshine, but gave it to his daddy to share with the rest of the adult men in the workforce. Maybe he was already taking seriously the new name, Emmanuel, which Aunt Lily had assigned to him.

Although the boys weren't allowed to drink any of the moonshine, it was generally understood that they'd slip into it when the grown-ups were paying attention to something else.

Apparently there was no red ear of corn in the crop. At least, no one reported having found one. Jimmie Sue wondered what that meant for the Bennetts in the coming months—but, then he reckoned that maybe the red ear he carried in his pocket would serve as a good luck charm.

He was a little anxious about the superstition to be able to substitute something to ward off any evil spirits what might be lurking as a result of the lack of a red ear of corn in their own crop. He felt sure that the red ear he'd been carrying around would somehow figure fortunate for his family or for himself.

At the end of the shucking and then the evening snack, while Uncle Levi was still helping with getting the corn shucks in the barn stalls, Aunt Lily had finished helping the womenfolk clean up the kitchen.

After Jimmie Sue had finished his chore of toting the baskets of corn to the corn crib, he sat on the back porch steps, feeling sorry for himself. He'd taken the red ear of corn out of his pocket and was examining it closely—whether contemplating it, counting the kernels or marveling at the variegated colors, even *he* wouldn't have been able to say.

Aunt Lily had stepped out on the porch where she discovered Jimmie Sue sitting there in such a dazed stupor. Fully aware of the reason for his dismay, she plopped herself right down beside him on the steps. It didn't seem to bother her at all that local social mores forbade whites and coloreds sitting down together.

People often use the phrase "marching to a different drummer," and it was true that Aunt Lily's marching beat came from a rhythm deep within her soul or somewhere out in the universe—probably a combination of both.

"Thet's a mighty nice year of corn, Jimmie Sue. Did you get to kiss a purty girl tonight? . . . Who might that be?"

Ignoring the question, he asked her, "Aunt Lily, if you was to have to tell what color this year of corn might be, what color would you say it is?"

"I'd say it's lotsa colors—red, yellow, even kinda purplish."

"Thet'd make it *colored*, wouldn't it?"

Aunt Lily hesitantly dug further into his concern. "Jimmie Sue, I see you ask a lotta oncomfortable questions."

"I didn't go to make you oneasy, Aunt Lily."

"Not oneasy atall . . . . Course you right, but folks can't always see whut some others—like yoahself—sees . . . . about colors I mean."

He then broadened his inquiry. "Aunt Lily, if you be a conjure-woman, what do you do to find out things?"

"You just let things come to you."

"Huh!"

"In Proverbs it says, 'But wait on the Lord.' When He come, he be acomin' in many shapes—at times He be a unexpected person, an' then maybe then jest a voice, an' sometimes a idea 'bout somethin' mighty important."

He wasn't finished yet. "Aunt Lily, how do you figure church things an' conjurin' an' healin' go together?"

"All things on God's green earth goes together. As you gets older and keep lookin' an' listenin' an' askin', then more of it starts comin' together."

"Well if all things come together on God's green earth, why cain't *folks* on God's green earth come together?"

Not directly answering his question, but knowing full well the implication of the question, she pushed back with a question of her own. "Do you know who be namin' Madeleen when she be borned?"

Shocked that she again was able bring up the subject of his inner thoughts, he answered, "No'm!"

"Clyde, who was three at the time, named her *Madeleen*."

"Why'd he name her thet?"

"He thought he wuz sayin' *Magdalene*. . . . You know who thet be?"

"Yeah she's in the Bible sommers—like with Jesus. But why didn't you give her the proper name of *Magdalene*?"

"*Magdalene* be too strong a name fer a livin' person. *Madeleen* be jest fine. You gotta be real keerful with God-words. You kin come up to the edge, but not get too close, particularly inside. Thet be too dangerous. *Madeleen* be as close as you wanna get."

He wondered, *How close am I ever gonna get to Madeleen?*

Instead of asking that question out loud to Madeleen's mamma, he delved deeper into the matter of Magdalene. "But wasn't Magdalene a good person?"

"Oh, Honey, she be a good person an' a knowin' person."

"Whatcha mean?"

"She know moah then than we know yet."

"Well, Aunt Lily, you know what I think?"

"Whut be thet, Jimmie Sue?"

"Well, I figure Madeleen is a good person an' a knowin' person!"

Aunt Lily was a little concerned where this conversation was headed and downright worried about the implications of what Jimmie Sue was questioning her about, "Yes, Honey, but sometimes I be skeered."

He didn't understand why she'd be scared of anything. "Skeered of what?"

"Even though it be good to know 'bout things, I sometimes be skeered if my chilren may know too much an' then it be dangerous like thet dynamite stuff they uses in the mines. Thet power might 'splode."

Almost as though he was beginning to get scared of the power of God-word names himself, he asked, "Then if her name be too close to the God-word name, somethin' pow'ful or dangerous might happen to her or to someone aroun' her?"

"Thet's whut I be afearin'."

"Aunt Lily, would you min' doin' somethin' for me?"

"Why, no, Honey, whut it be?"

"Would it be awright if you took this year of corn to Madeleen?"

"Acourse, thet'd jest tickle her to death."

Jimmie Sue, lightening up a bit, quickly quipped, "Oh, I certainly wouldn't want her to die over it."

Aunt Lily, chuckling, replied, "Oh I don't think there's no fear of thet. But I was put on notice by Madeleen to remin' you 'bout our revival next week. S'pose you could come?"

He, of course, was thrilled that Madeleen had been thinking about him in such a positive way. He thought to himself, *Maybe she be thinkin' a revival would cure my language,* but answered Aunt Lily, "I'd be much obliged. Should I bring my folks?"

"Bring whoever yoah a min' to."

She stood up slowly from the steps, as she saw Levi heading back from the barn with Great-Grandpa Robert. Aunt Lily said, "We better be goin' now, Jimmie Sue."

"Don't ferget the colored corn."

Aunt Lily took the ear of corn, examining the variegated colors, now fully realizing Jimmie Sue's connections of irony, as she mused, *Colored corn fer the colored girl.* "Take keer of yoahself, Jimmie Sue . . . . An' we'll maybe see you nex' week at the revival meetin'?"

It seemed appropriate for Jimmie Sue to say something kinda religious, "Yeah, . . . the Lord willin'."

That brought another chuckle from Aunt Lily.

* * *

CHAPTER 17

The Revival Meeting

Jimmie Sue thought of little else than the revival meeting at the colored church after Aunt Lily had extended, on behalf of Madeleen, an invitation to attend.

It wasn't that the prospect of the revival meeting itself had so absorbed his attention, as it was the overwhelming thought of being amongst all those colored folk (mostly unknown to him) in a completely different church (at least new to him) with strange proceedings (according to white folks' rumors).

Although Jimmie Sue didn't go to any church on a regular basis, his daddy did see to it that he and his siblings would read some scripture almost every evening. This resulted in all of them committing many Bible verses to memory.

Jimmie Sue would never be able to outquote Madeleen, but he felt, at any rate, he was somewhere in her proximity of scripture memorization. He would be the first to admit that he didn't always understand what some of his quotes might mean. They all sounded good; kind of like reciting poetry at the school functions

The colored church revival meetings started on a Monday evening, but Jimmie Sue that evening, while milking, figured that he still had a few nights left before he'd have to honor his commitment to attend.

Tuesday evening came and went without his going.

After school on Wednesday, Great-Grandma said, "Weren't you gonna 'tend the Hilton church revival meetin'?"

"Yeah, but the week ain't ovah yet."

On Thursday morning he and his siblings on their way to school saw Madeleen and Cletus and Clyde on the way to their school. They didn't say much to each other, aside from nodding hello.

They just ambled along until Cletus piped up, saying to Jimmie Sue, "Mamma tol' me thet you tol' her to tell Madeleen thet you be comin' to our revival meetin' this week."

With his siblings listening and staring at him with various expressions of wonder and humor, he asked Cletus, "Well, the revival ain't ovah yet, is it?"

"Nauw! Hit go on through Satiddy night."

It was time for Madeleen to contribute to the conversation. "Clyde, he got the Holy Ghos' las' night."

This bit of news could hardly be contained within the countenances of Thelma Lou and George Dowell, but it surely added a great deal of fuel to the blazing fear within Jimmie Sue's already fevered brow.

Is Madeleen expectin' me to get saved at the meetin'? I ain't perticularly scared of ghosts, as a general rule, but the Holy Ghost, itself, is a completely different and mysterious matter.

Madeleen glowed with an expression of divine satisfaction, while Clyde exuded an aura of wonderment. Whether their expressions of heavenly bliss or complete puzzlement over the previous night, Jimmie Sue couldn't discern.

He was surely greatly relieved to see that they were coming to the fork in the road, with one leading to the white school and the other to the colored school.

This would give him an opportunity to postpone a decision about the revival as well as some time to think over all the implications of the news Madeleen had just shared about Clyde's answering the call of the Lord to the altar the night before.

Madeleen said, "You comin' or not?"

Jimmie Sue answered, "This is the road to my school. You know I cain't come to yoah school. I think hit's agin the law."

Disgustedly, she asked, "Silly, I didn't mean come to the school. I meant are you comin' to the revival? There ain't no law 'bout comin' to a church."

"Oh yeah! I said I would . . . an' I will."

"When?"

" . . . Tonight!"

They all kind of waved goodbye to each other, as they went their separate ways. George Dowell and Thelma Lou kept up a barrage of questions, jibes and snide remarks all the way to the schoolhouse door.

Jimmie Sue had an unusually uneventful day at school, walked home without any mischief, milked the cow early and ate almost nothing for supper. Taking note of his behavior and demeanor, his mamma asked him, "I s'pose you be goin' to the colored revival meetin' tonight?"

"Yeah!" He didn't like at all the way the women in his life could always read his mind, and know what he was thinking.

George Dowell, having wondered for a long time about the services at the colored church, said, "I'd be happy to go 'long, Jimmie Sue."

This would be just another complication for Jimmie Sue, as he couldn't forget how George Dowell and Madleen had worked and sung together, so he declined by off-handedly saying, "I s'pose I jest as soon go this one alone."

Not completely understanding what he'd meant by that statement, George Dowell backed off without pursuing the matter any further.

Jimmie Sue had already put on a clean shirt and overalls. He'd even tried to polish his brogan shoes with a dab of lard from the kitchen cabinet. He saddled up ol' Pete, their most sure-footed mule for riding in the dark. He always seemed to find his way home even on a moonless night.

But the almanac had said that that night was meant to have a full moon, so he hadn't bothered to light a lantern or even to bring one. The moon hadn't yet appeared as Jimmie Sue headed out toward the colored church house on the far ridge right next to the colored schoolhouse.

He'd barely got started when the moon started rising over the eastern horizon to his back, lighting his way like a heavenly beacon. The farther he rode, the brighter the nighttime became, which began to spook him about some special meaning he was supposed to be getting with this heavenly attention.

As he tied ol' Pete to a sycamore sapling at the side of the church, he noticed the moon silhouetting a gnarly old stump of a dead oak tree.

The vision was so peaceful that he reckoned he could just stay outside, talk to ol' Pete and watch the moon play hide-and-seek behind the scudsy clouds, but that might not be religious enough tonight and besides, Madeleen wouldn't know that he was there fulfilling the obligation of his promise to attend. Staying outside, unseen, would hardly qualify for full attendance.

The church service had already started with the lusty singing filling the night air, completely drowning out the usual night sounds of crickets and frogs. One family was entering the church house, as Jimmie Sue was still considering if he should go inside or stay outside or ride ol' Pete back home.

But a promise is a promise.

Walking cautiously through the open church door, he saw an empty seating space on the back pew. He immediately sat and noticed that not only was he conspicuously the only white, he was also sitting on the wrong side of the church.

You see, it was the custom in the colored church, and sometimes in the white churches, for men and boys to sit on one side of the church house and women and girls on the other. Jimmie Sue had plopped himself right down on the back pew on the women's side.

Brother Peeples was standing behind the pulpit and Madeleen was next to the piano leading the singing. Sister Foster was playing the piano, and when I say "playing the piano," I mean she was *playing the piano* to a fare-thee-well.

The songs had different words from those at the juke joint, but the tunes were just as lively and jivey at the colored church as one might find at a roadhouse.

Madeleen was leading the song, "Love Lifted Me." Her voice soared over all the others, even the lusty bass voices. Jimmie Sue had never appreciated the first verse of that song which started with "I was sinking deep in sin, Far from the peaceful shore, Very deeply stained within, sinking to rise no more."

He was quite aware that he had some faults—even some unforgivable pranks—but he'd never felt he was sinking deep into anything aside from the swimming hole, and he knew he could always get out of that deep water all by himself.

Actually they were finishing the first go-around of the rousing chorus, ending with "Love lifted me."

Leading joyfully into the second stanza, Madeleen almost belted, "All my heart to Him I give, Ever to Him I'll cling."

It seemed to Jimmie Sue that she had seen him slip in and had even tittered at seeing him sit on the women's side of the church. He dared not change seats now, as it would just add to his awkward embarrassment.

"In His blessed presence live, Ever His praises sing."

Is she looking directly at me and singing especially for my benefit? He would like to think so, but he knew that when Madeleen was in the *rapture,* a person wouldn't be able to discern where her focus was or where her attention was directed. Also he knew deep down that the Him she sang for was a capital H and not a mere white boy.

At the end of the chorus of the last stanza she languorously held each note a little longer than normal in a sweet tremulous voice: "When nothing else could help, Love lifted me."

Jimmie Sue was jolted out of his indulgent fantasy by Brother Peeples announcing, "I see thet we got a visitor hyar from another of our neighborhood churches. I b'lieve it be one of the Bennett boys. Son, we shorely do welcome you into our midst in the Lord's presence, an' I know He'd want us to 'vite you down to set on the front banch clost to the seat of Jesus."

Jimmie Sue couldn't very well refuse, as he realized everyone was already fully aware of his presence and his error of sitting on the wrong side of the church. With straw hat in hand he walked awkwardly down the center aisle, the object of stares from the whole congregation.

"Now, son, which of the Bennett boys you be?"

"James Lafayette Bennett."

"Well we wants you ta know thet you or yoah fambly's welcome hyar now or any time the Lord directs yoah feet in the path to ouah door."

Jimmie Sue was used to Amens and an occasional Hallelujah, but he was surprised to hear so much toe-tapping and soft Amens as a kind of accompaniment to the preacher's intonations and the rhythms of the songs. The percussives might die down a little, but would never completely fade out completely, and would increase in intensity with renewed energy as words or music amped up.

Nodding politely as he sat down on the end of the bench, he recognized immediately that it was the mourners' bench. The mourner's bench was usually reserved for those persons under some kind of spiritual conviction or a soul on the edge of committing their heart to Jesus.

He was in troublesome deep waters again—this time maybe over his head where he couldn't swim out or by treading water or sweet-talking. But he sat down, nodded neighborly to the other mourners, and proceeded to listen and take in whatever was about to happen.

Sitting next to him on the mourner's bench was Rufus Jones, the Pierson town drunk, who reportedly got saved every year at revival. Ol' Rufus worked at the barber shop in town, polishing shoes and sweeping up the loose hair on the floor. He'd also been known to be the distributor for local moonshiners and could be counted on to supply prescriptions to the other town drunks. He, even on the mourner's bench, reeked with the stench of alcohol.

Jimmie Sue was amazed that three different offerings were collected: one for the graveyard funds, one for the painting of the church house and a love offering to give to the visiting preacher, Brother Connors, who had come all the way from the next county to preach the good news of salvation.

In addition to the number of collections, he was intrigued that the offering baskets weren't passed down the pews like at the white folks' church but stayed on the Lord's Supper table, where people would walk up and offer their contribution to whatever cause they felt compelled to honor. Everyone could witness your depth of charitable commitment.

Then there were several songs, all led by Madeleen: "Gonna lay down my burden, down by the riverside . . . ."; "Brightly gleams our Father's mercy, From the lighthouse evermore . . . ."; "On Jordan's Stormy banks I stand . . . ;" "Jesus, Saviour, pilot me over life's tempestuous seas."

The shouts and Alleluias and outright dancing accompanying the music completely flummoxed Jimmie Sue. He couldn't say he didn't enjoy the energy of the whole thing. He was almost tempted to get up and dance the way he would when musicians would stop by the general store on Saturday nights, but he held his enthusiasm in check.

Every once in a while he'd bring himself back to his reality of being a white boy in a colored church in the middle of a revival meeting.

It seemed that with all their music they had a thing for water—oceans, rivers, fountains. He wondered if Madeleen had chosen those songs or if she just sang them as though she really meant every word. Did these water songs remind her of their meeting *down by the riverside* at the swimming/baptizing hole?

As Brother Connors started his scripture reading from the book of Exodus, most folks had quit staring at Jimmie Sue, and even he started relaxing a little and enjoying the musical notes of Brother Connors' reading voice, intoning the sacred words, which ended with "And it came to pass that self-same day, *that* the Lord did bring the children of Israel out of the land of Egypt by their armies."

He preached fervently about the evil Egyptians and the horrors put upon the Hebrew children and how they wouldn't let them go on to their Promised Land. The preacher went on to excoriate those Israelites who, for one reason or another, didn't want to leave the reality of enslavement for the uncertainty of a long journey over deserts and up mountains and through the waters of the Red Sea.

After leading the believers on their own life journeys through hardships and fears of traveling in unknown waters, it was time to call them to repentance, not only for their sins and wrongdoings but also to upbraid them for their timidity to face the uncharted waters ahead and to challenge them to answer the call of the Lord to come unto Him and to join His flock.

Jimmie Sue tremulously realized that *It was time for the altar call!*

* * *

CHAPTER 18

Altar Call

Brother Connors was using his handkerchief to mop the sweat pouring down his brow. He'd already shucked his coat and loosened his tie and unbuttoned his collar. His shirt looked as though it had just come from the wash tub and hadn't got out to the clothesline yet. Even though it was past the heat of the summer, the closeness of all those people and the fulminations of the preachers and singers had generated quite a bit of warmth.

It was time . . . Preacher Conners' time . . . to call the sinners forward and deduce the effectiveness of his message and its delivery.

"Brothah Peeples, I call now upon you and yoah people to look forward to thet Promised Land, an' prepare the way of the Lawd.

"Thar still be Red Seas out thar afore us—seas deeper than we can even imagine.

"Thar still be deserts ahead of us—deserts as hot as the furnaces of hell.

"An' thar still be mountains we gotta climb—mountains so high with wild beasts so fierce and storms so harmful we cain't get our minds around it.

"But we be assured that the steady arms of the Lord swim us acrost thet ocean-sea. We been promised thet the comforting hand of Jesus cool ouah furrowed brow in thet hellish desert. An' the very wings of the Holy

Ghost carry us ovah them high mountains whut block our gates to ouah Promised Land.

"Who will come now an' join with me on the journey as we all hear the call of the Lord to come to His altar, confess ouah sins an' stamp the blood of the sacrificial lamb on our forehead fer ouah own personal key to unlock thet celestial gate?

"Who'll now come an' give yoah heart to the Lord, as we sing *Just As I Am?*"

Brother Peeples said, "Sistah Hilton, would you be so kind as to have Madeleen come forward agin an' lead us in this altar call hymn?"

During all of this time the amens, hallelujahs, toetapping and moans of penitential conviction almost drowned out the preachers' voices, but everyone knew exactly what was being asked and what the call to all of them meant.

The piano had kept a soft undertone throughout the altar call, and by time Madeleen got in place to lead the song, the piano was already banging out the musical prelude.

"Just as I am without one plea (the sanctified souls were already dancing in the center aisle) But that Thy blood was shed for me."

Rufus, the annual revival convert, had risen from the mourner's bench and had made his way down to in front of the communion table where he swayed back and forth while shaking the hand of Brother Peeples, who said, "Rufus, hit's good to see you back at this altar . . . once more."

Rufus collapsed onto his knees, whether from repentance for his waywardness or shame in front of the preacher or from the moving of the liquid spirits, one couldn't really tell, and probably no one would care to reason out.

Several people had come up to shake the preachers' hands by time Madeleen was singing the last part of the fifth stanza: "Because Thy promise I believe, O Lamb of God, I come, I come."

Jimmie Sue was getting to be a little fidgety and had some difficulty staying seated on the mourner's bench. The rhythm and energy were also getting to him, even in this strange place, but seeing Madeleen under the lamp lights and hearing her heavenly singing almost felt like a personal call to her own altar of blissful sanctification.

One young sister danced down the aisle, shouting and amening right down to take the preacher's hand, and when she grabbed Preacher Connors's hand, she was seemingly jolted by a bolt of lightning straight from heaven.

She swooned backward onto the floor just missing the arms of the young fellow who'd been walking right behind her.

He immediately knelt down beside her and administered mouth-to-mouth resuscitation. This was long before anyone knew about CPR, but somehow he knew exactly what to do.

She was surely being revived, both in body and in spirit. One of the older women opened up her purse to fetch a bottle of digitalis which she kept there for this very purpose. The young woman soon regained consciousness and began all over again, shouting and singing.

The Holy Spirit most assuredly had possessed her.

Rather than being critical, Jimmie Sue was impressed with all the contagious energy.

Brother Peeples called forth, "I know thet thar still be folks out thar under the influence of my voice, what be ready to accept Jesus in they heart but yet not ready to walk down this aisle.

"I feel in my heart thet thar's some soul out thar not yet prepared to answer thet last clarion call of the Lord when Gabriel blow on thet horn welcomin' all of us to come an' stan' afore the jedgement seat of Godamighty.

"Almost persuaded! Thet's whut it is—almost persuaded to heed thet inner voice in yoah heart an' answer the comfortin' voice of Jesus, callin' to you from the heavenly heights.

"Sistah Foster, would you strike the chord for *Almost Persuaded* while Madeleen lead us in the singin' of thet glorious revival hymn?"

Madeleen took her place beside the piano only a few feet from Jimmie Sue, and Sister Foster needed only to strike the first chord for Madeleen to stride wholeheartedly into the first stanza. "Almost persuaded, now to believe. Almost persuaded, Christ to receive; Seems now some soul to say, 'Go, Spirit, go Thy way, Some more convenient day On Thee I'll call'."

Enveloped in a sea of movement and sound, Jimmie Sue's head felt lighter than a humming bird feather while he looked at and listened to Madeleen. His body felt as though it might begin to float up off the mourner's bench in a swirling whirlpool of ecstasy. This wasn't one of his fantasy dreams—this was reality—a reality never experienced by him before—a reality calling his young innermost soul to the spiritual heart of an angel strumming the harp strings of her voice.

At the end of each stanza, Brother Peeples would call for that last, lost sinner, and Brother Connors would plead to "come forward now, afore it's too late to avoid the eternal grip of the devil nor be enclosed in the grasp of the death angel's arms. Thet ol' reaper be acomin' fer each of us, but why don't you come forth before the reaper gets to you, an' it be too late?"

Madeleen was finishing the third stanza, "Almost cannot avail; Almost is but to fail! Sad, sad, that bitter wail, Almost, but lost."

Before the song was ended, Jimmie Sue had jumped to his feet and, as the mourner's bench was so close to the altar rail, he was immediately in the midst of shouting new converts, whirling sanctified souls and toe-tapping reprobates under conviction.

All eyes reverted to the *white boy;* many hands reached to extend the "hand of fellowship;" an array of arms opened to embrace him into the "arms of the family of Godamighty."

A sea of sweaty ebony faces glistened with reflections of the flickering lights from the hanging oil lamps.

Countless pairs of piercing eyes were welcoming him from his own darkness into the light of Jesus.

The odors in the crowded church were almost oppressive: the scent of the burning kerosene in the smokey oil lamps, the smells of the perspiring bodies and more particularly the alcoholic fumes wafting from Rufus Jones, Jimmie Sue's mourner's bench companion.

And yet, even the unsavory combination of this odoriferous bombardment seemed to transport his own spirits.

Somehow the energy of all the movement and the rhythm of the music seemed to lift his feet from contact with the puncheon wooden floor, not unlike his dancing at the fiddlers' gatherings. He started moving to the accompaniment of handclaps and holy shouting.

Some weeks earlier at the general store Saturday night musicians, Madeleen had been crouching in a dark corner. But here she stood at the side of the piano in the full light of the hanging oil lamps, leading the heavenly choir of jubilation to the glorious throne of Jesus, where no one but the devil had to stand in the corner.

The rhythm beat into the pulsations of Jimmie Sue's brain, the pounding of his heart and even the cadence of his tongue, as he heard his own voice join the chorus of jubilee celebration.

As he stepped from the mourner's bench, the wave of celebrants moved aside as though Moses were there opening up the waters of the Red Sea. The rhythms of sound and movement picked up in intensity as he swirled inside the whirling waters of dark figures, circling within the pathway which opened up for him.

Then something quite unexpected happened—unexpected by both Jimmie Sue and everyone else.

His feet didn't lead him to the altar rail nor to the preachers' waiting hands nor to his knees in surrender at the altar rail. His feet looked to be leading him away from the destination where the rest of his being had seemed to be headed.

The sea of revivalists parted again to reveal a passageway down the aisle to the front door.

Was the devil in his feet leading him from the embrace of the Lord, or did he hear that little voice again?

As he exited the church house, there was a sudden explosion of quiet—almost as though the Lord had muffled the ears of the earth. Hush covered everything.

As he crept to the sycamore sapling where he'd left his patient mule, he looked back at the people in the church house outlined against the lamp lights—dark silhouettes frozen in time and space.

He cooled his heels and mind and heart, as he and ol' Pete made their way back home in the light of the full harvest moon.

He just gave Pete his head and didn't even bother to fasten the reins on his bridle. At that point he trusted the surefooted old mule more than his own feet or the dulcet sounds of Madeleen's music.

Jimmie Sue realized that Judgment Day, his personal Judgement Day, wasn't going to have to wait for the grave. The day of reckoning was near at hand, when he'd next encounter Madeleen.

The inner voice reminded him again, *But she's colored!*

* * *

CHAPTER 19

Back Home

Anyone seeing the two travelers along the road that night would have perceived them as outcasts from some nearby town. But they were simply ol' Pete, tired from a full day of work and an evening of standing immobile under the sycamore sapling, and young Jimmie Sue, carrying on his shoulders the burdens of the world in the form of early manhood with confusing visions of beauty and duty.

Why did it seem to be his responsibility to carry on the separated ways of coloreds and whites?

Neither his papa nor mamma had said that he had to do anything in a specific way. Somehow, a person just knew what was expected in certain situations. If you had to be told, you were either daft or rebellious. Jimmie Sue wasn't either one, but he couldn't sort out the things he felt for Madeleen, the sense of elation at the revival, or the accepted ways of both the whites and coloreds.

He was unaware they'd arrived back home, until ol' Pete stopped at the barn door. This jolted Jimmie Sue into his usual scolding of Pete when the obstinate old mule would balk and refuse to finish plowing or pulling the wagon. This time Pete had stopped because they were at the barn—if the mule had proceeded on into the barn, Jimmie Sue would have been scraped off Pete's back by the upper door jamb. Then he realized he'd been so busy daydreaming in the middle of the night that he had noticed neither the time nor the distance on the way back home.

He unbridled ol' Pete. He'd ridden bareback, so he didn't have to unsaddle. After a late night snack of fresh oats for his trusty steed, Jimmie Sue decided he'd not go into the house to bed. That'd just arouse everyone. As he really wanted to be alone anyways, he thought he'd take an old quilt, always on hand for a saddle blanket or for use at the tobacco barn, and climb up to the loft where he could be with his own thoughts, and maybe sleep. The full moon on the descent in the western sky cast a rectangular bright light through the haymow door.

This was long before the mountain farmers had haybalers. The hay in the barnloft had recently been mown with hand scythes and thrown by pitchforks into the top of the barn just like their haying over to the Hiltons'.

Jimmie Sue didn't bother to undress, except to take off his brogan shoes. The welcome softness of his barn bedding and the sweet fragrance of the lespedeza hay, transported him into a drifting stream of slumber.

The stream transformed into a leisurely creek on which he was somehow floating without a boat or without even getting wet. He felt quite relaxed and peaceful, though somewhat confused. As he attempted to figure out what was happening, the creek widened, and he could see Madeleen only a few feet away on the creek bank. He tried to call to her but no sound came from his mouth.

However, she saw him and turned slowly away.

The stream continued to expand and accelerate its speed. He saw her again, but she seemed to be a bit older. Again, he tried to call to her but couldn't make a sound, and again she saw him and this time deliberately turned away.

These events continued to take place with the expanding, accelerating river, his inability to speak and Madeleen's figure getting older and older. Until . . .

Jimmie Sue suddenly heard the roar of a mighty waterfall, which he knew must be just downstream ahead of him. When he then tried to scream, Madeleen appeared on an overhanging rock ledge. This time she was much older and pointing downstream, as though to warn him. The rushing water began to swirl amid huge boulders. Completely out of control, he was being carried in circles as though by some unseen cosmic hand.

Was he dreaming or was he still at the revival meeting or . . . was he somehow in a real river plunging headlong into disaster?

When he floated around a large boulder, he saw Madeleen lower her hands, then holding them together in front of her as though she were cradling something significant, but invisible, in them. As his body began a new onrush toward the waterfall sound, he could see a profound sorrow mask her usually calm countenance and tears falling into the cupped hands.

He found his voice at the top of the waterfall, and screaming downward toward the eddying pool below, he jumped up to discover that he was in the barn loft and in the meantime had aroused all of the barn inhabitants—probably even the field mice and certainly the barn owl, which began screeching.

The moon was now behind clouds, which had begun to release a torrential gullywasher. His face was wet, which he figured was from a drip in a hole in the roof—except no one had noticed a leak in the roof before that. It was probably the rain in the face which woke him so suddenly.

But then he recalled the image of an older Madeleen standing on the riverbank above the waterfall, holding something tenderly in her strong work-worn hands. He somehow knew that she was holding his heart and bathing it with her tears.

When he calmed down, listening to the rain rat-a-tat-tatting its percussive pings on the metal barn roof, Rufus, the barn cat, nestled next to his back and began purring. Jimmie Sue checked to make sure the cat hadn't brought a newly acquired mouse with him. Reassuring himself that Rufus was alone, he heard a new sound mixed with all the other sounds ringing through his head—a familiar human voice accompanied by the music of the rain:

Shall we gather at the river, Where bright angel feet have trod, With its crystal tide forever, Flowing by the Throne of God? Yes, we'll gather at the river . . .

The song faded gently away as his heart and mind drifted into a peaceful slumber.

* * *

CHAPTER 20

Breakfast at the Bennetts'

At breakfast the next morning, Jimmie Sue was bombarded with questions.

Simon was the first interrogator: "Did you git the Holy Ghost las' night, Jimmie Sue?"

"Aw shut up, Simple Simon."

George Dowell, who was increasingly interested in religious questions, asked, "Did they shout an' dance an' roll aroun' on the floor like the white pentecostal holy-rollers?"

"There was shoutin' an' singin' an' a kinda little dance-like thang, but there weren't no rollin' aroun' on the floor. What'd give you thet notion?" He wasn't about to tell them about the girl fainting and how the young fellow revived her with mouth-to-mouth healing.

"What kinda hymns did they sing?"

"Somewhat same as ours . . . . But they sung them a whole lot diffrunt."

"How?"

"You know real fast, livelier an' dancelike."

"Someone played the pianner?"

"Yeah, Mrs. Fowler, ovah . . . Sistah Esther Fowler ovah to Pierson."

"*Sistah* Fowler?" his mamma asked.

"You know Aunt Esther Fowler, who sometime play the pianner for the road show musicians?"

George Dowell persisted. "Was they a altar call?"

"Well, . . . yeah, it *was* a revival meetin'."

Thelma Lou wanted to know "Was there any snakes slung aroun' by the preachahs?"

"Don't be silly. The colored church ain't no snakehandlin' church."

Little Rosie asked, "Was Ruthie thar? If she was, I woulda wished I'd agone. "

Jimmie Sue answered,"Oh, yeah. She was real quiet all evenin'. Settin' between her mamma and daddy."

Great-Granddaddy Robert wanted to know: "Who was the preachah an' what'd he preach 'bout.?"

"Hit was Brothah Connors from over to Gilpin County. He preached mostly on gettin' saved acourse, but he talked a lot 'bout mountains an' deserts, but mostly 'bout watah . . . especially the Red Sea."

Jimmie Sue then realized that his dream about water that night was probably inspired by Brother Conners's water preaching.

Great-Grandma Sue was a little puzzled as to why he would call the preacher "Brothah" rather than "Preachah," him being colored an' all. She kept this little worry to herself and simply said, "Now yaw'l lay off of Jimmie. I'm sure he's tired—partickerly tired of so many questions."

But she had her own questions and concerns. "Jimmie, you seem to've lost yoah appetite of late. Honey, are you feelin' all right?"

He wasn't exactly feeling all right but reassured his mamma, "Yeah, I feel fine, Mamma, jest not very hungry this mornin'."

As the crops had all been taken in by that time in September, Great-Granddaddy said that after school the boys would be cuttin' up the oak tree blown down in the sudden storm that had come up last night. It was a huge hardwood tree, which would provide a great deal of stove wood and firewood for the winter.

On the way to school, the Bennett kids saw Cletus and Clyde, but Madeleen wasn't with them.

Jimmie Sue asked, "Where's Madeleen?"

The Hilton boys were particularly quiet and seemed to be reluctant to answer Jimmie Sue. "Oh, she be to home," said Cletus.

"Is she sick or somethin'?"

"Nauw, she jest not be feelin' too good."

Thelma Lou knowingly replied, "Oh, I know what thet's 'bout."

Cletus and Clyde just looked at her blankly.

After the children separated at the fork of the road to go their separate ways to their separate schools, Jimmie Sue said to George Dowell and Thelma Lou that he'd forgotten something important he needed at school but had left at home.

Thelma Lou wondered what he might have left, so she asked, "What'd you leave? You got yoah lunch box an' yoah book bag . . . unless you left yoah mind to home."

Jimmie Sue didn't bother to answer her sarcasm. He had already turned around and headed back toward home.

But he didn't go home. He'd made up in his mind to go to the swimming hole. It wasn't that he intended to go swimming. It was too cold for that then, in September. He was wondering if Madeleen might have gone down there to the baptizing hole.

Rattler, his favorite hound dog, joined him, even before he got down to the water. It was almost as though that perceptive dog understood Jimmie Sue's dilemma. He was always close by whenever there was some kind of trouble brewing.

When Jimmie Sue got down there, Madeleen was nowhere to be seen, so he just sat down on the diving-off rock and contemplated what'n'all had been happening to him. He sat there for nearly an hour just listening to the creek gurgling downstream and watching the multicolored autumn leaves falling in the water and floating like little boats down to the ocean-sea. He attempted to make some sense out of the dream he'd had the night before about the water—this water which he'd swum in many a time but had avoided as baptizing water.

Suddenly he saw, peering through the leaves of a bush on the north bank, the large brown eyes of a fawn. With a frightened look, it seemed to be focusing straight at him. Jimmie Sue wondered what *it* was wondering and as he wondered further if it was a small deer or a dear Madeleen. He recalled that the Hiltons had some Indian blood. Years earlier he had been told how certain Indians were known as shape-changers with the ability to change from the form of a human being into an animal and vice-versa.

Madeleen had assuredly transformed, or at least rearranged, something within Jimmie Sue, but would she have been that fawn looking at him with such a quizzical expression? He waited for quarter of an hour for the frightened deer to emerge from the brush, but all in vain, as it continued to stand there transfixed in a frozen state.

He stood up and turned away momentarily. When he looked back across the creek, the fawn had disappeared without making a sound into the forest thicket.

Following a new urge, he walked upstream of the swimming hole and crossed the creek on the footlog bridge with Rattler following close on his heels. *Why's Rattler not interested in chasing off in the bresh for a rabbit or somethin'?*

When he got in sight of the Hiltons' place, he could see and hear Uncle Levi splitting stovewood in the backyard. Jimmie Sue walked up on Uncle Levi's hindside and spoke, causing him to jump around to confront his unexpected visitor. "How're you, Uncle Levi?"

Cautiously Madeleen's old daddy answered, "I be fine."

"Is Madeleen to home?"

"Better ask her mamma."

By time Jimmie Sue had reached the porch, Aunt Lily had come out of the house.

"How are you today, Aunt Lily?"

"Jest fine." She continued, without giving Jimmie Sue a chance to ask about Madeleen. "But Madeleen ain't to home."

"Where would she be?"

"She not feelin' so good, so I say she didn't need to traipse off to school."

"You said she could stay to home, but then you say she ain't to home?"

"At her prayin' place."

"Where is thet?"

"She don't tell nobody, but I's sure it be somewheres close to the baptizin' hole."

He recalled to himself the deer eyes at the edge of the woods. "Do you s'pose she don't even wanna talk to me?"

"Even if she *don't* talk to you, hit don't mean she don't *wanna* talk to you . . . 'The Lord works in mysterious ways his wonders to perform'."

Jimmie Sue told Aunt Lily goodbye and retreated back down the hill toward the swimming hole, but instead of crossing the footlog, he decided to open his lunch bag and eat his biscuit and ham on Madeleen's side of the creek. *Maybe she'd show up.*

In fact, he decided to go to the spot where he'd seen those mysterious, penetrating deer eyes, less than an hour earlier.

There in a small clearing surrounded by mountain laurel was what appeared to be a playhouse or maybe a thinking place. The ground was covered with moss, which had evidently been brought there from somewhere else. A small table was made of rocks, carefully laid together without any mud daubing. He couldn't tell whether it was a play table or a table like in the church where the Lord's Supper would be prepared. Looking over the table, he had a clear view of the waterhole and the opposite bank on his usual side of the creek.

He stretched out there on the north bank, not sure what he was waiting on or looking for. Some freshly fallen leaves provided a soft resting place, and there was enough sun to keep a body warm. For a while he watched the clouds scurrying above the lacy tracery of tree branches before he fell asleep.

He hadn't been asleep for more than a few minutes when he was awakened by a commotion and conflagration of singing in full voice. Marching down from the direction of the Hiltons' on Sapling Ridge, was a celebrational group of dark-skinned marchers, singing *Shall We Gather at the River?*, with Madeleen leading the singing just as she'd done the night before at the revival meeting. She also was leading the whole procession in their jubilation march with tambourines, gourd rattlers and hand clapping, accompanying their marching feet.

Surprisingly the old hound dog completely ignored all the hoopla from that crowd of people.

Jimmie Sue soon recognized many of the folk, whom he'd seen at the revival meeting the night before, and some of the coloreds he'd seen over to Pierson or at the mule barn. What fascinated him the most were the colorful clothes they were all wearing.

That is everyone but Madeleen, who was wearing a dress and shawl and veil of pure white filmy cloth that billowed in the wind, making it appear that Madeleen was floating a few inches off the ground.

He supposed that when they got to the edge of the creek they'd all stop. But they waded right on into the water hole with Madeleen still leading them. The temperature of the water didn't seem to bother them at all. Everyone came a little way into the water, but Brother Peeples and Brother Connors waded in on each side of Madeleen until they were all into the water up to their waists. It looked as though there was going to be a baptism. Jimmie Sue remembered that the year before, Cletus had said that Madeleen didn't have the Holy Ghost but that she was trying to get it by tarrying.

Jimmie Sue thought *Maybe when I left the revival meetin' so quick las' night, maybe Madeleen answered the altar call, 'stead of me. Maybe she felt it was her place to take my place. But it's much too quick to now arrange for a baptizin' and lettin' all the folks know 'bout it—the nights of the meetin's not be finished yet.*

But that really seemed to be what was happening. The preachers stood on each side of Madeleen and with their hands closed over her nostrils, they immersed her once for the Father, once for the Son and once for the Holy Ghost. When she stood up straight with water running from her hair, her face looked as though it was a glowing lamp, even reflecting a path of light on top of the water over toward where Jimmie Sue's hiding place was. It seemed to make a renewed connection between them.

Then something really strange began to happen, just as Brother Peeples pronounced something which sounded like from the scriptures, "And now why tarriest thou? arise in the baptism that washeth away thy sins."

Slowly all of Madeleen's white garments began to melt, almost oozing as they flowed into the baptismal water. The marchers were all singing joyously, taking no heed to what was happening to Madeleen as she began—in slow motion—to wade toward the north bank of the creek, directly toward Jimmie Sue in his hiding place. By time she stepped out of the water all her white raiment was completely gone, almost as though her clothing was like the sin washing away when the preacher said, "washeth away thy sins." *Maybe that's what washed away all her pretty white clothing.*

Her whole body lit up with a brightness—not a brightness exactly, but a warm glow—with greater intensity than the usual brilliance of her bronzed face.

Thoroughly captivated by her heavenly beauty, he felt he should be ashamed to be looking on Madeleen's nakedness, but the whole scene was so other-worldly that no amount of personal negativity seemed to occur, as her clothing had begun to be replaced by a hazy golden glow, and as she drew ever closer to Jimmie Sue, his eyes began to lose focus. He'd remembered something scriptural about, *Now we see through a glass darkly, but then face to face,* as her face floated ever closer to his face, which was peering over the stone altar there in the laurel brake.

He closed his eyes momentarily in an attempt to clear them of any fogginess. While his eyes were still closed, water began to fall on his head like a gentle rain.

Is Madeleen brushin' the watah offen her hair onto my head or maybe she be bringin' the baptizin' watah up to me.

When he opened his eyes quickly to *behold this heavenly creature,* he saw old Rattler standing there and shaking the creek water off of himself, almost as though he was deliberately trying to get some message to Jimmie Sue. Apparently Rattler had gone for a swim and maybe was trying to wake up Jimmie Sue.

When Jimmie Sue realized that he'd been asleep and dreaming again, he still looked around for Madeleen, hoping to see her in person, even if she had all her clothes on. But she hadn't shown up—not even in the shape of a fawn, not where he could see her anyways—so he crossed the creek and went on toward home, arriving just about time Thelma Lou and George Dowell got back home from school.

No one said anything about Jimmie Sue playing hooky that day, until Great-Grandma said, "Well, how was school today?"

Thelma Lou looked at George Dowell, who looked back at her, then they both looked to Jimmie Sue, who simply said, "Hit weren't nothin' special."

After supper and the chores were finished, Jimmie Sue said, "I think I'll jest go an' sleep in the barn agin tonight, an' see if I can find out what's been raiding the chicken house ever' night." What he really had in mind was to go back to the revival, but he hadn't a notion in the world what he would do when he got there.

He decided not to ride ol' Pete, but would walk instead with ol' Rattler and take a lantern, as the moon was mostly hidden by some angry-looking clouds. It was getting late, and the service would already have started, but that would suit his purposes just fine. He could look in through the windows without anyone seeing him or even knowing he was anywhere close by.

Long before he saw the church house, he could hear the music. But it somehow seemed different than the night before. Instead of the fast upbeat kind of music, it seemed more like some of the music—a dirge—like he'd heard the coloreds singing last summer when he saw them toting the casket of ol' Mose to his resting place in the cemetery.

When he got in sight of the church house light, he doused the light of the lantern, so as no one would see him. It looked maybe like rain, so everyone was inside. Ordinarily, just like at the white church, most of the men and boys wouldn't go in—just stand around on the outside unless it looked like bad weather.

He slowly and silently slipped up to the window behind the pulpit. There was Madeleen standing next to the piano and leading the singing. She must have recovered from her bad feelings earlier in the day. As he continued to watch, he saw many faces he'd seen in his dream earlier in the day in that celebrational procession down by the baptizing hole. He particularly noticed that Madeleen had seemed to increase in spirit and liveliness as the preachers got closer to the time for the altar call, and he was surprised that she didn't answer the call to heavenly bliss. The only reviving sinner that night was Rufus Jones, the perennial convert, pleading for forgiveness at the revival altar.

Jimmie Sue, in this new configuration, was an observer and not a direct participant; however, he still felt some of the urges he'd felt the night before. But he had not yet figured out whether on the night before he'd been under the spell of the preachers' voices, the mesmerizing rhythm of the gospel music, or the continuing sorcery of Madeleen's whole being.

Ol' Rattler had laid down close by Jimmie Sue and had begun to whine softly, causing Jimmie Sue to wonder if dogs ever got to have the chance to *repent an' answer a altar call.*

After the service ended, the Hiltons started walking home. They hadn't come in the buckboard, so Aunt Lily and Ruthie had stayed to home. Uncle Levi had lit his lantern and was leading the little clan with Cletus and Clyde close behind him, and Madeleen following a little farther back.

It was usual in that day and time in the mountains for the men folk to walk ahead of the women in order to meet any challenges or dangers which they might encounter along the way. It was probably also as a symbol of being at the head of the household—whether white or colored.

Jimmie Sue waited until they'd gone a few yards down the road, before he started following a short distance behind Madeleen. He hadn't bothered lighting his lantern, because there was enough ambient light from the Hiltons' lantern and the intermittent moon to make his way.

Madeleen hadn't made any indication that she knew he was walking behind her, until she suddenly asked, "White Boy, why you be afollowin' me?"

"How you know it's me, what be . . . ?"

"An' why you peep inta th' church house winder an' not come on in?"

"Well, afta las' night . . . ."

She didn't let him finish. "We not be talkin' now."

"Could I 'splain? . . ."

"Ain't no need to be 'splainin' nothin'."

He insisted, "I'd like to talk with . . . ."

"We ain't talkin' . . . not right now anyways."

She didn't break stride while talking to Jimmie Sue about *not* talking, and she didn't even turn to look toward him. Well, they were too far behind Uncle Levi's lantern to really have seen into each other's eyes anyway.

Jimmie Sue stopped while the Hiltons continued on up the road. He struck a match to light his lantern, now that he was so far behind their light. Apparently Cletus must've turned and seen a light bobbing behind them, when he asked, "Madeleen, thet be a haint afollerin' us."

She acknowledged, "Yeah, thet be a sure 'nough early Halloween goblin."

Maybe because it was so close to Halloween that got Jimmie Sue to thinking about sure-enough ghosts seeming to be following Madeleen.

She had told him about the high-yaller mixed blood in her family, which seemed always to be haunting her. Everyone, both whites and coloreds, seemed to think that the mulattoes had more insight into the mysteries of the other world than either of the purebloods on each side of the racial line. For some reason he sensed a foreboding somehow hanging in the air, which had nothing really to do with Halloween.

It bothered him considerable that she had called him *White Boy* again and reminded him that they weren't talking.

But she didn't say we wouldn't be talkin' . . . ever."

* * *

CHAPTER 21

Talking or Not Talking

When Uncle Jimmie Sue was growing up in the mountains, no one used the expression "courting" or "wooing" and certainly not "dating." The term used was "talking." People would say, "So and so has begun talkin' to *whoever.*" And when a courtship was terminated, the rumor would be shared, "Did you know *he* and *she* have quit talkin'?" A fellow couldn't get very far in his courting if he didn't have a fair amount of pretty talk in him.

There was even a song sung about a fellow who came "acalling", but he and the girl sat up all night "and never a word did say." The song ends, "Now when he goes in company, the girls all laugh for sport, Sayin' yonder goes that ding-dang fool that don't know how to court, Ooh that don't know how to court."

Also, it was an interesting custom in the hills that in the wintertime whenever a fellow came "acallin'" to do some "talkin'", and when the fire had died down, and the cold had crept in under the door and seeped around the windows, there would be a bed where the talking couple would go with their clothes still on and a bundling board separating them from each other.

Some beds were made with a vertical slot in the headboard and footboard, which would accommodate a foot-wide plank to be put in place by the girl's parents before they, themselves, went off to bed.

Although they did have their clothes on, the girl's mother would make sure that the girl's petticoat skirt was tied in a knot. The old country's practice of chastity belts had nothing over the mountain people. However, it was known that some girls were rather adept at tying and untying slip knots.

It was told on Jimmie Sue that he had gone acallin' on a girl in the next county in the wintertime, and her folks had set up a bundling board, and he and the girl had climbed into bed and had continued talking until they both fell asleep; he on one side of the bundling board and she on the other.

When they woke up and had breakfast the next morning, the girl took him out to the barnyard to see the livestock. At the fence she pointed down toward the gate where she said Jimmie Sue should go to get to the other side of the fence, but that she was going to climb over the fence. It was said that he said, "I'm perfectly capable of climbin' thet fence, the same as you."

Supposedly she said, "I don't reckin you can climb a four-foot high fence, if you can't crawl over a one-foot-high bundlin' board."

That probably never happened to Jimmie Sue, but some of the boys enjoyed telling it on him.

Although Madeleen had told Jimmie Sue on the road back from the Friday night revival meeting that they weren't talking, she had said, "We ain't talkin' . . . *right now* anyways."

That was sufficient notice that things were different between them now, but, on the other hand, it was clear that neither one of them wanted to turn their back forever on the other one.

As Jimmie Sue was the one who had disappointed Madeleen so drastically, it seemed that it would be up to him to make amends, or at least to reach across the chasm which had now separated the two of them.

Actually, they never did share the bundling board experience, but they did do a lot of talking, though one couldn't say they were, in actual fact, a "talking" couple.

It would have been scandalous if they were officially talking . . . he being white and she being colored. That little fact always hovered over the star-crossed lovers, though at times it would seem that they were just simply good, close friends.

Usually when he'd go by the Hiltons' he would just sort of casually stop in and make out like he'd come to talk with Uncle Levi about a job of work or with the boys about going hunting. Both Jimmie Sue and Cletus had new—at least new to them—'possum dogs.

Madeleen would always be sitting close by, listening to whatever the conversation might be about. However, she usually didn't enter into the talking, except when the subject would be on—or at least touching on—religion.

Although this was a subject of which Jimmie Sue felt at a definite disadvantage, particularly with Madeleen, he would often, himself, broach the subject just to see if he could get her involved in the talking.

Of course, he was fully aware of the pitfalls of arguing with her; so instead of debating, he would agree on most points whether he understood them or not.

A subject they both avoided religiously (please forgive the pun) was the aborted revival meeting in September. It wasn't because they weren't interested. Actually it hovered over the consciousness of each of them, whenever the other one would come to mind.

Jimmie Sue still couldn't get straight in his mind what that revival meeting was really all about, and whether or not it'd always be a deep gulf between them.

Madeleen didn't understand why he didn't—or hadn't been able to—answer the call to the altar, and was it an unwitting sign that he was not only turning away from the Lord but rejecting her as well.

But it was the strangest thing that whenever Jimmie Sue kind of backed off from Madeleen, realizing the impossibility of their situation, why then, Madeleen would do something extra nice for him.

In the winter, as Christmas was getting nearer, Jimmie Sue spent less and less time over to the Hiltons', and even though the holidays were befitting times for special people in one's life, it didn't seem right to be giving a romantic-like present to Madeleen, regardless of what he might actually feel for her.

His sixteenth birthday was just two days before Christmas, and at supper that night his mamma brought to the table for dessert a meringue-covered pie in the place of a birthday cake. He, of course, wanted to know what kind of filling it had, because Great-Grandma was noted for all kinds of pies.

She said, "Why don't we just cut inta it an' find out whut its innards are like?" She let Jimmie Sue do the cutting.

He cut carefully through the high-peaked brown-tipped meringue and on into the filling and crust. He started to lick the cutting knife, but Thelma Lou said, "You bettah be keerful how you lick thet knife. Hit's got a sharp edge you know."

Simon offered a bit of useless information, "You know if you split a crow's tongue down the middle, hit'll know how to talk jest like people... an' speakin' of talkin', I ain't seen Jimmie Sue an' Madeleen talkin'...."

Jimmie Sue said, "Aw, jest shut yoah mouth, Simple Simon."

His mamma said, "Jimmie, I tol' ya befoah, ya shouldna oughter call Simon thet."

By that time, Jimmie Sue had tasted chocolate on the knife blade. "Mamma did you bake this chocolate pie?"

"Well, to be honest, Honey, hit was Madeleen what baked it an' brought it ovah for yoah birthday."

Simon and Thelma Lou started tittering and oohing and aahing in Jimmie Sue's direction, until their mamma said, "Now cut it out, you two. Let Jimmie Sue be. It's *his* birthday."

Everyone recalled the dinner on the grounds last August, but Jimmie Sue was particularly reminiscing on that bittersweet occasion.

He would now be compelled, indeed *im*pelled, to somehow return the favor of a gift to Madeleen, particularly at this Christmas time, but just as friend to friend. Wouldn't he have done the same for Emmett or Walt, that is if they were to have baked him a special birthday pie?

He tried to think of a favor he could give to her but then he reminded himself....

What I be thinkin', hit'd prob'ly be more a favor to me than to her, specially since she's been so stand-offish lately.

* * *

CHAPTER 22

Christmas Gift

It was only two more days until Christmas, and Jimmie Sue knew he dare not go to town to buy a present for Madeleen. Even if he'd wanted to, he didn't have enough money for a "fitten" Christmas present for anyone, and particularly a present for some one who was extra special .

Although the church his family attended didn't have any special Christmas celebrations, except some meetings for extra preaching, other churches had various Christmas events including caroling and pageants. The settlement school even had some pagan seasonal rituals, such as mummers' plays, that had been brought over from the old country.

Saturday was the day after Jimmie Sue's birthday, and the family had planned to go down the mountain to the Bowen's General Store, which carried groceries, feed and various kinds of supplies needed for farming and timbering. Mr. Bowen, the store owner, every year on the Saturday night just before Christmas, would have a kind of raffle, which they called a "drawing", to hand out a box of free groceries to some lucky family.

It wasn't a raffle in the sense that anyone had paid for a ticket, it was just that Mr. Bowen, prompted by his Christmas spirit and some good publicity for his usual customers, would donate a box of groceries to a family whose name would be drawn out of a hat by one of the smallest children present.

All the families made sure they'd bring in their wagon an empty wooden apple crate from their orchard, just in case they'd be the folks to take home a full box of free groceries.

After the chores and an early supper, all the Bennetts climbed onto the buckboard to head down the mountain. By time they got in sight of the store, they could already hear the musicians playing some lively fiddle tunes. Jimmie Sue's toes seemed to have a mind of their own as they began tapping the floor of the wagon, keeping to the beat of the music.

George Dowell was the first to jump down in order to run around and grab the mules' reins to lead them over to the porch railing, which served as a hitching post. The men and boys, as usual, climbed down and then helped the women and girls, who were somewhat hobbled by the long skirts of their dresses and aprons.

Everyone could hardly wait to get into the store, which was already filling up with neighbors, sharing news and gossip. Any one of the families could certainly use a passel of groceries just before Christmas.

Beside the front door was a large paper poke where each family was to deposit their family name on a little piece of paper. The Hiltons were already there, unobtrusively standing in the corner behind the pot-bellied stove.

It wasn't long before the musicians struck up such a lively danceable tune that Jimmie Sue's impatient feet transported him out of the crowd onto a small empty space where he had enough room to do the "buck and wing."

It was a space generally reserved for the mummers, who would arrive a little later, supposedly unbeknownst to anyone, to do their little St. George and the Dragon play. No one else had the nerve to get out and make a fool of themselves, even though there was a little extra space besides what Jimmie Sue was using, if he didn't kick up too high, "buckin' an' wingin'".

It was rather dark where the Hiltons were standing, which made it easier for them to kind of fade into the woodwork. However, when the beat of the music picked up so fast and Jimmie Sue was out there "cutting a rug," Madeleen started swaying with the seductive rhythm, not really unlike some of the revival tunes.

Aunt Lily saw her out of the corner of her eye, watching anxiously, and when Madeleen started tapping her toes it looked as though she might join Jimmie Sue. Aunt Lily didn't say anything yet, until she saw Madeleen's feet starting to float her toward the dance spot. Her mamma still didn't say anything, but firmly grabbed Madeleen's arm.

She then said, "No, Honey, we cain't be adoin' thet. We gotta keep 'memberin' who we be." Madeleen knew that her mamma was perfectly right and that she had scotched a potentially hostile scene, so she just scrouged farther back into the corner and let the music beat into her head and heart. *Maybe I kin dance in my inside space without nobody be noticin'. . . or carin'.*

Shortly after that, the mummers arrived with a lot of hoopla, yelling and stomping around, before they got down to the business of their little make-believe fight with wooden swords and the hobby horse and the attending doctor, who answered to the call, "Is there a doctor to be found to cure this deep and deadly wound?"

After the victim was dosed with outlandish concoctions, the actors asked for money or some goody, which they called a "soul-cake." There was even a song they sang, "A soul, a soul, a soul cake, please good Missus a soul cake." A few coins were tossed out onto the performance floor and Mr. Bowen gave the players a box of gingersnaps to be shared amongst them.

It was time for Mr. Bowen to have one of the boys fetch the paper poke holding all the slips of paper with the family names. He then poured all those names into an old high top hat he always kept on the shelf over the cash register.

Every year it was the custom to have the youngest child there (those past the crawling stage) to poke their hand in the hat and retrieve a slip of paper, naming the family winner of the batch of groceries. He looked around noticing . . . by the size of her . . . that Ruthie Hilton was probably the youngest, but after all *she was colored.* So he called Rosie Bennett up to do the drawing. Rosie knew that Ruthie was the appropriate candidate for the job and thus started to say something, but Mamma Sue said, "Shush, Honey, hit's a honor to pull out the winnin' name."

Rosie walked over to Mr. Bowen, who had stooped down to diminish his height closer to that of Rosie's.

She reached into the hat and pulled out a name. Before he read the name, he handed Rosie a gum drop as her own special prize. He pulled his reading specs down from off his forehead to read, then to announce, the name of the lucky family.

The Hiltons were being as unnoticeable as possible, but Ruthie, who'd been standing on their upturned apple crate in order to see, had got down just in case their crate might be needed for some welcome free groceries.

Mr. Bowen's expression of joyous magnanimity shifted to a troubled frown. "I'm sorry, but I can't read this name hyar. It's much too scribbly."

To Rosie, he said, "We'll just hafta go fishin' agin." He held the hat down toward her again, and she reached in for another slip of paper, which she handed to him, then held her open hand to him for another gumdrop for the extra work she'd done. Maybe she understood what working "overtime" meant.

He laughed uproariously, as he fetched another gumdrop from the candy bin. She deposited the second reward into the same apron pocket where she'd put the first one, as he announced, "Well, I be dadblamed if she didn't pull out her own family's name. Should we let the prize go to the Bennetts or should they be disqualified by havin' one of their own draw the name?"

There were a few mumblings until someone at the edge of the crowd, said, "If the family was automatically ineligible, whose child was gonna do the drawin', why thet shoulda been announced right from the start." There were lots of nods and general agreement, so Mr. Bowen started piling the groceries into one of his apple crates, as well as the one the Bennetts had brought.

In the meantime, Jimmie Sue, who'd been standing close by Mr. Bowen, picked up the crumpled, discarded paper, which the grocer had thrown on the floor. Jimmie Sue secretively straightened out the paper and read as clear as day, letters written in bold capital letters: H-I-L-T-O-N.

As the party started breaking up and folks began leaving, Jimmie Sue showed the paper to his daddy. Great-Grandpa Robert studied on the paper for awhile, mulling over in his mind what'd be the proper thing to do. He said to Jimmie Sue, "These groceries, by rights, belong to the Hiltons, so we'll just take them ovah to put in their wagon."

"Are you gonna tell them what happened?" Jimmie Sue asked, knowing full well that to let folks know what Mr. Bowen had done would have caused a great commotion with people choosing up sides.

"We'll just tell the Hiltons hit's a Christmas gift."

Jimmie Sue knew that the Hiltons wouldn't accept, in any way, a gift that smacked of charity.

"You know, Papa, the Hiltons are a pridey people an' won't like to take any charity—anything what they ain't earned."

"Why, yes, thet be the very thing. Levi helped out with some extra woodchopping las' week an' wouldn't take no pay, 'cause he said hit was jest a neighbor thing. I'll tell him, 'bout the groceries, thet he had them comin' to him, fair an' squar' fer all the work he's been helping with, an' hit's jest a neighbor thing."

That seemed to set Jimmie Sue's mind at ease. He'd already noticed Rosie taking the gumdrops from her apron pocket and after examining them closely giving the green one to Ruthie. She kept the red one for herself.

When the groceries were first offered to the Hiltons, Aunt Lily declared, "No, we ain't the winnahs in this."

Great-Grandma Sue explained to her that it was the Bennetts' neighbor thing for Christmas.

Aunt Lily then said, "I reckon we's all winnahs this Christmas."

Christmas was already starting with some challenges as well as a spark of genuine Christmas spirit.

Jimmie Sue still hadn't figured out yet what gift he could give Madeleen.

* * *

CHAPTER 23

Snow Cream and Snow Angels

On the way home from the grocery-drawing at the general store, Rosie was still excited about the gumdrops, but she couldn't understand why the Hiltons got the groceries when the only name read out by Mr. Bowen was the Bennetts. Her papa said, "Hit was kinda like a Christmas gift from us to Ruthie's family."

"Oh, and the gumdrop was my Christmas present to Ruthie?"

"Why, yes, I s'pose it was."

Rosie asked, "Did you see what Ruthie give me?"

Great-Grandma said, "I didn't see Ruthie give you anything."

"Didn't you see the cornshuck doll what she was playin' with?"

Thelma Lou said, "I saw thet cute little doll jest made outta cornshucks."

"Yeah, she give it to me."

Her mamma said, "Are you sure she give it to you or did you jest kinda take it an' ferget to give it back to her?"

Rosie was mortified for her mamma to suggest such a thing. She would never do a thing like that and particularly to Sistah. She couldn't say anything, but she started crying—sobbing so hard you could hardly hear the mules' metal shoes clopping on the hard-frozen road.

Great-Grandma felt terrible. She had no intention of accusing Rosie of stealing, but she knew how attached a child could get to a toy and want to hang onto it. She was always on the alert to make sure her children didn't take undue advantage of anyone and as much as possible to be assured that they were traveling the "straight and narrow." She was particularly cautious about this with their treatment of the Hiltons, " 'cause bein' colored they already got too much hassle to deal with."

Jimmie Sue rode to the rescue of his little sister—and to his mamma as well. "Rosie, why don't you and me go over to Ruthie's tomorrow mornin'? Mamma, could we take some of yoah Christmas cookies?"

Relieved to be past that little moment of misunderstanding, Great-Grandma answered, "Yes, acourse thet'll be jest fine. I'd intended to send them some anyways."

The next morning was brisk and frosty with about a two-inch snow cover. Even before breakfast, Jimmie Sue asked Rosie, "You *sure* you wanna go over to Ruthie's in this snow?'

She answered excitedly, "The snow will jest make it thet much more funner."

"Well, I gotta get the milkin' done first."

Rosie, jumping up and down, said, "Kin I go with you Jimmie Sue with yoah milking? Bossie not be skeered of me."

Jimmie Sue cautioned."Sure, you kin go, but you gotta be real careful 'round the cow an' not get underfoot."

"Oh, I can do thet."

At the barn, just before he started the milking, Jimmie Sue was still concerned about Rosie's safety, so he picked her up and set her on a shelf right beside Ol' Bossie. He said, "Now you an' yoah new doll set real quiet up there jest like a flowerpot, an' a flowerpot don't move none does it?"

"Nauw, but we don't have flowerpots in winter."

"Let's jest say thet you an' me know you be a special unusual Christmas flowerpot. Thet be okay with you?"

"Yeah like Mamma's Christmas Cactus thet be bloomin'."

"Yoah right, an I'll call you my flowerpot."

Jimmie Sue finished the milking in record time, and both he and his little flowerpot rushed through breakfast.

Of course Jimmie Sue would be happy to have an opportunity to see Madeleen again, and maybe to talk a little. He got the little sled out from under the back porch. "Flowerpot, me an' you can ride down the wagon trail to the swimmin' hole on the sled, but I guess I'll have to pull you up the face of the Sapling Ridge slope to the Hiltons'."

The rest of the Bennetts wondered why Jimmie Sue had called her "flowerpot", and George Dowell asked, "Why'd you call her thet?"

Rosie answered quickly, "Jimmie Sue set me up on a shelf an' I was real quiet jest like a flowerpot."

Their mamma said, "Jimmie Sue, why would you do a thing like thet?"

"Well, Mamma, it kept Rosie out from in under the cow, an' she acted real good, jest like a pretty flowerpot."

No one pursued the matter any further, but they were fascinated by how quickly Rosie was eating her breakfast and didn't have to be prompted to finish her milk.

After breakfast she was so excited, she was fairly dancing, which took Thelma Lou that much longer to get her winter clothes and boots on her. She was thrilled to get to go over to Ruthie's, and especially pleased that only she and Jimmie Sue would be going.

She'd been finagling a way to spend some time alone with her favorite brother, but the way this was turning out, she didn't have to do anything sneaky.

Grabbing her new cornshuck doll, she tucked it in the front of her coat with just the face showing. Jimmie Sue said, "Why'd you do thet fer, Little One?"

"You know the baby always has to be kep' warm."

"What did you name yoah new baby?"

"Her name be Hildy 'cause thet kinda like Rosie's las' name."

Jimmie Sue smiled and put the two of them, the little mother and her doll-baby, onto the sled. He had to give the sled a little push to get the trip started. He then jumped on behind Rosie and they fairly flew down through the woods, picking up speed all the way down toward the creek, spraying snow in their faces, much to the delight of Rosie.

When they approached the edge of the swimming hole, Jimmie Sue thought about brakes, which he realized he didn't have—not like on the wagon, which would have a block of wood on a lever to push against the back wheels. He could have simply put his heels down, if they hadn't been going so fast. Instead of trying to stop, he kept praying that the ice on the pond was thick enough to hold them and the sled.

They hit the ice with a heavy thud and Jimmie Sue could hear a crack in the ice creaking all the way upstream to the mouth of the pond, but the ice held. They fairly sailed across the frozen swimming hole; and even up a small distance on the opposite side, safely above the creek.

Rosie was squealing with delight, while Jimmie Sue was thanking his lucky stars that they didn't get a baptizing in the dead of winter.

The snow had covered the doll's face, and as Rosie started dusting off the doll, she said, "Hildy be much too white. She need look moah natcherl."

The trip up the other slope to the Hiltons was rather uneventful, but Rosie was so anxious to be there that she didn't want to slow down the hike up the ridge, so instead of riding the sled, she tried to help her big brother pull it. As a matter of fact, it probably took them longer that way than if he had actually pulled her in the sled, but she wanted so much to help, and she was tired of being called "Little One."

Ruthie came running out onto the porch when she heard the dogs barking that company was coming. Madeleen rushed out after Ruthie. "Sistah, yoah gonna ketch youh death of cold. Hyar, Honey, wrop this quilt aroun' yoah back. An' cover up yoah head, now." She caught up to Ruthie and draped the quilt over her shoulders, as she caught sight of Jimmie Sue.

Although Madeleen wasn't often confused or perplexed in whatever situation presented itself, so much had transpired between her and Jimmie Sue, and unusual circumstances had seemed to beset them from all sides, that she wasn't sure about this new visit. They'd never had a chance to just talk, even in just a friend-like manner, let alone in a boy-girl way.

Ruthie immediately invited Rosie into the house, jabbering about how Aunt Lily was getting ready to make some snow cream.

Jimmie Sue wasn't quite sure what to say or what to do, so he just asked Madeleen, "You got yoah Christmas tree up yet?"

"We don't evah put up a tree."

"Why?" He pursued the matter a little further.

Madeleen answered. "Well you know we ain't got no pine trees nur neither no cedars. 'cause don't be fergettin', we be sharecroppers "

"Why they's a sight of pines and cedars all over these ridges."

"Yeah thet's right, but they be on somebody else's place."

"Well, yeah, but all you gotta do is go with a ax, an' when you fin' a good one fer a Christmas tree, why you jest chop it down an' bring it on in home."

"What would the white folks do if they seen a Hilton, cuttin' down one of theah trees—even iffen hit's jest a teensy-tinesy one?"

Jimmie Sue quickly responded. "Oh . . . I see what you mean . . . cause you be *colored* . . . I ferget."

"You seem to keep on fergettin', . . . but *we* can't never ferget."

He wasn't going to let that be the final word. "Well, fer the time bein' why don't we keep on fergettin'. I'll fetch a ax an' we'll jest go . . . ."

He was interrupted by Ruthie yelling, "Come on inta the kitchen. Me an' Rosie have done scooped up a whole bowl of snow fer some snow cream." Of course in those times and in the mountains there wouldn't be any ice cream, but snow cream was a really good substitute.

Aunt Lily had already mixed up some fresh sweet cream with the bowl of snow. She then added a teaspoon of real vanilla extract and a cup of sugar that she'd bought down to the general store.

Ruthie said, "Mamma, could we open one of yoah jars of canned peaches, whut you put up las' summer?"

Aunt Lily said, "Sure, Sistah, but why would we wanna do thet?"

Madeleen said, "Mamma you teasin' Sistah now. You know how silly she is ovah canned peaches and 'pecially when they be put inta snow cream."

Aunt Lily said, "Madeleen, would you go to the root cellar and fetch a pint jar of peaches?"

"Acourse, Mamma."

When Madeleen closed the door behind her, Aunt Lily turned to Jimmie Sue—Ruthie and Rosie were both playing with their cornhusk dolls in front of the fireplace. "Jimmie Sue, how you be adoin' these days?"

"I be fine, Aunt Lily."

"Well, they's times when I worry . . . ."

"No need ta worry 'bout me."

"Well, they's times you know when I sees signs. Hit was only las' night when I seen a lotta watah, an' hit was red as blood. I couldn't tell whether it be a river or a ocean-sea. Mebbe hit coulda been the Red Sea of Moses."

"Well, what would thet have to do with me?"

"You be standin' on the edge of the watah, . . . but I don't allus onderstan' everthing 'bout . . . ."

Madeleen came hurrying in, brushing the snow off her coat. She looked suspiciously at both Jimmie Sue and her mamma. "Here's the jar of . . . ."

Aunt Lily interrupted her as she had interrupted Aunt Lily. "Yeah, Jimmie Sue, I don't allus onderstan' . . . all 'bout this hyar weather."

Jimmie Sue wasn't sure what Aunt Lily was getting at about him at the edge of the Red Sea, but by that time the jar of peaches had been opened and everyone was pouring them liberally over their snow cream. Jimmie Sue had had snow cream before and also plenty of canned peaches, but he'd never had them combined this way.

The combination of the cold snow, the vanilla in the cream and sugar mixed with the tartness of the peaches was a flavor he wasn't likely to ever forget. Maybe the seasonal flavor of the occasion, itself, would assist with that memory.

The Christmas cookies Great-Grandma had sent over were the perfect accompaniment to the snow cream.

As soon as everyone had finished their snow cream, Madeleen said, "Why don't we go out in the yard an' make snow angels?"

Ruthie said, "What be snow angels, Madeleen?"

Rosie excitedly said, "Let's go an' find out."

The four of them: Rosie, Ruthie, Madeleen and Jimmie Sue, put their coats back on and traipsed in a line to the outside. Madeleen immediately laid down in the snow and started waving her arms back and forth, brushing the snow up and down. When she got up she said, "You see, hit's real easy to make a snow angel, you jest bresh the snow away from the ground, an' thet bare groun' be the shape of angel wings."

The two little girls looked on in amazement, but Ruthie appeared mesmerized.

"Madeleen, whut color do angels be?"

"Why they be white, jest like the snow."

Pointing to the dark, bare ground, Ruthie said, "But, Madeleen, the angel you jest made is dark, with the white be all aroun' it. Does angels hafta be white? Can they be dark too?"

The implication of what Ruthie was saying was an emotional overload for Madeleen, as she scooped up Ruthie in her arms and headed into the house with Ruthie beginning to cry and yelling, "But why can't me an' Rosie make snow angels too?"

Neither Rosie nor Jimmie Sue completely understood the burden Madeleen carried on her shoulders of constantly being aware of her and Sistah's personal unacceptable darkness.

* * *

CHAPTER 24

Mistletoe

As things were still a little awkward between Jimmie Sue and Madeleen, Jimmie Sue said, "Well, Little One, hit's gettin' a little late an' 'bout time fer us to be headin' on in home. Mamma'll start worryin, an' hit'll soon be dinnah time."

"But I left Hildy on the kitchen table."

Jimmie Sue said, "Why don't we plan to come back tomorrow? We can get her then."

Rosie didn't say anything anymore, she just followed Jimmie Sue to fetch the sled. He tried to put her on the sled, but she kicked and yelled, "No, I won't." Although she loved to sled and, particularly, if Jimmie Sue was pulling her, but now all of a sudden the sled, the hill slope, the creek at the bottom of the hill—everything—had an ominous aspect to it. She surely wished she knew how to ask a question, and especially why folks act so funny when they grow up and even when they start growing up like Jimmie Sue and Madeleen.

The darkening clouds didn't help any—either for Rosie or for Jimmie Sue.

They silently pulled the sled down to the creek, but Jimmie Sue decided to use the foot log to cross the creek. He wasn't sure he could count on the ice on the swimming hole supporting them again after the sun had probably warmed it up a little. Leaving the sled on the north side, he carried Rosie across the little bridge. "We can get the sled tomorrow, Rosie, when we go back to Ruthie's fer yoah doll and with a big surprise."

"Oh what'll the surprise be?"

"I'm not sure yet. It might even surprise me."

Realizing he'd need to carry Rosie up the slope, due to the deepening snow, it was apparent that the morning had tired out the Little One who was about to fall asleep. The warm, comforting arms of big brother seemed to be just the thing to lull her off to into dreamland, especially when he started singing a lullaby, "Good night, good night, beloved mine, good night, sleep well, my dear . . . ."

Rosie didn't hear the last words of the song.

The next morning, the day before Christmas, Rosie was already bugging Jimmie Sue at breakfast about his plan to go back to see Ruthie—*and Madeleen.*

"What's the surprise we're takin', Jimmie Sue? Can we start right now? Can we make snow angels?"

"Maybe we'll be fergettin' th' snow angels this mornin'. We can start as soon as Thelma Lou can get yoah wraps on. I'll tell you 'bout the s'prise, jest as soon as we get to the footbridge acrost the creek."

Great-Grandma said, "Rosie, did they like the Chris'mas cookies, what I sent yesterday?"

Rosie responded, "Oh, ever'body liked them real good. I used mine to dip inta the snow cream."

Thelma Lou said, "Did Aunt Lily make some snow cream?"

"Yeah an' with peaches."

Thei mamma said, "Thet sounds like a real tasty idea. We'll have to try it our own self sometimes."

By that time Rosie was fully winterized, protected from the snow and cold winds. Jimmie Sue picked her up, put her on a kitchen chair and backed up to her. "Okay, now, Little One, grab aholt on my back."

"Oh, we gonna play horsie?"

"Yep, at least as far as the footbridge. You might have to save yoah stren'th fer crawlin' up Saplin' Ridge."

"We gonna have to crawl?"

"Nauw, but there'll be places, you know, like yesterday, where we hadda go on all fours fer a ways, acrost some of them big rocks."

When he stepped off the back porch he walked over to the chop block and picked up the ax embedded there.

Rosie jabbered all the way down toward the creek, constantly asking Jimmie Sue, "Do you know yet what the s'prise gonna be?"

"I've got a real good notion."

She answered, "Well, I wanna know, right now."

"When we get acrost the footbridge, I'll tell you fer certain."

As soon as Jimmie Sue had stepped off the foot log onto the snow-covered north bank, Rosie demanded, "Well, we's hyar now."

"Yep we's hyar."

"Well?"

"Well, what?"

"The s'prise! You promised."

"I'm sorry, Little One, fer keepin' on teasin' you. You see the sled yonder we left hyar las' night?

Well, we gonna get a Christmas present so big fer Ruthie, thet we'll hafta tote it on the sled."

"Where we gonna get somethin' thet big down hyar at the creek?"

"You see thet big stand of pine trees up the creek thar?"

"Yeah."

"Thet farm b'long to Mr. Bowen down to the general store."

"He give me gumdrops."

"Yeah, an' I think he wants us to take one of his pine trees as a special Christmas present to Ruthie."

"Oh, goodie!"

It didn't take Jimmie Sue long to cut down a full-limbed pine a little more then six feet tall. He took some twine out of his pocket, tying the tree securely onto the sled. Rosie jumped up and down, constantly encircling the project, while begging to help in some way. Jimmie Sue did have her hold the end of the twine a couple of times.

Rosie said, "Jimmie Sue, why does the pine tree smell like Chris'mas?"

"Maybe 'cause we always put a fresh pine tree, what smells like this in our house ever' Chris'mas."

"An' what's this sticky stuff hyar where you cut?"

"Thet's jest pine rosin, but you oughten not touch it, 'cause hit'll stick to yoah fingers."

It was too late as she'd already touched it with her pointing finger, and when she touched that finger to her thumb, they stuck together. She started crying, "Jimmie Sue, my fingers're stuck. Kin I evah get 'em unstuck.?"

Jimmie Sue started laughing and assured her they'd come unstuck with a little bit of warm water and some lye soap.

The trek up the Sapling Ridge slope was rather strenuous for both of them, as they were lugging the sled with its cargo. When they were about halfway up the slope, they felt that they ought to stop and catch their breaths. Sitting down on a rock outcropping, Jimmie Sue looked up into a white oak tree and saw a large growth of mistletoe with lots of white berries.

He said, "Now, Little One, set real still right hyar, while I go climb thet tree."

"Why?"

"I'm gonna get some of the mistletoe up thar."

"Is it good to eat?"

"Nauw, they's poisonous, but they be good fer other things."

"Like what?"

"Like a kinda magic."

"Oh, I wanna see thet."

"You need ta set real still hyar on this rock ledge, jest like a pretty little flowerpot."

"Okay!"

Jimmie Sue shinnied up the tree just like a squirrel and retrieved a huge sprig of mistletoe loaded with berries.

He lodged the mistletoe branch down in under the tied-up pine Christmas tree, and they hurried as fast as they could go on up to the Hiltons. The dogs welcomed them again, but Ruthie didn't come to meet them that time. Jimmie Sue looked over to where Madeleen had made the snow angel the day before, but the new snow had covered it with new white stuff.

However, he could still see the indentation where an angel had landed earlier, but it had transformed into a white angel now.

Madeleen came out onto the porch, and said, "Whatcha got there?"

Ruthie peeked around Madeleen's skirt and said, "Hit looks like a tree to me."

"Acourse, silly, hit's a tree, but whut's it fer?"

Jimmie Sue looked at Ruthie and said, "Sistah, this hyar is a special Chris'mas tree 'specially fer you."

Rosie said, "Mr. Bowen wanted us to bring it *specially* fer you."

As innocent and guileless as this whole event was, Jimmie Sue realized that Madeleen would really appreciate any act of kindness to her little sister. His realization was rewarded with a huge smile from Madeleen, who declared, "Why, Jimmie Sue, thet's the most thoughty thing I evah 'member 'bout Chris'mas gifts from unexpected places like white neighbors. Hit's a whole lot like the gifts of the wise men, don't you think? How nice of

Mr. Bowen, 'cause he's never shown thet kind of neighborliness twarge us afore."

Jimmie Sue wasn't quite sure how to set things right, so hesitantly he tried to explain. "Oh, we didn't wanna bother Mr. Bowen directly, so hit was jest like his piney woods contributed the Chris'mas tree fer Ruthie."

Madeleen looked appreciatively at Jimmie Sue, acknowledging with her eyes that she understood completely. She simply said, "I thank you, Rosie an' Jimmie Sue . . . an' Mr. Bowen."

Jimmie Sue took charge of fastening the tree onto a cross-planked stand. Aunt Lily showed them where to put it in a corner of the small living room, away from the fireplace, so it wouldn't dry out too quickly. Uncle Levi and the boys, Cletus and Clyde, had come in from chopping up firewood in the backyard.

Ruthie said, "Look, Papa, whut Rosie an' Jimmie Sue brung ovah fer Chris'mas."

Everyone stood back and admired it, until Uncle Levi said, "Thet sure is a thoughty thang to do."

Aunt Lily said, "Hit sure smells up the house real good. I always liked the fresh scent of a new-cut pine."

Rosie and Ruthie, who'd been playing under the tree, started giggling.

Everyone wondered what was so funny under there. Aunt Lily said, "Now what're you girls doin' down there?"

They emerged from under the tree with their right hands stuck together, as Rosie said, "I showed Ruthie 'bout thet pine juice, an' it stuck our hands together. Does thet mean we be sisters now we stuck together?"

Everyone ignored the question, but Madeleen hurried the two little girls into the kitchen to wash off their hands.

Right over the front door was a little nail sticking out, which Jimmie Sue regarded as an appropriate place for the sprig of mistletoe. He said, "I'll be back in a minute."

He left and did return quite quickly with the bunch of mistletoe. Reaching above the door, he balanced a fork of the mistletoe sprig right on that nail head sticking out. "Now," he said, "Thet's jest a little more Chris'mas decoration."

Madeleen and the girls had returned from the kitchen and looked at the new greenery.

Cletus said, "But Jimmie Sue, whut's it fer? Whut does it mean?"

"Well, I jest think it's kinda pretty with little white berries an' leaves still green in the middle of a snowy winter."

Madeleen knew exactly what it meant, because she'd been reading books about Old Christmas and all the kinds of celebrations that went with it, but she wanted Jimmie Sue to say more about what the mistletoe meant. "What did it usta mean in the old country?"

He wasn't quite sure whether or not she knew the traditional meaning of mistletoe, so he just said, "Well, hit's supposed to bring real good luck an' lots of love to ever'one in the house where it be hangin'."

Although Madeleen knew full well that Jimmie Sue was leaving out the most important part of the meaning and symbolism of mistletoe, she was overwhelmed with his generosity of spirit. She also recalled the scripture he'd quoted so often before, *Faith is for things hoped for, the evidence of things not seen.*

She was still concerned about *things hoped for,* but she certainly had *seen the evidence* of Jimmie Sue's Christmas spirit and kindness toward her little sister.

As Jimmie Sue was explaining his interpretation of the meaning of the mistletoe, he wandered casually over to the door right beside where Madeleen was standing, directly under the love symbol.

He turned toward the others, who were focused on this bit of decoration. Madeleen was sure that Jimmie Sue knew the traditional use of the mistletoe and was a little uneasy that Jimmie Sue might embarrass her right there in front of her family.

When it became obvious to her that he was not going to honor the mistletoe tradition, she startled him by quickly reaching up, and with her hands on his arms, she kissed him on the cheek.

Everyone gasped, as the two of them stood there for a moment, transfixed in a flood of emotional uncertainty.

"Well," she said, "Thet's what people in some countries usta do under the mistletoe."

Uncle Levi said, "Was thar any call fer you to go an' do thet?"

"I was jest follerin' what it said in a book 'bout Chris'mas thangs, 'specially mistletoe."

Jimmie Sue was so overcome with the whole situation that he said, "Jest 'cause hit's the *usual* thing to do when a body might be under the mistletoe?"

She cautiously added, "Hit might also mean to express thankfulness an' gratitude fer Chris'mas kindnesses."

This was more than Jimmie Sue had dared to hope for, but with Madeleen and her family and even Rosie standing there, there was nothing more he could say or do, except to appreciate this revelation of *things hoped for*.

Madeleen realized that she had taken a far bigger step than she was able to follow, knowing that the kiss was a kind of unspoken promise, which Jimmie Sue would welcome and for which she wasn't prepared to continue.

She looked up to Jimmie Sue with fearful eyes, filled with wonder and brimming over with translucent dewdrops. Not knowing what else to do, she hurriedly left for the kitchen, leaving everyone in a daze.

Jimmie Sue said that he and Rosie needed to get on back home. Aunt Lily invited them to stay for dinner, but Jimmie Sue declined, knowing that it would be too awkward for both him and Madeleen for him to sit down with her and her family to a casual meal because of their different colors and after her innocent display of affection.

They all, except Madeleen, said their goodbyes, and Jimmie Sue and Rosie with Hildy headed on in home. Rosie was excitedly recounting the happenings of the morning, even the kiss under the mistletoe, while he quietly mulled over in his mind the implications of all those little details of the day.

When they fetched the sled, Rosie said, "Jimmie Sue, why didn't anyone answer my question?"

"What question was thet, Little One?"

"'bout me an' Ruthie bein' sisters iffen we be stuck together with pine juice."

"Well, now, maybe the pine rosin 'mind us what the scriptures say thet we s'posed to be like brothahs to each othah, an' I'm sure hit means also *sistahs* too."

Rosie said, "Then me an' Ruthie be sistahs whetha nobody likes it or not."

* * *

CHAPTER 25

A Long, Cold Winter

Christmas at the Bennetts' was as wonderful as every other year, with church services, Santa Claus presents and even the boys participating in the mummers' plays over at the settlement school. The Hiltons had come over for caroling, but they didn't call it that. They just said they wanted to share some of the church songs at the time of Old Christmas, which was January sixth—Twelfth Night.

Great-Grandma Sue had baked up some soul-cakes with raisins and some sweet potato pie. They always had plenty of fresh sweet cream from the daily supply of milk provided by Bossy, so it was no problem to have whipped cream for everybody on their generous portions of pie.

Everyone—both families—sat down for the sweets as though it was just an everyday thing for coloreds and whites to sit down together at the same table to eat.

Both Madeleen and Jimmie Sue acted as nonchalantly as possible, not really trying to ignore the mistletoe kiss a few nights back, but not wanting anyone to focus on it. They acted like a couple of birds, pretending they weren't interested in each other but making little movements and glances meant to attract the other one.

The little girls, Ruthie and Rosie, certainly remembered the kiss, as they, themselves, glanced at each other and snickered at this shared remembrance of their adored older siblings. Rosie would glance at Jimmie Sue, then

Madeleen, and cast a knowing grin at Ruthie who had simultaneously choreographed her own dancing eyes to duet with Rosie, then they'd both try unsuccessfully to muffle their giggles.

Great-Grandma said, "What you girls titterin' 'bout?" Of course, she hadn't seen the mistletoe kiss, and Jimmie Sue certainly hadn't told her about it. Aunt Lily simply said, "Lots athings get shared by little ones, what we, sometimes, don't know nothin' 'bout."

Of course the Hiltons knew the cause of the girls' amusement, but they didn't want to embarrass Jimmie Sue nor expose Madeleen's forwardness under the mistletoe a few nights earlier.

After Christmas, Jimmie Sue didn't see very much of Madeleen, as the winter was unusually cold and snowy. Oh, once in a while, he'd drop by the Hiltons', pretending to visit with the menfolk. He would attempt, as usual, to bring up some question about religion, but Madeleen seemed to be engrossed in her own inner world—not really ignoring Jimmie Sue, but somehow detached from conversation with anyone.

On one of his visits to the Hiltons', when the usual topic of the weather was broached, Jimmie Sue said, "Hit's been so snowy an' sleety an' cold this winter, I doubt if spring will ever come this year."

Madeleen rose to the occasion by affirming, "You know the Lord always provideth; maybe not in ways we want but in ways we need. An' don't be fergettin' yoah favorite scripture quote: 'Faith is the substance of things hoped for, the evidence of things not seen'."

He countered, "I'm afraid thet my faith has become feeble, as the 'substance of things hoped for' keeps tricklin' through my fingers. An' maybe the 'evidence of things not seen' is still too far away."

"Don't be blasphemin' the Word of the Lord," she said as though she thought Jimmie Sue was talking about spring 'still too far away', but she knew precisely what he was talking about, but she wasn't about to acknowledge his true meaning of the fruition of their relationship being 'too far away'.

Only a couple of weeks later, his doubts gave way to "substance of things hoped for," as within only those few days the winter weather had retreated to give way to the smiling sun rays of spring.

Even some of the sarvisberry trees were beginning to bloom., and the red bud trees were budding, Could it be that the altar call at the revival last October had had some religious effect on Jimmie Sue, inspiring some heartfelt praying? If spring could appear so unexpectedly, perhaps other "things not seen" could become more apparent, as well.

The spring in the air inspired a lilt in his walk and renewed hopes in his heart. He reckoned that that night might be just the right propitious time to trek over to the Hiltons'. Dinner was over, but the milking still needed to be done. If he hurried over to the Hiltons' he'd be able to get back before pitch-black dark. Anyways, it wouldn't be the first time he'd done the milking by lantern light.

So he scurrried down the slope toward the creek and swimming hole, which was completely free of any leftover ice from the winter. He fairly scampered up over the rocks to the Hilton ridge.

As luck would have it, Madeleen was the only one on the front porch, sitting almost as though lost in thought, gently rocking back and forth on the porch swing. Her silhouette against the whitewashed porch wall, lighted by the setting sun, exhibited the budding figure of a maturing sixteen-year-old young woman. Even though it was apparent that spring was at last arriving, she was wearing too skimpy a dress for that time of year.

Jimmie Sue was grateful that there was no one else around, and not wanting to disturb her but hoping to gain her attention, he sat down quietly on the porch floor in front of the swing, leaning leisurely against the porch post and looking directly into her mysterious dark eyes. He too had pushed the season a little by venturing out without a coat.

Still in her own inner world she began singing softly, "Shall we gather at the river?" Pleased that he knew the first verse of that hymn, he joined in the next phrase, "Where bright angel feet have trod." She paused for a moment, studying the message in Jimmie Sue's eyes. As she continued, he joined in, "With its crystal tides forever, Flowing by the throne of God?"

The sweet countenance on her face seemed to him to be an invitation to join her on the swing, though he hesitated. She started singing again, but instead of the chorus, which he knew, she sang the last verse, which he didn't know. That was just fine, as he loved to hear her compelling voice. "Soon we'll gather at the river. Soon our pilgrimage will cease. Soon our happy hearts will quiver With the melody of release."

He joined her on the chorus, "Yes, we'll gather at the river, The beautiful, the beautiful river, Gather with the saints at the river That flows by the throne of God."

Although he certainly didn't know the song as well as she, he thought she had changed the last word of the last verse from "With the melody of peace" to "With the melody of release." He wondered if she'd knowingly changed the wording or had simply forgotten. It wasn't likely she'd forget a single word of that hymn, but "peace" was a whole lot simpler to understand than the various interpretations a person might have about "release". *Was she trying to tell him something? If she was, what would it have been? What kind of release was she singing about?*

Her moment of quietude *released* him from his seated position on the porch floor, softly inviting him to sit beside her on the swing. Rather than sitting all the way on the other end of the swing, he sat rather close to her, yet not quite touching. He didn't wish to push his luck.

"White Boy, you be scrougin' me much too uncomfortable."

Without moving away, he replied, "Why you callin' me ag'in, 'White Boy'?"

"If I be callin' you different than thet, I be thinkin' different than thet . . . an' thet cain't be."

"Whatta you mean, *thet* can't be? Hit's jest you and me . . . we's hyar ain't we?"

"We hyar, but there be a fence atween us . . . . We got a fence song:
'So high we can't get over it,
So wide we can't get around it,
So deep we can't get under it.'"

Jimmie Sue knew the song and sang the last line with her:

"We gotta come in at the door."

After another awkward moment of silence, Madeleen explained, "Thet door be locked."

Jimmie Sue countered, "A lock kin be unlocked."

"Not this lock. Yoah folks—white folks—locked it an' throwed away the key a long time ago; so long ago thet even if a key be found, the lock be rusted tight shut 'til Jedgement Day—thet great gettin'-up mornin'."

"Madeleen, when you s'pose Jedgement Day be comin'?"

She answered, not recognizing the contradictions of her statements, "It be hyar ever' day."

"You mean I'm to be jedged right now fer what I be doin' an' what I be thinkin' . . . right now?"

"In one way or nother you be jedgin' yoahself."

"I'm not jedgin' myself. . . . How I be jedgin' myself?"

"You be thinkin' things right now?"

"Uh . . . yeah." There she was, somehow knowing what he was thinking.

She pushed it even further. "You be thinkin' 'bout what you be thinkin'?"

He suspiciously agreed. "Well, yes, I guess so."

"Then you be jedgin' what you thinkin' an' what you doin' when you be thinkin' 'bout it."

Really puzzled then, he said, "I don 't see as how . . . ."

"To be thinkin' an' jedgin' don't mean you be condemnin'. Hit jest mean you considerin' what you be thinkin' an' what you be doin' an' what thet all mean."

He said, "You jedgin' what you be thinkin' an' what you be doin'?"

She agreed, "An' what I already might've did."

Jimmie Sue was stunned for awhile, while he conjured up in his mind how to ask, "What do you mean, might've already did?"

Hesitantly, she said, "We has to answer not only to ourselves, but sometimes also to others an' maybe even afore we answer to the Lord."

Slipping over a little closer to her until the edges of their bodies touched, he asked, "Does answering to others might could mean somethin' to me?"

"Hit might could've."

"Well, I'm a big boy now. I can take it."

Not wanting to reveal her own mystery, she became a little playful by jumping up on the swing.

"Okay, Big Boy, you might be able to take a lot, but I'm as big now as you, an' you might take a lot but you ain't atakin' me."

This action and statement of hers took him by surprise, as he couldn't tell if she was teasing him, challenging him or defying him. He didn't have time to figure out her scheme, because she began to teeter on the swing and would've fallen over the back of it if he hadn't caught her by wrapping his arms around her knees. Her body stiffened at first, seemingly to resist.

He heard her gasp for breath almost as though he'd clinched his strong, young arms around the fullness of her breast. She was surprised by his action, but grateful, as she realized he'd prevented her from toppling off the back of the swing and over the edge of the porch.

They were locked in that position until she slowly lowered her hands to his shoulders to help him in steadying her. He then gently lifted her off the seat of the swing and turned to lower her to the porch floor. As she slowly descended down the front of Jimmie Sue, she knew he was holding her much too tightly for mere support. His arms around her continued contact with each curve of her body as she slipped on toward the floor.

She didn't want to encourage him further, but she certainly wasn't discouraging his helpful arms, as they seemed to caress every inch of her legs and back on her descent. The pressure between their bodies strained the buttons on the front of her cotton dress. The hem of the dress lay on the top of his arms, so that by the time her feet had reached the floor the bottom hem of her dress was above her waist.

He could justify his holding her so closely to keep her from falling, but if truth be told, his arms had their own mind as they staked out their claim, holding her ever closer to him and causing even one of his overall galluses to unsnap.

Their disassembling garments appeared to be conniving to reveal the "substance of things hoped for, the evidence of things not seen." They had never been so close since the encounter in the baptizing hole the summer before. She slid her hands off his shoulders around his head, clasping tighter than even he would have dared.

When her feet touched the floor, they both continued the descent to their knees; and then almost as though being lowered slowly by an invisible repelling rope, their entwined bodies continued down the slippery emotional slope until they lay facing each other on their sides on the broad worn boards of the porch.

Such an opportunity had never been presented to Jimmie Sue ever before, and their lips conjoined in the feverish space between them. Madeleen was no longer resisting any amorous moves initiated by Jimmie Sue, even though they both knew, in their ecstasy, that they were advancing toward forbidden territory.

His mind was no longer contemplating *but she's colored,* and for that brief but eternal moment her mind didn't call him *White Boy.*

Just as Joshua in olden times had commanded the sun to stand still, their time stood still as their trembling bodies gave way to a calm stillness . . . until the reality of time began to tick.

Then without warning or a word of explanation, Madeleen scrambled awkwardly to her feet, clasping the front of her dress and brushing it straight with her agitated hands, as she scurried into the house.

Jimmie Sue could hear her soft sobs as she hurried away from him.

He thought, *So close and yet so far away but tomorrow will be another day.*

She hadn't said, "Goodnight!",

He didn't realize she was saying, "Goodbye!"

* * *

CHAPTER 26

Gone

Even though bewildered as he was by Madeleen's actions on the porch the night before—her passionate embracing kiss and her sudden exit into the house—Jimmie Sue, ever the optimist, fairly skipped home and barely slept at all that night with fanciful dreams of exotic places and dancing to unfamiliar music, not like the roadhouse or revival meetings, but played on instruments previously unknown to him.

It was his last year in school, and he expected to see Madeleen that next morning on their way to their respective lessons. He was at the fork in the road early and waited a long time to see her; but neither she nor any of her siblings showed up. This worried him, fearing that they might all be down with some kind of ailment. He knew that Aunt Lily would see to it that her children would get all the schooling they could get, so it didn't stand to reason that they would miss school unless something drastic may have happened. So Jimmie Sue tried to figure where they all were.

He went on to school, but after school let out, instead of going straight on home, he decided to go to the Hiltons' to find out what was wrong. He told Thelma Lou and George Dowell to go on home that he wanted to go check something down by the swimming hole but that he'd be home in time for milking.

When he came in sight of the Hiltons', Ruthie came running out the door onto the porch, crying, "Madeleen be gone. Jimmie Sue, Madeleen be gone!"

"Gone? Gone where, Sistah?"

"Don't know. You better ask Mamma."

About that time Aunt Lily and Cletus joined Ruthie and Jimmie Sue on the porch.

Jimmie Sue turned his attention toward Ruthie's mamma. "Aunt Lily, what did Sistah mean thet Madeleen be gone?"

"Cletus, you take Sistah an' go on back in the house. Me an' Jimmie Sue need to have a little talk hyar on the poach. You can give her some of the cookies I baked earlier . . . . You might take a couple yoah own self."

Aunt Lily sat down on the porch swing and patted the other side of the seat, inviting Jimmie Sue to sit down. He obliged by carefully sitting on the spot where he'd sat the evening before, but only momentarily—almost as though the swing was a hot seat from memories of last night's interlude with Madeleen.

Opening the discussion, he immediately wanted to know about Madeleen. "Aunt Lily, I waited fer Madeleen at the fork in the road this mawnin', but when she didn't show up, I went on to school. Only a few more weeks, an' we both be through with school."

Aunt Lily wanted to help Jimmie Sue understand. "Yeah, I know, Chil' . . . . Madeleen not be finishin' school."

Incredulously he asked, "Why not?"

"She say she don't need the school learnin' to do what she gotta do."

He wondered, "What she gotta do?"

"She gotta find work."

"Why?"

"Ever'body as they's growin' up gotta fly outta the nest."

"But fly where?"

Attempting to scotch this conversation from going any deeper she said, "Jimmie Sue, you be astin' too many questions."

Becoming frustrated and not a little irritated, he said, "But I'm not gettin' any answers. Madeleen was fine las' night . . . *really* fine, an' now she be gone today, an' I don't know why, an' I don't know where. She must of hated me so much to jest up an' leave without no word atall."

Madeleen's mamma answered haltingly, "She left like thet 'cause she cared much too much for you, an' I know she kep' tellin' you, thet hit never can be . . . . But she give me somethin' to give to you."

This surprised him. "What kind of somethin'?"

"A letter," as she handed an official looking letter to Jimmie Sue.

He hesitantly took the letter and opened the flap, which obviously had already been torn open. It had been addressed to "Miss Madeleen Hilton,

Pierson, Virginia" with a return address: "Office of the Attorney General, 900 East Main Street, Richmond, Virginia."

Taking out the folded piece of paper, he read:

Dear Miss Hilton:

Pursuant to your inquiry concerning marriage between the

White and Negro races, let me assure you that this practice is strongly to be avoided. The Commonwealth of Virginia, even as a colony, made it illegal to practice miscegenation, as we want to protect the distinction of white, black, yellow, Malay and red races as God had intended. He put those races on different continents and therefore there is no cause for such marriages.

Just as buzzards and crows do not crossbreed, God did not intend for the human races to interbreed.

If you or a friend may be contemplating such an action, let me assure you that the persons involved will not go unpunished.

Sincerely, yours,

. . . .

Jimmie Sue could not read the name of the sender, as it was smudged, apparently by drops of some kind of moisture.

He looked at the date which was January 5, 1877—shortly after Christmas and the mistletoe kiss but before the wonderful kiss on the front porch, when he rescued her from falling off the porch swing where she was standing.

He was stunned. "Aunt Lily, how did Madeleen know where to write sech a letter?"

Aunt Lily answered,"You know thet new young lawyer down to Pierson?"

"Yeah."

"Well he be real good to me an' my fambly. Kinda like yoah fambly. An' she ask him 'bout who an' where a person be who be knowin' 'bout the legal law."

"Aunt Lily, I still don't understan'. Why would Madeleen do sech a thing?"

"Sech a thing, as what?"

"As to write sech a letter to sech a big important person in Richmon'?"

Attempting to put the whole matter in the proper context, she answered, "Well, she does know how to write. I made sure all my chil'ren learn to read an' write. My daddy, what was the grandson of a plantation owner, wanted to make sure thet none of his chil'ren, nor gran'chil'ren let they circumstance in life keep them from knowin' how to read an' write."

"She tol' me 'bout all thet, but why would she . . . ?"

"'cause she figgered that even though she can't vote, she bein' too young, an' bein' too colored and she a female, she's still got the right to find out things from those folks who knows 'bout sech."

Jimmie Sue then came right to the point. "As marryin'?"

"Don't you s'pose Madeleen wrote to Richmon' to find out what the legal law is 'bout marryin' up in this state with somebody of a different color?"

The situation became quite clear to him then. "Yeah! . . . You mean she was tryin' to find out if a white boy an' a colored girl might could marry here in Virgnia?"

"Thet's what she said she done."

"She was thinkin' maybe we could . . . ?"

"An' she find out you couldn't. Like you read in thet letter, it's illegal for you an' Madeleen to marry up in this state."

"Why would she need . . . why would I . . . why would we need a sheet of paper to love each other?"

Aunt Lily put some extra nuance on the circumstance. "What would any chil' be called who had parents not blessed by the Lawd?"

He understood where he argument was going. "Couldn't God bless without a county jedge blessin'?"

"The legal law in Richmon' don't think so."

Jimmie Sue thought of other situations. "Emmett's folks was never married under the law."

She countered. "Don't the boys call him, 'Bastard'?"

"Not no more, 'cause you know he'd beat the . . . you know what out of 'em."

"Does anybody call him a mullato, a half-breed, a octoroon?"

"'Course not!"

"How 'bout 'high-yaller'? Anybody call him 'high-yaller'?"

Jimmie Sue had no answer for Aunt Lily, as she had provided the answer by the thrust of her own question.

"Where she be goin' then?"

"Richmon'."

He still wanted to know why she would be going to Richmond. "Is she gonna be lookin' up thet feller, what wrote thet letter?"

"Nauw, 'cause she know she already got all the answer he gonna give her. She be goin' to help my sistah take keer of her four little ones, until she kin find work her own self with one of the white famblies there."

He was afraid she'd stay away forever. "Will she be comin' back to visit?"

"I certainly be hopin' so."

"Do you s'pose I could write to her?"

"If you kin write, she kin read it."

"I mean, would she mind and would she likely write back?"

"I'm sure she'd write somethin' back. But you need be careful not to write sweet stuff. She past that now . . . now thet she's made up her min', an' you know she be stubborn."

Laughing, he answered, "Like a mule, but where would I send a letter to her?"

"I wrote her address down on a little piece of paper I put in thet letter envelope."

"Okay, but don't you want thet letter back?"

"Oh, pshaw no! She wanted you 'special to have thet letter. She thought it might mean somethin' to you. Or to 'splain how things really are, whether they oughta be or not."

He looked at the envelope, containing the letter and Madeleen's address, then tucked it into the pocket of his overalls bib, before he thanked Aunt Lily, and slowly turned to trudge toward home.

It may be that Aunt Lily wasn't his blood relative, but there was something between them that surely felt like kinship to him.

She hadn't told him what had already transpired that day before Jimmie Sue showed up at her place on Sapling Ridge, asking a whole heap of probing, unanswerable questions.

Actually, the day started in earnest the night before when Madeleen retreated into the house while Jimmie Sue was still on the front porch. By time she had opened and closed the front door she ran into the embracing arms of her omniscient mother.

"Mamma, I be troubled."

"Troubled?"

"I mean really troubled."

"You mean 'bout Jimmie Sue?"

"'Bout Jimmie Sue an' me!"

"Yeah, Honey, I know."

Madeleen asked quizzically, "You already know?"

Her mother reassuring her answered, "I know that the both of you have feelin's. I'm yoah mamma."

Trying to explain, she said, "But awhile ago . . . ?"

"On the poach?"

Trying to ferret out the complete implications of the matter, Aunt Lily asked further, "What about awhile ago . . . on the poach?'

Madeleen blurted out, "Jimmie Sue kissed me."

"Uh . . . Huh an' did you kiss him?"

Then Madeleen's story began burbling forth, "I did kiss him, an', Mamma, it seemed like the most natural thing in the world to do, an' nothin' else in the world seemed important, an' I didn't consider what nobody nowhere would say nor care."

"An' then you ran inta the house?"

"There was nowhere else to run."

"Why you be runnin'?"

She tried to understand, herself. "If I'd stayed with Jimmie Sue one moah minute, there'd be no turnin' back from where we be headin'."

Madeleen's mamma then asked the crucial question. "Does you love him?"

Madeleen answered as truthfully as she knew how. "If I understand love, I know I love him, but I know it nevah can be. .. Why did the Lawd put these burdens on us, Mamma?"

"This ain't the Lawd's doin's. He gives folks the rights to make their own decisions, whether they be the right choices or not."

Madeleen retorted, "But somebody ain't gonna 'low me to make no choice nor Jimmie Sue nuther."

Aunt Lily agreed. "It's the way of some folks to keep other folks from goin' where they wanta go an' do what they feel like doin'. The Lawd tell us we need to follow our own mind an' heart an' be responsible for that."

This gave Madeleen the opportunity to declare her deep feelings for Jimmie Sue. "My heart be yearnin' for Jimmie Sue, but my mind tell me that there's lots of other things I need to consider . . . like that letter from Richmon'."

Her mamma counseled, "Well, Honey, hit seem like you need to go to the desert an' pray for moah understandin'."

"An' where would thet be, Mamma?"

"You know my sister, Lucy, be in Richmon' an' could use some help with her four little chilren."

Madeleen understood. "Oh, yeah."

"Yoah papa an' me will go down to the train depot with you in the mawnin' an' catch the train for Richmon'."

"But, Mamma, the money!"

"We allus have some money saved up from the crops for such things, what may need fixin'.. 'specially with fambly."

That seemed to settle the matter, at least for the time being, but Madeleen understood that she would simply be buying some time and grieved for what she knew the feelings of Jimmie Sue were, as well as for her own interpretation of the *substance of things hoped for, the evidence of things not seen.*

* * *

CHAPTER 27

Retracing the Path

Neither Jimmie Sue nor Madeleen's mamma could know what transpired in her life after she boarded the train that day for Richmond.

The train was hauling coal and cattle as well as people, who were ensconced in the car right behind the tinder-car, which was right behind the train engine.

There were a few compartments where some folks—those who could afford the higher ticket prices (mostly whites)—had safe closed-in places. However, Madeleen and those others who could barely afford a ticket price at all, sat on wooden benches that ran down the edges of the coach, as well as a long bench right in the middle of the car.

Madeleen found herself a place at the front end of the bench on the right side of the car. Various other people (mostly colored) placed themselves and their belongings . . . and in some cases, their children, all around them.

The sounds and smells were nearly overwhelming. The crying children, two yapping dogs, gossiping neighbors and the puffing sound of the locomotive accompanied the clanging of the steel wheels on the iron rails. Each of those elements seemed to emit their own odors topped off by a whiskey-imbibing passenger and the overwhelming stench from the cattle car.

In her safe corner, holding on dearly to her small carpetbag of clothes, writing materials and Bible, she settled down as comfortably as possible. When a large colored man, seeing that she was alone, came to sit next to her and seemingly with nefarious intentions on his mind, an older colored woman said to him, "I'm sorry, mistah, but you gotta move elsewhere, 'cause I gotta sit here nex' to my granddaughter."

Madleleen had no idea who the woman was, as she had never seen her before in her life, but she was grateful;—and said so—for the rescue. And she could surely use a grandmotherly person in her life at that point.

Even though there was a continued jostling with other folks, Madeleen took out her Bible and started reading softly aloud, but to herself. She knew where the scripture was that Jimmie Sue seemed to be quoting often enough to her. It was Hebrews 11:1. *Now faith is the substance of things hoped for, the evidence of things not seen.*

Surprisingly this hadn't comforted her at all. It simply reminded her anew of Jimmie Sue and the strong feelings they had for each other. As she went over again in her mind the encounters they'd had in the previous year and months, it even brought a slight smile to her face, particularly when she recalled the several times he'd stumbled or fell backwards whenever they would meet.

Leaving the book of Hebrews, she turned to the Psalms, as they seemed always to put her mind into some ease. So she thought she might just as well start right at the beginning with Psalm 1.:

1. *Blessed is the man that walketh not in the counsel of the ungodly, nor standeth in the way of sinners, nor sitteth in the seat of the scornful.*
2. *But his delight is in the law of the Lord; and in his law doth he meditate day and night.*

Madeleen ceased her reading for a moment to meditate—not on the "law of the Lord", which she knew quite well, but—on the law of people, particularly the law people in Richmond . . . . the one who had written her that letter about the law on *miscegenation.*

The older woman sitting next to her had listened to her quiet reading and said, "Honey I likes yoah readin' the scriptures. It sounds real good and makes a person feel kindly twarge the Lawd. Could you read a little bit moah befoah we gets outta the light?"

Madeleen was pleased for this response and the earlier rescue this strange woman had given her.

It was also the only real comfort she had felt since leaving her mamma and daddy on the platform at the train depot.

She opened the Bible again to continue with the first chapter of Psalms.

> *3. And he shall be like a tree planted by the rivers of water, that bringeth forth his fruit in his season; his leaf also shall not wither; and whatsoever he doeth shall prosper.*

She couldn't read any further as these scripture words brought up more images of Jimmie Sue . . . particularly the reference to *rivers of water,* recalling the many times that water, particularly the swimming/baptizing hole, had been referenced in their meetings. She also wondered about the meaning of *bringeth forth his fruit* and *his leaf shall not wither* and *whatsover he doeth shall prosper.*

She focused on that last phrase and prayed softly, while tears began dripping on the pages of the Book of Psalms. "I do pray dear Lawd that whatsoever he doeth shall prosper, even though I not be in that whatsoever."

Her traveling companion thanked her again for the scripture reading, and even though she didn't know the exact impetus of the tears and the prayer, she said, "Honey, I knows you's tired, so if you wanna rest yoah head on my shoulders, yoah welcome to do so."

Madeleen, reckoning that those shoulders had been leaned on numerous times before, looked deeply into the older woman's eyes and said, "I'd sure be much obliged."

She leaned and slept on the comforting shoulder of the stranger and in the embracing arms of Jesus.

When she woke her new friend was gone, apparently having gotten off the train at an earlier station. She realized that they had not introduced themselves to each other—at least they had not told each other their names. Madeleen realized names sometimes get in the way of real person-to-person feelings.

The train was stopping in the Richmond Depot and Madeleen could see her Aunt Lucy through the train window.

The beginning of another chapter in her young life.

For Jimmie Sue that next day was Saturday, and even though the sun didn't need to contend with any clouds, in the early morning it hadn't yet taken much of the chill out of the air. Easter was still a couple of weeks away.

After the morning chores and breakfast were finished, Jimmie Sue started walking. It was the time of year when there wasn't a lot of demanding work to be done. Cold weather was receding, so no extra firewood was needed. The tobacco plantbeds had already been sown; everyone would just be waiting until transplanting time. It was also a little early for using the turning plow for breaking the ground for the crops.

Strangely enough, Jimmie Sue had turned down the opportunity to go into town to the hardware and feed stores. In fact, Great-Grandma asked him if he was feeling all right. "Yeah, I'm feelin' fine . . . as fine as to be expected." He'd often heard the grown-ups using that expression.

She responded, "Expected about what?"

He answered, "Oh, you know . . . jest expected 'bout things in life."

She was genuinely worried about him. "Jimmie Sue, hit sure beats me what to think 'bout you sometimes."

Trying to reassure her as well as himself he said, "Well, you know there's sometimes little things what happen." He hadn't bothered telling anyone yet that Madeleen was gone.

"This little thing you aint' talkin' 'bout must be pretty big, an' if there's somethin' I oughtta know, you kin jest tell me."

"Okay Mamma! I'll do thet.", as he put on his coat and hat and headed out the door.

He had no plan—no rhyme nor reason—to go to anywhere in particular. It was just that he felt he needed to walk and let his feet take him wherever they might. It even brought to mind a little song that his mamma had often sung to him and his brothers and sisters at bedtime: "Little feet, be careful where you take me to, Loving things for Jesus only let me do."

He didn't understand much about Jesus, but he wondered, *"How's Jesus let bad things happen, when he tells us 'to love one another?"*

When the word, "loving" popped up in his reminiscence, he realized where his feet were propelling him—the backfield tobacco barn where he and Madeleen had argued about "living the rest of your life," not quite eight months earlier. He then recalled that he had already met her earlier last year when her sharecropping family had passed down the public road. They were on their way to moving their things into the rent house on the Goins' sharecropper farm. It was then that he had realized there was something frightfully appealing and mysterious about her.

But he didn't know then, and wasn't completely sure now, whether that foreboding was for good or ill—particularly for his own best interest.

The barn, of course, now looked abandoned, as it wasn't the season yet to be using it. It even appeared lonely, in the grove of beech trees, themselves just coming alive with new shoots of leaves.

The door was half-open with, for some reason, a loose hinge which no one had bothered to fix. There was a great deal of evidence of recent animal activity in the ashes and loose dirt at the edge of the flues.

However, when he went into the empty barn the wonderful familiar smell of cured tobacco, embedded in the very fiber of the hand-hewn logs, permeated the air. He was so grateful it was the perfume of cured tobacco and not the nauseous smell of the green leaves.

Outside the barn he sat on the long bench they'd been using the summer before for laying out the armfuls of tobacco leaves to then be bunched in small hands [handfuls] for the stringer, who'd tie the bunches onto the tobacco sticks. As he sat there, he glanced over toward where he'd remembered Madeleen had been seated.

The early morning mist, infused by the light of the rising sun, enveloped a figure of Madeleen, who just stood undulating in the ambiguous haze. Of course she didn't say anything, but he wouldn't have been surprised if she had, as he recalled with great admiration how she'd shown such spunk when unexpectedly she had jumped into a religious discussion.

As he recalled, it wasn't really a religious question, but the subject of the discussion wasn't important. What was memorable was the nerve and determination of this colored girl to have her say—not necessarily her *way*—but her *say*.

Walking a few steps down the hill to the beech tree where he'd surprised her a couple of nights after the tobacco-stringing meeting, he stood facing the tree almost as though it were standing there as a palace guard for some royal personage. Stepping carefully around the beech, he moved closer to stand exactly in the spot where she'd been standing before he'd slipped up behind her to play "guess who."

Without understanding why, he moved closer to the tree and embraced it, just as she'd done. For a moment he stood there with surprising tears welling up in his eyes, lost in thought, when he was suddenly slapped vigorously across the cheek.

Reeling backward, he stumbled again against that same rock that had sent him tumbling last summer. Then lying on the ground he squinted to see if she were standing, irately against the tree. Instead he saw a tree branch dancing strongly in the wind against the tree trunk at the spot where he'd been standing.

He decided there was really no point in staying there at the barn, so his feet, following the force of least resistance, took him downhill toward the swimming/baptizing hole. Finding himself on the diving-off rock, he sat down to look across to where he'd seen Madeleen last summer. The water was crystal clear, as there were no freshly plowed fields above the waterhole to muddy it, and, as is usual in the spring, the creek was swollen with recent rain and melting snow.

Looking down through the translucent water, he saw a face looking up toward him. Was she laughing or frowning? Maybe she was crying over recent happenings. He couldn't really tell, as the water plants beneath the surface kept waving and changing expression.

It was too cold to jump into the swimming hole, but he would have loved to. *Maybe thet shock of cold would give me some answers.*
He wanted to walk to the Hilton but instead headed toward the schoolhouse. Why would he do that? He was there only yesterday. Instead of going on to his school, he took the fork in the road to the colored school and didn't even stop there, but continued to the colored church house right next door.

Turning the door handle, he discovered that it wasn't even locked, which wasn't unusual for any mountain church. It was almost as though mountain church folk—whether colored or white—kept the church house open for spiritual needs or a haven from a storm for any passerby.

Timidly, fearfully, apprehensively, he walked slowly up the center aisle toward the preacher's pulpit. The altar rail looked receptive to accept the contrition of any sinner, regardless of age, station in life or color.

It wouldn't hurt a thing to rest himself on the end of the mourner's bench where he'd sat just last October next to Rufus Jones, the perpetual drunkard and regenerated revival convert.

As he sat there, he thought if those apparitions and appearances of the morning were any omen, surely he would now hear Madeleen's clear voice singing.

Quite unexpectedly, the church became dark, accompanied by a rumbling of thunder, which raced back and forth across the ridges and echoed up and down the hollows of Baucus Mountain.

The early spring thunderstorm spattered softly at first on the tin roof of the church, then heavier swaths of rain propelled by intermittent gusts of powerful winds drummed on the roof, slapped on the weather boarding outside and splattered on the window panes.

Gradually the rain diminished; the rumblings of the thunder receded to distant ridges. He was always amazed at how the sound of thunder seemed to roll up the hollow, almost as though it had become a physical being. The rain slowed to a simple pitter-patter before vanishing altogether.

Jimmie Sue wasn't particularly surprised by the sudden rain, but he did listen carefully for any indication of Madeleen's voice, either in pitch or in rhythm. His creative imagination heard nothing but the usual storm sounds, which now in its silence calmed his soul. Not only could he feel his heartbeat against his ribs, he could also hear it pound against his eardrums.

Then he found that his feet had led him to the altar, where he knelt only—he supposed—to rest. It did give him an opportunity to listen to the quiet inner voice that preachers often talked about.

The inner voice was no longer saying, *but she's colored.*

What he did hear distinctly from the inner voice:

Madeleen's gone!

He wasn't about to have that be the last word, so he then deliberately left and headed over toward the Hiltons', where he'd really wanted to go earlier.

Of course, he had to cross the creek, but had no intention to stop there, as he'd already seen her face shimmering at him beneath the surface of the water. Halfway across the footlog some strange force or urge stopped him. *Was it a sound or another apparition?*

Actually it was both sound and appearance, as he listened to the gurgling of the creek and watched the clouds scud across the tops of the trees. It looked as though the swaying tree branches were sweeping the clouds across the blue linen of sky.

He no longer was seeing or hearing Madeleen in this little pilgrimage, but he realized that her spirit had so completely infused his soul, that whatever he saw or heard reminded him of her face and voice. *Why? After all, we'd shared only one little kiss on the front porch—well, there was also the mistletoe at Christmas.*

Continuing on up the steep incline toward the sharecropper cabin, he wondered what reason he'd give the Hiltons for traipsing over that morning. Apprehensively approaching the front porch, he saw Aunt Lily standing on the front porch and Ruthie standing behind her, peering around her starched apron. They were both staring across the south ridge where the Bennetts lived.

Without distracting her glance, she said to Jimmie Sue, "What you be lookin' fer, Jimmie Sue?"

Startled by the question, he hadn't been aware that he was *looking* for anything, but answered straight out, "Well, you know, I be lookin' fer Madeleen."

She replied, "Ain't thet the Lord's truth? But no body can find Madeleen. She gotta find her own self. An', Jimmie Sue, you gotta find yoah own self."

"Yeah, an' I wonder where thet self might be."

"Whatta ya s'pose, Madeleen'd say?"

He thought for a moment before he answered. "She'd say, 'Call on the Lord.' But I'm not sure I know how to do thet."

Aunt Lily, attempting to console him, said, "Mebbe if you be not too anxious, the Lord be callin' on you."

He couldn't figure if that was a comforting or a warning.

* * *

CHAPTER 28

But Not Forgotten

    Jimmie Sue was determined to honor the urge to contact Madeleen, but he couldn't find a place to hide away from his siblings to write to her. He knew any attempt at letterwriting to her would result in a great deal of hoopla and teasing. So he decided the only place was the barn loft, a favorite place of his, anyways. That was his retreat when trying to sort out in his own mind what was going on within him at the time of those nights of revival-going to the colored church, and the kisses under the mistletoe and on the front porch, and Madeleen's abrupt departure.
    The more he thought about it the more clearly he recalled that whenever Madeleen seemed to be in a tight spot which she couldn't manage, she'd just up and leave without a single word. He remembered, as a child, he had playfully tried to jump away from his own shadow. He wondered if Madeleen was trying to run away from her shadow. While realizing that in order to escape your shadow, you have to turn off the light or get away from the sun, he wasn't sure of the implications of that thought.
    He knew he had plenty of time to concentrate on a letter, as it was Sunday afternoon after dinner, so he climbed the ladder with his tablet and newly sharpened pencil in his bookbag. Settling down into the comforting loose hay, he was amazed anew at how cozy it always was in the barn loft even as it had been in the dead of winter.

He knew, of course that the hay against the walls was great insulation to keep out the winter wind, and the body heat from the barn animals provided a welcomed warmth to the floor. Somehow the sweet odor of the hay and the shared animal breaths as well as the sounds of the cooing pigeons helped to alleviate his feeling of aloneness. He may have lost touch with Madeleen, but he was embraced by many other living creatures of God's grace. *Am I beginning to feel more religious, or am I jest feelin' lonesome?*

Taking out his tablet and pencil, he tried to compose a beginning of a letter. He checked the sharpened tip of his pencil, giving it a couple of whacks with his jackknife. Looking up toward the fluttering pigeons, he stuck the pencil point onto his tongue. He always did that whenever he wanted to make the pencil mark a little darker. It might also loosen up some words, not readily at hand . . . or I should say "readily at mind."

But he started without figuring exactly what to write, unthoughtedly so to speak: *Dear Madele . . . No, no, no the word "dear" may be too . . . friendly . . . maybe. Hello Madeleen, but isn't thet jest too off-handed?* There just didn't seem to be any good beginning. He crumpled up that sheet of tablet paper and threw it down the chute where the ladder was. One attempt after another ended in another wad of crumpled paper, only to be discarded down the ladder chute.

It was most unusual for any of the Bennett children to waste anything, particularly store-boughten things like a tablet of paper. You might say that all the folks around there were careful to make do with whatever was available and to practice recycling before that was even a recognized word or concept. But the trashing of these pieces of paper with his noble yet feeble attempts at communicating with Madeleen were worth the sacrifice to be made to the ardor of his heart.

Just impulsively to express his true feeling, he wrote, *My Dearest Darling Madeleen, The moon can no longer glow, my feet go ever so slow. And since you went my life now seems spent. What I must know is why you had to go. Was it maybe the kiss that made things amiss? My only hope . . . .*

He didn't dare go any further with that line of thought and surely couldn't have sent it anyway, even though it was a relief for him to express how he really felt, which he hadn't been able to acknowledge even to himself in his wildest dreams.

Down the chute that crumpled-up love note flew. He'd pick up all those papers later.

Although the letter was not destined to be delivered to Madeleen, it was intercepted by an interloper. Rosie and Thelma Lou had come to the barn looking for Jimmie Sue. Rosie was always wanting to go on his adventures like those times over to the Hiltons'.

Thelma Lou yelled up, "Jimmie Sue, you up there?"

"Yeah!"

Rosie called up, "Kin we go ovah to Ruthie's?"

He said, "Not today, Honey."

"Why not?"

Jimmie Sue started to answer. "Well, you know Madeleen's not . . . ."

Rosie countered with, "Ruthie's to home, I'll bet!"

Thelma Lou picked up a crumpled piece of tablet paper. Even though there were several papers on the ground by that time, the temperature of that special one must have directed her eye and hand directly to it. "Jimmie Sue, is this yoah tablet paper layin' hyar on the ground?"

He jumped up, heading toward the ladder. "Yeah, give it hyar, Thelma Lou."

In sensing the compromising importance of that little piece of paper, Thelma Lou went running to the outhouse which was the only place where she knew she'd be safe from Jimmie Sue's interception. She latched the inside hook of the door, although she knew he wouldn't follow her in there.

Standing on the outside and pounding loudly on the door, he yelled, "Thelma Lou, come out hyar, an' give me thet letter. Hit's mine an' it ain't got nothin' to do with you."

"I'll give it to you jest as soon as I satisfy my curiosity thet you not writin' no nasty things down on papah."

"I kin tell you already thet there ain't no nasties at all writ down on it."

Teasingly, she said, "I'll jest check thet out fer my own self."

As it was obvious she was going to start reading it, Jimmie Sue slouched against the side of the outhouse and slid down until he was sitting on the ground. By that time little Rosie had caught up with him, and sensing that something terrible was bothering him, she sat down in his lap with her arms flung around him.

That gesture was some comfort to him but not nearly enough to balance the discomfort he began feeling as Thelma Lou started reading . . . slowly, deliberately and loudly.

"My Dearest Darling Madeleen."

By this time she was laughing loudly enough to draw a crowd of other family members.

Seeing that he had attempted to write in a rhymed verse, she started singing the next lines:

The moon can no longer glow
My feet go ever so slow

"Jimmie Sue's a poet an' he don't know it but his feet is Longfellows." George Dowell and Simon started laughing.

Great-Grandma Sue said, "What's goin' on?"

"Thelma Lou's got my letter I'd writ."

The recitation continued.

And since you went
My life has been spent

Great-Grandma said, "You wrote thet?"

Embarrassed, he answered. "Yeah!"

"To who?"

He didn't really want to let his mamma know, but did answer truthfully. "Madeleen."

Not really wanting to know, but asking anyway,, she asked further. "You mean the colored Hilton girl?"

"Yeah!"

Thelma Lou continued:

What I must know
Is why you hadda go.
Was it the kiss
That made things amiss?

My only hope . . .

Although that was the last line of Jimmie Sue's poem, Thelma Lou finished it with,

Though I'm a big dope.

Jimmie Sue groaned, as Rosie held him even tighter. She couldn't understand what was going on and particularly why they were picking on Jimmie Sue that way.

Great-Grandma rebuked Jimmie Sue. "James Lafayette Bennett, I never figgered a boy of mine would take sech a shine to a colored girl, even enough to write a romantical poem, when 'you know very well hit never can be."

Trying to defend himself, he said, "Yeah, I do know, an' she kep' tellin' me. Thet be why she's gone."

His mamma delved further. "An' what kiss is it, thet you be writin' 'bout? You know you not s'posed to be kissin' no girls . . . an"specially no colored girls."

Innocent-like, he said, "Well it was jest under the mistletoe, where a body is s'posed to . . ."

That was not reason enough for her. "Not no colored girls, even under a sprig of poisonous mistletoe."

Great-Grandpa saw how much Jimmie Sue was hurting, so he announced to the whole audience, "Now leave him be. Thet's enough. Thelma Lou come outta there an' give Jimmie Sue what's rightfully his. You had no call to go an' take what really belonged private to him."

They all started dispersing, except Rosie, as Thelma Lou came out of the toilet and sheepishly handed the crumpled up paper to Jimmie Sue.

Rosie said, "Jimmie Sue, I love you."

Responding gratefully, he said, "I love you too, even if nobody else in the world loves me."

Rosie, sensing the reality of the situation, countered Jimmie Sue's assertion. "Madeleen does."

The honesty of his little, innocent sister was just too much for Jimmie Sue, and although he was a big boy of sixteen by then, he started sobbing quietly—crying for both the naïve love of his little sister and the unrequited love of the colored girl.

"I know Rosie, an' I 'preciate thet, an' I love you too."

He had a lot he could include in a letter to Madeleen then, but when he went back to the barn loft and retrieved his pencil and paper he wrote just one short sentence filled with a lot of meaning between those lines—the lines that weren't even there.

Madeleen, I miss you.

* * *

CHAPTER 29

An Answer

Jimmie Sue waited anxiously each day for an answer—some kind of response to his letter, as brief as it was. A couple of weeks passed without any answer at all. He had almost given up hope for a reply. He reckoned that Madeleen may have been offended by such a short letter or maybe she was figuring it would be best for the both of them if they had no more contact with each other, because, as she had reminded so many times before, such a relationship couldn't go anywheres, anyways.

It could be that he had the wrong address, and besides that, his handwriting was not the best in the world. Maybe the mailman couldn't read it, even though Jimmie Sue had taken great pains to write as legibly as he could, realizing that at times even he couldn't always read his own writing.

Still, every day he'd make sure he got down to the mailbox at the end of the lane, not just because he was so anxious to hear from Madeleen . . . as exciting as that may be . . . but also to prevent one of his siblings from intercepting his mail. He still didn't trust Thelma Lou, even though Great-Grandpa Robert had admonished her about messing into other people's things.

Every day Mr. Colvard, the mailman, would arrive on his mule about noon. He didn't know, of course, what Jimmie Sue might have been expecting, but it became quite clear to him that it must have been something rather important . . . maybe an anticipated catalog. Each day he'd greet Jimmie Sue, "Nothing with yoah name on it today, Jimmie Sue. Sorry 'bout thet."

Jimmie Sue would begrudgingly thank Mr. Colvard for the disappointing news, "Well, much obliged anyways," as he'd turn and mope back up the hill toward home.

Spring somehow shifted into early summer, and Jimmie Sue continued his daily ritual of traipsing to the mailbox. "Well," he'd say, "somebody's gotta pick up the mail anyways."

Then six weeks after his letter to Madeleen, Jimmie Sue was greeted by a smiling mailman. "Well, Jimmie Sue, I still don't have anything fer you."

Jimmie Sue's jaw dropped, as he must have misinterpreted Mr. Colvard's cheerfulness as good news.

Mr. Colvard quickly added, "But I do have a letter here, nicely addressed to a Mr. James Lafayette Bennett. Any notion of who thet might be?"

Jimmie Sue snatched the letter out of Mr. Colvard's hand and turned to run up the hill.

"Don't you wanta take the letter to your mamma from her sister over in Carolina?"

He said, "Yeah! Sorry 'bout thet." He took Great-Grandma's letter and hurried up the hill.

He ran into the house and Great-Grandma asked, "Was there anything in the mail today?"

He hastily replied, "It's on the table!" As he deposited her letter on the kitchen table and proceeded to the barn loft. No one followed him that time, as they had all given up any hope that Madeleen would ever answer.

When he climbed to the loft and plopped himself down into the soft inviting hay, he noticed for the first time the beautiful handwriting on the letter. He'd never seen anything before that Madeleen had written. Settling himself into his safe spot, he opened the letter carefully with his jackknife, unfolding timorously the neatly folded paper as he began to read.

June 15, 1877
Dear Jimmie Sue,
    I'm sorry for not answering your nice letter sooner. I no longer take care of my aunt's children. They're most big enough to take care of themselves. The oldest one, my cousin Betty, is only a year younger than me. Of course the youngest one, Teddy, is just four and still needs a whole heap of looking after. The

main reason I'm not staying at my aunt's house now is that I got a job. It's real nice. Doesn't pay much, but I have a little uniform type of thing with a cap that looks like a nurse's hat. I guess that's all right, as I'm kind of like a nurse taking care of people, and getting them whatever they want.

I don't think I ever told you why I'm so skittish about being a high-yellow. It is that my grandma worked in a plantation house down here near Richmond and she couldn't keep the master's boy from bothering her. He just wouldn't leave her alone. She didn't live where the other slaves lived, even her own family. But she had a little room right behind the big kitchen, so as she would be real handy right there where the food would be fixed and cooked.

One night they had, what they called a cotillion, and there was a lot of liquor and whiskey being served to all the white folks. When midnight come around, everybody but the boys went off to bed. Well the young bucks kept on raising quite a ruckus with their drinking and cussing and yelling. Grandma Nancy was only sixteen, but she was to look after the young folks, so she took it upon herself to quieten down the boys. When she did that they thought they'd just have a little more fun. They all picked her up and covered her mouth. That way no one could hear her when she might be hollering. They took her to her room and threw her on the bed and had their way with her.

She didn't tell anybody for fear of being sent away, but when it became for certain that she was great with child, the master and mistress made her leave the house and the farm, altogether. My granddaddy, Sam, took pity on her and married up with her, and they ran away from the plantation and went there to the mountains to get away from all that. The white folks didn't try to get them, because they didn't want any scandal in their own family. Grandma Nancy was taught to read and write, because she was working in the big house with the white children. She made sure all her children and grandchildren on down would learn to read and write. I am grateful for that or I wouldn't now be able to write you this letter.

I don't know why I'm telling you all this, since I didn't bother to tell you face to face when I was to home. But I thought it might help a little for you to know kind of why I have the feelings I do about high-yellow.

Also I need to talk to somebody, but I can't do that here 'cause I'm only colored help. So writing you helps a lot, even though we're not talking, I mean talking direct.

There's a boy here in this family who is just a little older than me and, wouldn't you know it, he has red hair and blue eyes. Even though he looks somewhat like you he's not the least bit like you. Well, he's not a farmer, and he's not saved. But I shouldn't say anything to you about that after what happened at the revival meeting. He's mean to everybody and got into a lot of trouble at the military school where his folks had sent him, but his teachers there made him come back home. I wish they hadn't of done that. I'm afraid of him. He scares me because he looks at me in a funny way.

I miss you too,
Madeleen

Jimmie Sue folded the letter carefully, tucking it back into the envelope before looking for a safe place to hide it. Not many people, aside from himself, came up to the barn loft, but he had to be sure this letter would remain for his eyes alone. He found a place for it in the corner where two logs dovetailed, leaving a crack, right above the chinking.

He thought, *Madeleen's got herself right in the same kinda fix her grandma got herself into. Maybe I could go to Richmond, an' get her outta thet place. But she prob'ly wouldn't go with me, 'cause she done told me so many times there be no place fer her an' me to go, 'cause I ain't colored an' she ain't white.* He also wondered about the real meaning of that song Madeleen sang at the revival, *Love Lifted Me*.

Then he remembered that he'd heard the preacher say, "Jesus commanded that we love one another."

I s'pose thet since Madeleen and me are "one an' another," thet then if I love her, an' she love me, why then we must be obeyin' the commandment of Jesus.

I'll be sure an' write thet to Madeleen next time I write. We jest be obeyin' the commandment of Jesus, if we kin love one another, an' if down at Richmon', they'll jest allow us to do it.

* * *

CHAPTER 30

His Answer to Her Answer

This time, Jimmie Sue wasted no time in writing the letter with his answer to her answer to his earlier letter. He still had his tablet and pencil in the barn loft so, after retrieving Madeleen's letter from its hiding place, he placed it on the hay beside him and started his letter. Using an old plank to support his tablet he wrote:

Dear Madeleen
    Jesus command us to love one another so if I love you and you love me then we be keeping the teachings of Jesus.
    Then he realized that he wasn't supposed to write anything sweet-like to her, but as he had considered the matter a little more thoroughly he figured, *This ain't no sweet talk; it's scripture talk, an' Madeleen'll 'preciate thet.*
    He continued to sit and think, but his mind was as blank as the sheet of tablet paper—that is except for that one sentence he'd already written. *Maybe she'd like to hear 'bout the crops. Nauw, thet'd jest remind her of work. Aunt Lily had surely already written her 'bout goin's-on over at the Hiltons'.*
    An' she prob'ly wouldn't be innerested in the new calf we got (which he could hear bleating, downstairs) *or how many eggs I found yestiddy* (as he hears a hen cackling). *I could tell her 'bout*

the dead snake I found floatin' in the swimmin' hole. Oh gosh, no! Thet'd remind her all ovah agin 'bout our meetin' down there las' summer, an' the snake whut nearly skeered the religion outen her.

 Having considered what he would write her but couldn't, or at least shouldn't, he simply poised his moistened pencil (having touched it to his tongue again) and wrote at the bottom of the tablet page.

 I still miss you.

James Lafayette Bennett

 He figured that if folks sometimes can read between lines, as some grownups claimed to, why then Madeleen would have plenty of empty space to read a lot between the lines at the top of the page and those at the bottom.

 The very next day, he was down by the mailbox to hand his letter directly to Mr. Colvard, so there'd be no chance of its being intercepted. "Why Jimmie Sue, there was no real necessity to bring the letter to me, 'cause the new mailbox yoah daddy put up has a little flag there on the edge, what you could just raise up as a signal to me thet there was a letter in there fer me to pick up an' send on its way."

 Jimmie Saue answered, "Yeah I know thet, but there're varmints in these hyar parts, whut could make off with an important letter."

 Mr. Colvard understood exactly what Jimmie Sue was alluding to, but he continued to rib Jimmie Sue some more. "But I don't see howsomever a critter could open . . . ."

 Jimmie Sue interrupted him. "Oh, Mr. Colvard we got varmints hyar at our place, which you wouldn't hardly believe." . . . thinking of course about Thelma Lou.

 The mail man realized that Jimmie Sue was not referring to four-legged varmints. "Well, now maybe you're right, so I'll jest deposit this here epistle right into the safety of my mailbag, an' you can rest assured thet it'll be on its journey to its proper destination. Thet'll be two cents fer the stamp"

 Jimmie Sue handed him the two pennies. "Much obliged, Mr. Colvard."

 Jimmie Sue had an ominous feeling about that letter, although he assured himself that there was nothing unsuitable that he'd written. Maybe he'd left too much space in the middle of the page for Madeleen to fill in with her own feelings, but in her answer to his earlier letter she told a lot of things which he appreciated knowing. She had shared more family information in that letter than she'd ever told him outright before. But she hadn't included any special sweet-talk, except at the end to say that she missed him too. Still, he worried.

There was a great deal to worry about, though Jimmie Sue had no way of actually knowing any of the details. He hadn't even had a dream outlining the dire predicament of Madeleen's situation. Her letter was enough to put him on edge and his mind to be troubled.

Her situation with the white boy in Richmond was troublesome, indeed. He continued to leer at her whenever she was in his proximity, and when they were together alone, he would even make threatening comments to her and telling her to get naked for him.

As he became more aggressive, Madeleen became more cautious, avoiding, whenever she could, having any direct contact with him. However, she was compelled to serve him at the dinner table along with the rest of the family.

Whenever she would walk by him, he would tease her in what seemed an innocent manner, such as untying her apron strings.

His mother would say, "Now, Percy, leave the colored girl alone."

He'd answer, "Aw, Mamma, I'm just a-funnin'."

"I know, Honey, but you know the colored help could so easily get ideas thet you were interested in them . . . I mean in a more social way than just havin' a little innocent fun." She talked as though Madeleen wasn't even in the room.

Instead of him calming his attention toward her, he simply increased abusive tactics toward her; even touching her inappropriately whenever she would pass his chair. She didn't have the nerve to say anything, but once when he pinched her on her buttock, as she leaned over to serve him some hot biscuits, she let out a little yelp.

His daddy laughed uproariously and said, "Percy, you better be careful or you'll have her followin' you to bed like a little black puppy dog." He laughed wholeheartedly again at his own witticism.

After that pinching incident, Madeleen was in her small bedroom next to the pantry off the kitchen. She knew she couldn't tell anyone about this, and shouldn't write Jimmie Sue about it. But she thought that she might feel better just to write to Jimmie Sue but wouldn't have to send it. *Thet's jest what I'll do.* So settling herself beside the table and the kerosene lamp, she began,

Dear Jimmie Sue,

    Taking pen and paper in hand I begin this epistle to you. Of late I've begun to study the book of Exodus, because you might recall that's where the Hebrew Children were being led out of Egypt where they had been held in slavery. My people like that story of being led out of bondage. But there's a verse there that bothers me a bit in just trying to understand what it means, I mean what it might mean if things was different for us, for you and me. It's in Exodus 22:16. "And if a man entice a maid that is not betrothed, and lie with her, he shall surely endow her to be his wife." If things had been different with us and I had been more agreeable with you, I would have to marry you and be your wife, and the state couldn't do anything about it because it would be according to scripture. Maybe things might could have been better if I had not have been so one-minded, and if I could of said that I loved you. Even though I couldn't let on to you that I loved you, like being married in mind and body, I feel we were married in mind even though I couldn't bring myself to marry you in body. But I was following what the state told me to do and not what my heart . . .

She had no time to continue the letter or even to sign it as she was interrupted by Percy slamming her door open. It hadn't been locked, because the hired help were not allowed to lock their doors in case they were needed in a hurry by some of the white family who might have some special needs.

Obviously Percy was in a hurry, and obviously Percy had been drinking.

Startled, Madeleen turned quickly toward the door. Realizing the condition Percy was in, she slid the letter off the table and finding no where else to hide it she slipped it up over her knees under her dress.

"Whatcha got there, black bitch? . . . You writin' somethin' down? . . . Where'd you learn to write? . . . I s'pose if you can write, you must be able to read. Right?..I ask you who taught you to . . . ?"

"My grandma."

"That's the damndest thing I ever heard of. Not only are the niggahs learnin' to read they're even teachin' it to their pickaninnies."

Madeleen sat as quietly as possible, diverting her eyes from those of the intruder.

He started in again. "Bitch, look at me when I'm talkin' to you."

Moving only her eyes, she looked directly beyond his own eyes into his very soul.

"Don't think you can beguile me with those dark brooding eyes of yourn.... I asked you what'd you slip under your skirt?" Without waiting for an answer, he grabbed the hem of her dress, lifting it over her knees, exposing not only her letter but also her bare legs.

"Well I see the black bitch has been writing almost like a real person. Let's see what that writing is about."

Reaching for the letter with his right hand, he let his left hand rub across her knees while jerking them apart.

"Well, well, well! I see that you tryin' to write a letter. 'Dear Jimmie Sue', is it a boy or a girl or a 'morphadite like at the circus? Or maybe it's just a mule which is a half-breed, high-yaller?", as he glared at her in her shame.

Before he could read any further, she grabbed the letter, saying, "You got no call..."

He retracted his left hand from her legs, slapping her across her face with his right. Before he could retrieve the letter from her, she crumpled it quickly, stuffing it into her mouth.

Prying her teeth apart, he pulled the wet paper from her mouth. "You black bitch!"

Throwing the letter on the floor, he angrily yelled, "I'll be god-damned if I'm gonna let a niggah whore get the better of me. Let's see what else you got up under that skirt.... I'll bet it's much better than a ignorant niggah letter."

He grabbed the hem of her dress, as she stood up to run. Still holding onto the skirt of her dress with one hand, he grabbed her around the waist before throwing her onto the bed. He wasted no time in tearing off all of her clothes.

"Well, you know, I been tellin' you to get naked for me, but I see I have to do everthing myself."

"Percy, please don't do what you set out to do with me. I ain't been baptized."

While deliberately undressing himself, he continued, "What's baptizin' got to do with it. I ain't gonna kill you. I just aim to take my delight.... You know that's why the Good Lord put the coloreds on the green earth... for the work and pleasure of us Christian folks. So we'll just pleasure ourselves right here... right now."

Knowing that no amount of protesting or screaming would stop him, Madeleen sobbed softly, diverting her mind as much as possible to other places and times and another person. *The baptizin' swimmin' hole would be so nice.*

The crumpled-up sodden letter to Jimmie Sue lay on the floor, and the scripture passage from Exodus didn't seem to apply—*And if a man entice a maid that is not betrothed, and lie with her, he shall surely endow her to be his wife.*

Jimmie Sue resumed his earlier practice of meeting Mr. Colvard every day at noon and maintained his vigilance the last time for several weeks, but this time the weeks were evolving into months, as summer had blown into fall.

He occasionally stopped by the Hiltons'. Actually the Hiltons' place was not where one would just "stop by", because the road didn't go any farther than where they lived.

In fact, he deliberately went over a couple of times—once on the anniversary of the mistletoe kiss—and he would get around to asking kind of offhandedly about Madeleen. Each time no one, not even Aunt Lily, seemed inclined to share any information with him except to say that she didn't write often, but that she was fine, so far as they knew.

The last time he went by was in March a little while after a tremendous blizzard had passed through, but most of the snow had already begun to melt. Before he'd had a chance to inquire of Madeleen, Aunt Lily brought up the subject. "Jimmy Sue, I had a dream jest las' night, an' I seen Madeleen awalkin' right down the public road an' like in a victory parade up to the front door of our church. She was singin' in her most pretty voice."

He asked, "What was she singin'?"

She answered wihan upbeat. "We'll Shout the Jubilee!"

Jimmie Sue in quired further. "Thet song's 'bout 'when we all get to heaven' ain't it?"

"Thet's right."

He was curious. "Well, what does your dream mean?"

She wasn't interested in meaning. "Mean? Mean 'bout what?"

"'bout Madeleen?"

She came to the point. "It mean she be comin' home triumphantly jest like Jesus ride into Jerusalem with the wavin' of leaves offen the palm trees,"

He wanted to know more. "When will thet be, Aunt Lily."

"We won't know fer sure, but the Lord be assurin' me thet Madeleen's homecomin' won't be long from now. Maybe she be back fer Easter."

Jimmie Sue, said his goodbyes and wearily headed toward home. He'd heard the good news from Aunt Lily that Madeleen was coming home, but he was troubled in mind and heart. Maybe he was beginning to get conjuring abilities like Aunt Lily, but as a beginner in such unfamiliar territory for him, he could be reading the tea leaves wrong.

In less than a month, Cletus came to the Bennetts' and asked immediately to see Jimmie Sue, who was out at the barn mucking out the mule's stall. Thelma Lou, as curious as ever, nonetheless didn't ask Cletus what news he had but told him that Jimmie Sue was out to the barn.

Seeing Cletus headed toward the barn, Jimmie Sue walked out to meet him. "Cletus, hit's been a month of Sundays since you been ovah hyar."

"Yeah, well I come to tell you. Mamma wanted me to special tell you thet Madeleen'll be comin' home."

Jimmie Sue was overwhelmed to hear the news. "Cletus, thet be wonderful good news, but why you look so downtrodden?"

Reluctantly Cletus answered, "When I say she comin' home, I mean to say Madeleen's body be comin' home."

This answer was much too incredulous for Jimmie Sue. "Whatcha mean by thet?"

"Jimmie Sue, Madeleen is dead! Mamma wanted you to know right away, 'cause she felt she give you some wrongful hope 'bout Madeleen."

An awkward pause stood between them as Jimmie Sue choked back the tears.

"Mamma say the funeral be this Saturday an' she' want particular for you to come."

Still in shock, Jimmie Sue asked, "What she die of, Cletus?"

Cletus was reluctant to share any more details, but Jimmie Sue insisted on knowing. "She be dyin' of childbearin'."

"What? I didn't even know she's married, Cletus." Then angrily, " Why didn't youall tell me she was married."

"Thet be the trouble, Jimmie Sue."

He began to decipher the truth. "Oh, I see. But they still gonna bury her in the church graveyard?"

"Yeah. Preacher Peeples say we can't turn nobody away what needs a final restin' place, but we'd have to bury her way back at the back corner right next to the woods an' acrost the fence from the white folks' graveyard. You welcome to come to the funeral, Jimmie Sue, if you likes. They won't be many folks there, 'cause we ain't tellin' many folks."

"What 'bout the baby?"

"He died too . . . . You ever go to Richmond?"

This was taking a different direction for Jimmie Sue. "No, why do you ask?"

"They say the baby have blue eyes." He said this deliberately as he looked directly into Jimmie Sue's blue eyes.

"Thet son-of-a . . . . ?

Now Cletus was asking, "Who you swearin' at?"

"Madeleen tol' me in the only letter I ever got from her, thet she's skeered of the boy in the family where she worked. He had red hair an' blue eyes. If I could get my bare hands on him right now, I'd kill him. This wadn't somethin' she did of her own free will. There's not many things certain in life, but thet's one thing thet's fer damn sure certain."

Jimmie Sue inquired further, "Did Madeleen have a name picked out fer the baby?"

"Yeah . . . Moses."

Jimmie Sue thought of Red Seas and dreams and fences and "colored" and "White Boy" and revival meetings, and snakes in swimming/baptizing holes. He even remembered that Madeleen told him that Moses was the grandson of Levi.

Cletus just stood there shuffling, the way he'd learned from his daddy to shuffle backwards in front of a white man when no one's saying anything. He didn't know whether he should wait for Jimmie Sue to say something or just scoot on back home and tell his folks he'd done what it was his mission was supposed to accomplish.

Jimmie Sue collected himself, started to shake Cletus's hand, but then thought better of it as he remembered that he wasn't supposed to do that, and it might embarrass Cletus, so he merely said, "Much obliged, Cletus. I 'preciate you comin' ovah hyar to tell me. Tell your mamma and daddy I'm real sorry 'bout Madeleen, an' I be grievin' too"

Their painful shared moment held them both in limbo for several moments until Jimmie Sue moved deliberately toward the startled Cletus and took him in his arms, embracing him like a long lost brother. The two of them—the white boy and the colored—stood there sobbing tears of deeply felt hurt and reconciling hope on each other's shoulders—*for a lost sister and a forbidden sweetheart.*

* * *

CHAPTER 31

Last Rights

Jimmie Sue's sorrow hovered over and penetrated into many different levels—much deeper than he dared let on to his family. He attended the funeral . . . the only "white boy" there.

Standing beside the front door of the colored church, he was surprised to see two caskets unloaded off the funeral wagon. He was expecting a full-size casket, but the small infant-size casket stunned him. When he went into the church he sat in the back pew, where the colored would have had to sit if they were to attend the white folks' church.

Miz' Hilton invited him down to sit with the family, but he declined, feeling in some way unworthy.

He did go up to look on Madeleen when they opened the casket lid for their last goodbyes. In the eighteen months since he had seen her, she had matured into a beautiful woman with an expression of acceptance now on her calm, dark face and of course, she had become a mother. However he was surprised to see in her right hand a red ear of corn—the red ear he'd sent to her by Aunt Lily from the corn shucking—what seemed like a lifetime ago.

As he viewed those forbidden lips for the last time, he thought of the moments when she and he had touched quite by accident, resulting in disastrous results but encompassing passions each time for him.

And there were the times that touch was no accident at all: the time she kissed him deliberately under the mistletoe, surprising both him and her family.

Then there was the last touch . . . the kiss on the porch floor the night before she left for Richmond. That touch overwhelmed them both, binding them together, yet releasing them forever—at least in this lifetime.

Gently he kissed his own fingertips, then reaching toward her peaceful countenance he transferred the moisture of his lips to the cold full lips of Madeleen.

As he turned, he was immediately confronted by the other coffin and for some reason it was even more difficult to view the remains in the small casket. The baby was obviously a mixture of two races. His hair was curly and light brown—not red at all—and of course it wasn't possible to see his blue eyes. *Was this the child the contorted 'ways of the world' denied him and Madeleen?*

Jimmie Sue didn't follow the casket procession into the colored cemetery, but walked through the whitefolks' cemetery and stood across the fence right next to where they'd dug the hole for Madeleen. The rusty old iron fence reminded him anew of fences and locks, she'd talked about, seemingly a century ago. He sat down on a white oak tree stump there across the fence from her grave site, listening to their singing and prayers and strained blessings.

He was still sitting there when everyone had left the colored cemetery. As Aunt Lily left the side of Madeleen's grave she walked up the hill to the front gate then over to the white folks' cemetery gate and down the hill, heading directly toward Jimmie Sue, who didn't see her coming.

"Jimmie Sue," she said, "I's so sorry. I knowed how you cared for her. An' you must know how she cared for you . . . . I s'pose you prob'ly want your grave dug right ovah hyar."

"Why you think thet, Miz' Hilton?" He was always amazed—sometimes alarmed— at the wisdom of this woman; her knowing all about herbs and healing and at times seeming to be able to read a person's thoughts.

That was exactly what he'd been thinking, so he assured her, "Yes, Aunt Lily, I thought I'd be put to rest right hyar, planted by this ol' oak stump. Mebbe if they plant me real close here, then I be rooted by this tree an' in this mountain fer sure."

They both chuckled at his feeble attempt at humor before they said their goodbyes. He watched this bereaved, colored woman stand proudly, turning slowly to leave this time and place of loss to walk back through the burial grounds for other folks—white folks.

He thought again of Madeleen, aware not only of her youthful exuberance but also realizing for the first time that she had already attained a great deal of the wisdom of her colored mother, who now hesitated at the graves of white people she'd known, saying a quiet blessing or a muted goodnight to each one as she made her way to exit the white folks' burial gate.

Uncle Jimmie Sue didn't go by the Hiltons' so much anymore, but he would stop by every day at the cemetery and sit on that old stump, looking through the rusty fence at a small fieldstone, marking the resting place for Madeleen.

Her younger brother, Cletus, had placed it there and had written her name MADELEEN HILTON with some black paint, made from tobacco tar and a small brush he'd made from a sweet gum tree branch.

Beside Madeleen's headstone was a smaller stone which had MOSES inscribed on it, but with no last name.

Jimmie Sue's daily ritual of sitting on the old oak stump was somewhat similar to those times, day after day, he'd waited down by the mailbox for a letter from Madeleen. Could he still be waiting for a word from Madeleen—a word from beyond this "veil of tears?"

Anyone might have wondered what he might be pondering, while sitting there. It became apparent after some subsequent action of his, that he was figuring how he might provide more "fitten" headstones for both Madeleen and her baby, although he'd appreciated the effort Cletus had made on Madeleen's behalf.

Later, Uncle Jimmie Sue married Lydia Smith, whom we all knew as Aunt Lydie. They had several children, but he never forgot Madeleen or his daily ritual, whenever possible, of visiting the grave yard. The home he and Lydie had bought was only a short distance from the cemeteries.

Many years later, when I visited the cemetery with Uncle Jimmie Sue, I noticed that Cletus's fieldstone head markers for Madeleen and her baby had been replaced by simple, but tastefully engraved granite stones. Knowing that the Hiltons couldn't afford them, I asked Uncle Jimmie Sue who would've had those headstones placed there.

He answered so quickly, "Oh I ain't got no notion in the world." that I knew he had saved money from various odd jobs until he could afford those monuments. It was then I realized too that he'd continued over the many years to put money into his own burial insurance to make sure he was "put away decently."

It seemed that the older Uncle Jimmie Sue aged the more cantankerous he became. He was particularly critical of vehicles like cars and tractors. In many ways they'd ruined his blacksmith business of buggy repairs and shoeing horses. Also earthmoving equipment was a real bone of contention with him, as they had begun to remove whole mountaintops to get to the coal a little easier. He said that backhoes were the work of the devil, particularly when they were used to dig graves.

Gravedigging was what neighbors did as a kind of last respects for a person. He just wasn't ready for the twentieth century and yet lived through the first half of it.

After the second world war—he'd also lived through the time of the first world war—he seemed to get more tired as that last summer wore on. We'd begun to worry about him a lot.

In early fall I saw Virgil Needham at the filling station. He said that he'd seen Uncle Jimmie Sue a few days before, looking awfully weary. He said he was taking a short cut into Pierson across Chestnut Ridge when he looked up the path and saw an old man walking with a cane, pretty much depending on it.

Virgil went on to say, "When I got up behind him and spoke, he stopped and turned around and said, 'Son. I hadn't seen you acomin'. How's yoah mamma doin' after thet spell she had?'

"I answered, 'Oh she's doin' fine, got over the last sickness.' I hadn't recognized him as I was comin' up behind him, 'cause I'd never seen him so bent over an' slow."

I asked Virgil, "So did Uncle Jimmie Sue make it over the ridge all right? My Lord, he'll be ninety, if he lives till Christmas."

"Oh he made it over the ridge. Whenever I stopped him, it kinda startled him, but he started straightenin' up an' picked up his walkin' stick an' commenced whittlin' on it like it was just an old stick he'd picked up side of the road."

"Yeah, he's still as proud as a Philadelphia lawyer."

Shortly after that as Old Christmas was coming on, one morning Uncle Jimmie Sue said that he and Ol' Trailer, his favorite rabbit dog then, had decided to go for a little hunt across the ridge where the Hiltons used to live.

Their little sharecropper house had been empty for years and had nearly completely fallen down—sunk in from the insides.

We cautioned him about the weather, but he merely said, "Well we might jump a rabbit or two." We noticed when he left he didn't take his gun, but he did take his walking stick. As he stepped off the porch, Ol'

Trailer came loping out from under the house, where he usually slept. He was also getting on up in dog years, which showed up as his lope turned into a walk.

Uncle Jimmie Sue was wearing a worn-out army coat, he'd won in some kind of card game over to Pierson. Although he was a tall man, over six foot, the coat came down nearly to his ankles. Ol' Trailer was following him right close behind, and whenever Uncle Jimmie Sue would slow down a bit or maybe stop, Ol' Trailer would run halfway under his coat.

At noon they weren't back for dinner, but nobody said anything. You could see the worried looks on everyone's face. On toward supper time, Cousin Bill and I said that we thought we'd just step out a little early to feed the stock and then to do the milking.

Of course, we both intended, without letting on to anybody else, that we'd better go check on Uncle Jimmie Sue. Everybody knew that he wouldn't like at all for anybody to be worrying about him; certainly not his ability to get back home in a timely fashion.

It was in the dead of winter, so we put on our boots and winter coats and gloves. As we went on past the barn, where we hung up the milk bucket, we started calling Ol' Trailer, who didn't even bark back at us.

We also brought along the 'possum horn, (used to call the 'possum dogs) made out of an actual horn taken from a cow carcass. Whenever we'd blow that 'possum horn, we'd usually get all of the dogs to answer us. Ol' Trailer was always real good about responding to the horn, but we couldn't hear even a whimper from him now, until we got to the top of the ridge, over toward the Hiltons' old place.

It was real quiet up there as everybody'd all left years ago to find work somewhere when sharecropping days were over.

Bill blew another long, mournful blast on the 'possum horn, and we began to hear a soft whimper or whine, almost like somebody crying. Going toward the sound, we began to understand that it was Ol' Trailer's voice sobbing, instead of his normal barking that we'd been listening for.

Then we saw them.

Uncle Jimmie Sue was lying on a slope next to a huge rock. He was on his back with his arms outstretched. Ol' Trailer had his head on Uncle Jimmie Sue's stomach and looking toward us with those big, mournful hound dog eyes.

We called to Uncle Jimmie Sue, but with no answer. I think we both knew at the same time that he was gone; but not without his having the last word, or at least the last laugh.

Bill said, "Look at that; he's made a snow angel with those outstretched arms."

It reminded me of what he'd told me about him and Rosie and Ruthie and Madeleen making snow angels somewhere close to that same place so many years before. His appearance was as though he was welcoming someone or maybe not a snow angel, but a real one.

Bill also noted the smile on his face, but I think it was a downright grin.

That was about three months ago from what I'm telling you now.

In a couple of hours time I have traveled in my own mind over many years and several ridges with the remembrances of Uncle Jimmie Sue within his lifetime. I've been sitting here daydreaming and recounting all those things he had told me about his life and several things other people had told on him.

The monument truck has come with the memorial headstone for his grave, and they're already lowering it into place. It's a beautiful black granite stone with his name and dates of birth and death, a span of ninety years from before the civil war through the first world war to past the second world war.

There's a figure cut into the headstone—a figure of an angel with outstretched wings.

I notice the fence where Uncle Jimmy Sue had put a gate with a clasp of embracing angels. In his blacksmith shop he had pounded out the angel latches from braised steel, and although the angels were naturally black from the fire of the blacksmith forge and the pounding of the hammer on the anvil, he painted one of the angels white.

That reminded me of the time that Madeleen had told Uncle Jimmie Sue of the fence between them and when they sang "You gotta come in at the door."

When I looked across the fence at the two headstones in the colored cemetery, I saw on the small one the single name, MOSES. There was no last name. Beneath the name was the single date of his birth and death: March 15, 1877. Below that was a short statement, "A little child shall lead them."

On the other stone was the name, MADELEEN HILTON, and underneath that were her dates: b. September 29, 1860, d. March 15, 1877. And there was an engraved key—the key that Madeleen had told Jimmie Sue would be too rusted to undo the lock on the gate separating them. Underneath that was the first phrase of her favorite song, "Shall we gather at the river?"

Glancing back at Uncle Jimmie Sue's headstone, which was now in place, I wondered if he might have chosen some scripture for his memorial and was not really surprised that he had selected the second phrase from Madeleen's song, "Where bright angel feet have trod."

It had seemed that water had been a strong motif in their relationship. And although Uncle Jimmie Sue hadn't ever received baptism by water, I felt that he had truly been baptized the day he and Madeleen had encountered each other in the swimming/baptizing hole so many years ago.

I suppose water continues as an element of their relationship, as now it's beginning to rain. It's a fortunate thing I brought an umbrella, having noticed some rather threatening rain clouds to the west.

Rather than leave quickly, I watch the rainwater begin its rivulet down the side of Uncle Jimmie Sue's fairly recent mounded earth and flow hurriedly toward the swag under the gate. Water from the other side of the gate, apparently from Madeleen's weathered grave mound, has joined in the rush toward the creek.

The gurgling water is making an almost distinct laughing sound as though it has a mind of its own to hurry downhill to the swimming/baptizing hole.

Trying to avoid the rain, I decide to leave Uncle Jimmie Sue and Madeleen and the little one to rest in peace.

But I'll be back I'm sure—particularly when I need to meditate on the meaning of "Love that passeth understanding."

* * *

EPILOGUE

The rain falling on the sarvisberry bloom
Also nurtures the roots of the oak.
The intensity of the rain accelerates
As it descends on both graves, white and colored,
Separated now by only an unlocked gate
Almost as though an unseen hand
Had lifted the double-angel latch.

Shortly the accumulation of
Raindrops on the earthen mounds
Begin to flow swiftly toward each other,
Then seemingly laughing
As the commingling water
Gurgles happily down the hillside
Toward an old swimming hole
Where rejoicing souls
Were once refreshed
In the spiritual baptism
Of childhood romps.

E. Reid Gilbert

Edwards Brothers, Inc.
Thorofare, NJ USA
October 10, 2011